The Politics of Millennials

Today the Millennial Generation, the age cohort born from the early 1980s to the early 2000s, is the largest generation in our nation. This generation exceeds one-quarter of the population and is the most diverse in US history. Millennials grew up experiencing the terrorist attacks of September 11, the global proliferation of the internet and smart phones, and the worst economic recession since the Great Depression of the 1930s. Their young adulthood has been marked by rates of unemployment and underemployment surpassing those of their parents and grandparents, making them the first generation in the modern era to have higher rates of poverty than their predecessors at the same age. *The Politics of Millennials* explores the factors that shape the Millennial Generation's unique political identity, how this identity conditions political and policy choices, and how this cohort's diversity informs political attitudes and beliefs. Few scholars have empirically identified and studied the political attitudes and policy preferences of Millennials, despite the size and influence of this generation. This book explores politics from a generational perspective, first, and then combines this with other group identities that include race and ethnicity to bring a different perspective to how we examine identity politics.

Stella M. Rouse is Associate Professor of Government and Politics and Director of the Center for American Politics and Citizenship at the University of Maryland.

Ashley D. Ross is Assistant Professor in the Department of Marine Sciences and Fellow at the Center for Texas Beaches & Shores at Texas A&M University at Galveston.

The Politics of Millennials

Political Beliefs and Policy Preferences
of America's Most Diverse Generation

Stella M. Rouse and Ashley D. Ross

University of Michigan Press
Ann Arbor

For questions or permissions, please contact um.press.perms@umich.edu

Published in the United States of America by the
University of Michigan Press
Manufactured in the United States of America
Printed on acid-free paper

First published August 2018
First paperback edition published August 2020

A CIP catalog record for this book is available from the British Library.

Library of Congress Cataloging-in-Publication data has been applied for.

ISBN 978-0-472-13107-5 (hardcover)
ISBN 978-0-472-12441-1 (e-book)
ISBN 978-0-472-03787-2 (paperback)

Contents

List of Tables

List of Figures

Acknowledgments

This project has been a number of years in the making and has drawn upon numerous professional and personal resources and support of which we are most grateful. First and foremost, we are grateful to family, friends, and colleagues who encouraged us to pursue our curiosity about the political attitudes and policy preferences of the Millennial Generation and how the topic might have broader appeal that was worth exploring. Second, we are thankful for both the formal and informal support we received to compete this project. Ashley Ross would like to specifically acknowledge funding from the Department of Political Science at Sam Houston State University and the Department of Marine Sciences at Texas A&M University at Galveston. Stella Rouse would like to express gratitude for the financial support received from the University of Maryland, College of Behavioral and Social Sciences Dean's Research Initiative.

We are extremely thankful to our professional colleagues, Dr. Mirya Holman at Tulane University, Dr. Walter Wilson at University of Texas at San Antonio, and Dr. Karen Kauffman at University of California, Los Angeles who facilitated the recruitment and logistics of focus group interviews. Their willingness to help us advance our project is a great example of the generosity within our academic community. Other colleagues at our respective institutions also helped bring this project to fruition. In particular, Stella Rouse would like to thank Mike Hanmer, Irwin Morris, and Rich Engstrom for intellectually stimulating conversations that helped refine survey questions and improve the arguments of the book. Stella Rouse is especially grateful for the guidance provided by Shibley Telhami, who, through the Anwar Sadat Chair for Peace and Development, helped underwrite one of the surveys used for this project, and also made us realize the importance of cosmopolitanism to the Millennial identity. Stella Rouse also thanks the faculty, graduate students, and undergraduate students affiliated with the Center for American Politics and Citizenship, a number of them who provided research and editing support for the book.

Finally, neither one of us would be able to do what we do and embark on this project without the unwavering love and support of our families. Ashley Ross thanks her husband, Gabe Wootton, for his steadfast support of her professional work. Stella Rouse owes a perpetual debt to her husband, Rodney Rouse, who unconditionally supports her endeavors with little regard for time and schedule constraints. And a special acknowledgement to her sons, Carson (a young Millennial) and Riley (a post-Millennial), who still do not quite understand why their mom spends so much time writing, but who provide love, support, and encouragement, nonetheless. They both embody the faith and confidence we have in the rising generations.

CHAPTER I

Millennial Generation Persona: Who Are Millennials and Why Should We Care?

"Young people understand they are the future of the country and they intend to shape that future."

—from Bernie Sanders' speech in California on June 8, 2016,
after the California Democratic primary.

In the presidential primary elections of 2016, an incredible phenomenon emerged—the tremendous appeal of a 74-year-old white Jewish man from Vermont to young adults who are part of the Millennial Generation (those born between the early 1980s and the early 2000s). At first blush, this pairing seems quite odd, given the age and generational gap between the Democratic candidate, described as having a "cranky grandpa vibe" (Burns 2016) and his most ardent followers. However, Sanders' message resonated deeply with Millennials and continued to do so late into the primary election season. A Gallup Poll from April 2016 showed that 55% of Millennials still favored Sanders over the presumptive and eventual Democratic Party nominee, Hillary Clinton (38%), or her Republican counterpart, Donald Trump (22%) (Norman 2016). A closer examination of Millennials reveals why their support for Bernie Sanders was so strong, and perhaps even inevitable. This phenomenon is both a starting point and an ending point (in Chapter 10) to understanding the politics of Millennials, a journey we embark on in this book.

To appreciate the appeal of Bernie Sanders and his "Social Revolution" to the now largest generation in the United States, exceeding one-quarter of the population (US Census Bureau 2015a), we must begin by understanding the context in which Millennials have come of age. Imagine a world without cable TV, without cell phones, without computers, and without the ability to instantaneously and constantly communicate. Also, imagine a world without September 11, 2001 as the literal and figurative ground zero for homeland security and foreign policy decisions and debates. Furthermore, imagine a world (or more precisely, a country) where ethnic minority groups like Latinos and Asian Americans make up a very small proportion of our communities. If you were born before the early 1980s, you can certainly envision this world, because you lived in it. However, for the Millennial Generation, it is nearly impossible to fathom, as they are the most digitally connected (Experian 2014) and demographically diverse group in the nation's history (Pew Research Center 2014a). Millennials have also reached adulthood in the midst of the worst economic recession since the Great Depression of the 1930s. Despite a rebounding economy and job growth in recent years, rates of unemployment and underemployment for Millennials surpass those of their parents: 40% of the nation's unemployed in 2015 were Millennials, and the number of employed young people making less than $25,000 a year is higher now than it has been in more than a quarter century (McHale 2015). A recent report by a British think tank found that Millennials are at risk of becoming the first generation to earn less in their lifetimes than their parents (Intergenerational Commission 2016). Many Millennials have no health insurance, live at home with their parents, and are burdened with massive student loan debt (Pew Research Center 2014a). This economic hardship has been difficult, protracted, and unexpected. Millennials are, after all, the best educated generation in American history with a third of older Millennials (ages 26–33) having a four-year college degree or more (Pew Research Center 2014a).

While Millennials' education, like other generations before them, opens opportunities for increased political information, knowledge, and engagement, they are distinct from older adults in that information today is largely digital and global in scope. Millennials are also different from older generations in that they prefer to engage in political problems directly, see issues from a cosmopolitan (or global) viewpoint, and seek to affirm principles of social justice and tolerance (Zogby and Kuhl 2013; Dalton 2016). Against the backdrop of recent economic difficulties, we have seen this expressed in their frustration that the rich get richer off the backs of the young and poor and that political and economic institutions are at best complicit about their struggles, or at worst rigged to exploit them. This strong sentiment brought about the Occupy Wall Street (OWS) movement in 2011–2012 against social and economic inequality that was largely led by Millennials. This same current pushed Millennials' over-whelming support for Bernie Sanders, whose Democratic socialism agenda seemed like a better alternative to the economic and political status quo. As Nikhil Goyal, a Millennial author and activist states:

> When a disheveled old white dude comes along and says our society is rigged for the rich, perpetual warfare is not the answer, and that people of color should not be slaughtered by police—and then asks for our help and a few dollars to bring about a revolution—you're damn right we are going to stand with him.[1]

This brief overview of Millennials provides a preview of how their genera-tion persona, frame, or identity—based on a multitude of factors—helps us understand and evaluate this generation's political beliefs, attitudes, and policy preferences. One important question to consider in this evaluation is whether Millennials are distinct, compared to other generations, or if their attitudes and beliefs are a product of a lifecycle effect. Conventional wisdom has often noted that young people, regardless of generation, are more liberal and anti-establishment than other age cohorts but rarely has research supported such generalizations (c.f. Campbell and Strate 1981; Fullerton and Dixon 2010). In fact, studies have demonstrated that ideo-logical differences between older and younger adults are attributed more to the unique experiences of a particular cohort than it can to age itself (Braungart and Braungart 1986; Ghitza and Gelman 2014). As we will argue in this book, Millennials are indeed different from other gener-ations, based on a number of factors, and while it is still too early to fully demonstrate (only time will tell), these characteristics are likely to have a lasting impact on their overall political outlook. We begin to make this case below, as we detail who Millennials are, what their persona is composed of, and what experiences set them apart from other genera-tions. This is particularly important, given that Millennials will likely be the largest voting bloc in America by the 2020 presidential election (Fry 2017).

Who are Millennials?

The Millennial Generation[2] refers to the age cohort that was born from the early 1980s to the early 2000s.[3] Described another way, Millennials are those that experienced a varying number of their formative years around the turn of the century (2000 AD). Although it would seem appropriate and perhaps even useful, generational boundaries are not defined by the government; rather, they are determined by popular writers, marketers, the media, and generational scholars who make somewhat arbitrary decisions about when generations begin and end, sometimes, but not always, marked by some dramatic event. Often, at least a partial consensus forms around generational classifications (or becomes the popular lexicon) as it did for: the Greatest Generation (approx. 1900–1924)—those that spent formative years during the Great Depression and fought and died in World War II; the Silent Generation (approx. 1925–1945)—those that grew up during the Dust Bowl and in part, the Great Depression and are known for working hard and keeping quiet (as the name implies); Baby Boomers (approx. 1946–1964)—those born during the post-demographic "baby boom" after soldiers returned from World War II; Generation X (approx. 1961–1981)—those born after the post-World War II baby boom and sandwiched between two much larger cohorts (Baby Boomers and Millennials); and the Millennial Generation—the generation we focus on in this book.

The Millennial political identity is borne out of a number of factors. These include value shifts on issues including family, institutions, religion, culture, and prospects about the future, as well as shared experiences at the same point in life. These factors are encompassed under what generational theorists refer to as a "core persona" or a "generational frame" that define the unique characteristics of a generation (Howe and Strauss 2000; P. Taylor 2014). Every generation may be understood to have a unique persona, frame, or identity. This generational identity should not be viewed in the same way we understand minority group identity (i.e. Latinos, African Americans, Asian Americans, members of the LGBTQ community, and other historically disadvantaged groups) where a specific set of values, issue priorities, and policy preferences may be assigned based on shared group interests. However, this persona is as real and relevant as race and gender in understanding group differences (Campbell et al. 2015).

Generational identity is fundamentally rooted in cultural shifts resulting from social, economic, and/or political events or phenomena (Braungart and Braungart 1986; Erkulwater 2012; Twenge 2014; Campbell et al. 2015). As Lyons and Kuron (2014) put it, generations are people born within the "same historical and sociocultural context, who experience the same formative experiences, and develop unifying commonalities as a result" (140). For example, Generation X came of age at the end of Cold War, and witnessed the collapse of the Soviet Union and the fall of the Berlin Wall. Gen Xers also experienced the AIDS epidemic, the space shuttle Challenger explosion, the advent of video games, and the popularity of MTV and music videos. In contrast, Millennials have experienced the events and ramifications of rapidly changing demographics, the terrorist attacks of September 11, 2001, and the Great Recession. Millennials are also the first digital natives, coming to age surrounded by technological advances, online information, and digital connectedness (P. Taylor 2014). These events and trends are accompanied by new and different values—another hallmark of generational identities or frames (Twenge, Campbell, and Freeman 2012), ranging from rising distrust of traditional institutions to extreme tolerance for same-sex marriage. These values distinguish Millennials from other cohorts, helping form a generational imprint that is likely to transcend age-only effects.

When we speak of generations, we speak of averages (Twenge 2014); individuals within a generation, therefore, may deviate from others in their cohort. Shared experiences are complex phenomena whose interpretation and impact on values, beliefs, and behavior vary across individual factors, including race, ethnicity, gender, and religion (Beier and Kanfer 2015). The Civil Rights Movement of the 1960s and 1970s, for example, was a formative experience for the Baby Boomer Generation; however, its impact on personal ideas of equality, justice, and fairness is dependent on the individual. While older generations are primarily white and of European immigrant descent, Millennials are increasingly nonwhite and have emigrated largely from non-European countries. These demographic shifts have significantly contributed to Millennials' divergent political philosophies, social views, and policy preferences (P. Taylor 2014). As we will examine in more detail in ensuing pages and chapters, the diversity of Millennials is a strong catalyst for political attitudes and policy preferences that differ not only from other generations but vary within this cohort as well. For example, partisanship, ideology, and policy priorities are not the same for white, non-Hispanic Millennials, as they are for Latino Millennials, or African American Millennials. Thus, Millennials are far from the monolithic group portrayed by pundits and the news media.

Diversity is one of multiple factors that have shaped the Millennial generational frame and differentiates this cohort from other generations. As we will argue in this book, the traits that comprise this generational frame help define and explain Millennial political attitudes, policy preferences, and levels of engagement. We start with a discussion of the Millennial generational frame, but, importantly, this is explored through the lens of group identities including race, ethnicity, and cosmopolitanism and collectivist worldview. Therefore, we will examine both inter- and intra-generational group differences throughout this book.

Millennial Demographics: The Crucial Tale of Growth, Diversity, and Tolerance

Demographer William Frey (2016) has said, "Racial diversity will be the most defining and impactful characteristic of the millennial generation." This diversity is a product of an incredible shift in the makeup of the US population during a relatively short time span, from 1960 to 2010, and encompassing the birth years of Millennials. White non-Hispanics have gone from 88.6% of the US population in 1960 to 72.4% in 2010. In contrast, Latinos or Hispanics comprised 4% of the population in 1960, but by 2010, made up 16.3% of the population (more than quadrupling in size during this time).[4] During this same time frame, African Americans and Asian Americans have also seen a growth in their population size (African Americans: 10.5% in 1960 to 12.6% in 2010; Asian Americans: 0.6% in 1960 to 5.3% in 2010). Figure 1.1 below visually depicts the demographic shift that has occurred in the United States over the last fifty years, as well as population projections by race and ethnicity for 2060.

If projections hold, the population shift will result in a negative change for whites and a continued growth for other groups, especially Latinos and Asian Americans. This shift is so significant that non-Hispanic whites, the dominant, majority group since the inception of the country, will become

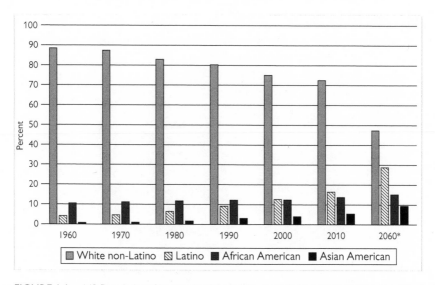

FIGURE 1.1. US Population Changes by Race and Latino Origin, 1960–2060

Note: "Asian American" includes Hawaiian and other Pacific Islanders; data obtained from US Census Bureau 2015a, decennial census population; *2060 projections are from the US Census Bureau, 2014 National Projections.

the minority group in the United States in a matter of a few decades. The US Census Bureau estimates that by 2044, the United States will become a majority–minority nation, meaning that there will be no single dominant group; rather, the compilation of minorities will comprise the majority of the country's population (Colby and Ortman 2015).

One major factor driving this population change is the large influx of Hispanic and Asian immigrants to the United States in the past half century, and whose US-born children are now aging into adulthood (Drake 2014; P. Taylor 2014). These two groups now make up a large part of the Millennial Generation. In fact, when we examine the Millennial population by race and ethnicity, the distribution is even more dramatic, compared to the overall population breakdown. Figure 1.2 below shows the composition of the Millennial population by race and ethnicity in 2014. Whites comprise 57% of the Millennial population, compared with 21% of Latinos, 13% of African Americans, and 6% of Asian Americans.

Minorities, particularly Latinos, are younger than the rest of population—further contributing to the demographic strength of

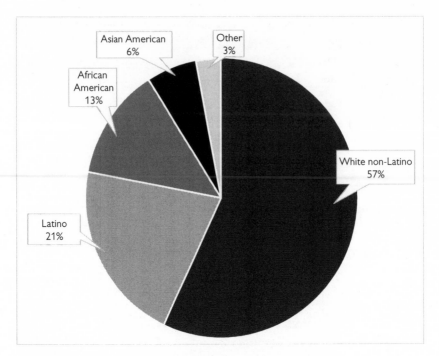

FIGURE 1.2.   Millennial Population in 2014 by Race and Latino Origin

Source: Pew Research Center 2015e. "Comparing Millennials to Other Generations."

Millennials. To place this in perspective, 37.9% of Latinos are part of the Millennial Generation, compared to just 25.9% of non-Latinos (Rouse, Kawashima-Ginsberg, and Thrutchley 2015). Millennials will spearhead the transition of the United States into a majority–minority nation (Frey 2016), with 44.2% of this age cohort being part of a minority race or ethnic group (US Census Bureau 2015a). The Public Religion Research Institute's (PRRI) Chief Executive Robert P. Jones aptly summarizes the implications of this trend: "Millennials really have rubbed shoulders with difference in a way that older Americans did not have an opportunity to, just sheerly by composition of their generational makeup."[5] The racial and ethnic diversity that has been part of the demographic landscape of Millennials' lives not only sets them apart from older generations in terms of population composition but also in terms of the values they support. As Dalton (2016) argues: "Generation is a surrogate for the different socialization experiences of individuals" (p. 98); for Millennials, diversity has been a formative life experience.

Perhaps not surprising, given their diversity, Millennials are also highly tolerant of people of different races, ethnicities, religions, and sexual orientation. While racial and gender tolerance has increased among Americans as a whole (Schwadel and Garneau 2014), studies have also shown that young adults are more tolerant than older adults (Brooks and Bolzendahl 2004; Dalton 2016). As an example, a Pew Research Center poll (2011) found that 60% of Millennials are more likely to say that people of different races marrying each other is a "change for the better." This compares with 47% of Gen Xers, 36% of Baby Boomers, and 29% of the Silent Generation. Similarly, 35% of Millennials are also more likely than older cohorts to say that the growing population of immigrants is a "change for the better." In contrast, 30% of Gen Xers, 23% of Baby Boomers, and 22% of the Silent Generation express the same. Overall, the Millennial Generation appears to be more accepting of the changing face of America.

Millennials' racial tolerance has garnered attention in the news in the past few years with some claiming that this generation is "just as racist as their parents" (Clement 2015). However, polling data reveals that there is variance among Millennials in their expressed racial tolerance. This variance emphasizes the importance of disaggregating the attitudes of Millennial subgroups and not treating this cohort as a monolithic unit. We see these differences among Millennials in their perspectives on how minorities are treated. When asked how much confidence they have "in the US judicial system's ability to fairly judge people without bias for race and ethnicity," the Harvard Public Opinion Project 2014 reports that 59% of African American Millennials say they have no or not much confidence, while 52% of Hispanic Millennials and 42% of white Millennials say the same. Despite this, we see Millennials, as a whole, actively aware of and concerned about racial issues, expressed most recently in young adult participation in the "Black Lives Matter" movement and high-profile protests over racial insensitivity and discrimination at college campuses (Foran 2015).

Diversity and tolerance does not stop at race for Millennials. This cohort is also more open-minded about sexual orientation. Millennials are twice as likely as older adults (7% to 3.5%) to identify as lesbian, gay, or bisexual (Gates 2011; Jones and Cox 2015). Also, 70% of Millennials support same-sex marriage compared to 59% of adults aged 35–50 years and 45% of adults aged 51–69 years (Pew Research Center 2015a). These numbers indicate that for Millennials, now or in the near future, being LGBTQ is "no big deal" (Allen 2015).

Remarkably, Millennial tolerance has bloomed in a garden that is overrun with seeds of hate and fear. In the aftermath of 9/11 and the ongoing war on terrorism, Millennials are supportive of religious expression and the culture of American Muslims. More than six in ten Millennials say they would be comfortable with a mosque being built near their home, and 73% are comfortable with a Muslim teaching elementary school in their community. In contrast, just 37% of those 65 and older are comfortable with a mosque and 36% percent with a Muslim teaching elementary school (Cox et al. 2011). Moreover, despite a crushing economic depression that hit the employment prospects of their generation the hardest, Millennials remain supportive of immigration and do not view immigrants as their competition for jobs (Ross and Rouse 2015).

Diversity and Minority Group Identity

The narrative of Millennial diversity dovetails into an important discussion about the role of minority group identity. As mentioned at the onset of this chapter, minority group identity differs from generational identity. Minority group identity—most often tied to racial and ethnic identity—refers to the commonality an individual feels toward others based on their shared experiences, interests, beliefs, and traits that result in a sense of belonging to a community or group (Tajfel et al. 1971; McClain et al. 2009). An extension of group identity is the concept of group consciousness, which refers to the recognition by group members that they belong to a deprived group or class (Miller, et al. 1981). The commonality individuals in a group feel, coupled with their sense of being disadvantaged, manifests itself in a lack of access to resources that leads to collective action in pursuit of common interests (Stokes 2003). Research on group identity and group consciousness has primarily focused on the plight of African Americans (Dawson 1994), Latinos (Sanchez 2006), and Asian Americans (Wong, Lien, and Conway 2005). As a result, these concepts play an important, although latent, role in our study of Millennials because of the disproportionate number of minorities that comprise this cohort. While exploring the underlying psychological attributes of group identity and group consciousness is important, it is beyond the scope of this project. We acknowledge the impact of these concepts on the attitudes and preferences of Millennial subgroups, but we do not have the data to test them directly. Diversity not only influences Millennials, compared to other generations, but racial and ethnic identity help draw political distinctions *among* Millennials as well. This work provides a baseline for understanding how generational identity can be included as part of broader research into the effects of multiple identities on political attitudes.

Global Citizens: Millennial, Cosmopolitan Identity, and Worldview

Millennials have come of age in a globalized world where goods, services, people, information, and cultures largely flow freely across both real and virtual borders. The world Millennials live in is much smaller and closer than the world experienced by previous generations. Just a few decades ago, communication between people across the country or across the world occurred either via phone or through written correspondence that took days, if not weeks, to receive. Now, communication and interaction are instantaneous, either via email, through social media sites, or with a video connection available on small, hand-held devices. While many non-Millennials have integrated into this "modern" world (some more reluctantly than others), it is Millennials who are the first digital natives and who are the adults most immersed in this new global environment. These characteristics have led some scholars to dub Millennials the "first globals" as a reflection of their strong global sensibility (Zogby and Kuhl 2013).

Interconnectedness with the global environment contributes to a larger identity known as cosmopolitanism or being a "citizen of the larger global community" (Nussbaum 1996). As Hopper (2007) explains, ". . . global communications and information technologies, the modem and the mobile phone in particular, are facilitating the stretching of social life across time and space, and this again means that intercultural contact is likely to be happening more often and more quickly in the contemporary period" (160). This connectedness provides opportunities to develop understanding and empathy for cultures, traditions, and ideas from around the world and, perhaps, adopt certain aspects into our personal outlooks and lifestyles, thereby experiencing integration into global processes and phenomena (Vertovec and Cohen 2002; Hopper 2007). We observed technological connectivity sparking a sense of cosmopolitanism with Kony 2012, a video created by the non-profit group Invisible Children to raise awareness about Joseph Kony, a warlord known for his forces' recruitment of child soldiers in Uganda and Central African states. Millennials' social media feeds were flooded with messages of "Stop Kony;" the film spread virally and received over 100 million views, and the non-profit raised $28 million in 2012 (A. Taylor 2014). While the film was criticized for oversimplifying the issue and the movement stagnated, it underscored the connection of Millennials with the global community.[6]

Cosmopolitanism derives from a number of experiences beyond the connectedness afforded by technology, including travel abroad, fluency in foreign languages, tolerance of others, and, of course, diversity (Zogby and Kuhl 2013). Afforded these opportunities and valuing these experiences, Millennials are much more likely than other generations to identify as cosmopolitan (Zogby and Kuhl 2013; Telhami 2015; Telhami and Kishi 2015). The result is that as many as one-third of Millennials see themselves as "citizens of planet Earth" rather than as citizens of a particular country, and US Millennials prefer a cosmopolitan identity only next to being a "citizen of the United States" (above religious and other group identities) (Zogby and Kuhl 2013; Telhami 2015). The prevalence of a cosmopolitan identity among Millennials is a product of social modernization, globalization, and associated changes in social, economic, and political landscapes; these same forces contributed to the deconstruction of traditional institutional boundaries as Millennials know them (Dalton 2016).

A sense of global civic responsibility accompanies the cosmopolitan perspective, as nearly two in three Millennials say it is important to contribute time and money to an international charity (Zogby and Kuhl 2013). Cosmopolitanism also affects Millennials' views on domestic policy and foreign affairs, which have recently involved increasingly nationalist proposals, ranging from building a wall along the United States–Mexico border to banning Muslims from entering the country. According to CNN analysis of recent polls, Millennials are more open to outsiders and less likely to perceive foreign entities as threats than older generations; in short, they simply are not scared of the outside world (Thrall 2016). This reinforces what we already know about Millennials—they display high levels of social tolerance.

Related to cosmopolitan identity is collectivist worldview—the belief that society as a whole is paramount to individual interest and responsible for securing the shared welfare (Oyserman 1993; Tieku 2012). Both consider the larger collective and are components of the Millennial Generation persona as Millennials want the world to be a better place and see the government playing a large (or larger role) in that mission. Millennials "intrinsically understand 'government as a platform'" (Ben-Yehuda 2010); a platform, according to a recent study by the Center for American Progress, that can and should do more to solve both national and international problems, ranging from improving schools to developing new clean energy sources to reducing poverty (Molyneux and Teixeria 2010). While Millennials' perception of the role of government in bringing about global change is, at first glance, contradictory to their lack of trust in political institutions, it speaks to a view among young adults of what government could be (and do), rather than what it presently is (and does). Research shows that the majority of Millennials believe that government should improve its efficiency and effectiveness but not reduce its size—a position a majority of older adults maintain (Molyneux and Teixeria 2010). Overall, Millennials are more positive and trusting about the role of government than non-Millennials (Pew Research Center 2015b, 2015c) and favor a strong federal government in society (Pew Research Center 2014a). As described in the report *Government By and For Millennial America*, Millennials view government as "nothing less than the greatest tool at society's disposal to address the collective action problems of today" (Roosevelt Institute 2013: 8). This belief that government can be a positive force of change is at the heart of liberal ideology, a defining characteristic of their shared persona that we turn to next.

Left and Left-Out: Millennial Political Ideology, Party Affiliation, and Attachment to Traditional Institutions

Millennials often encounter the criticism that they are lazy, unengaged, and uninformed when it comes to politics (Twenge 2014). But Millennial politics is not as simple as that. Dalton (2016) sums up what is missed about Millennials: "It isn't that the young are apathetic and unconcerned about politics—they are often involved and they show their concern in different ways than their elders. It isn't that the young are disaffected and cynical about politics—they are cynical about politicians and how the political system currently functions, but supportive of the democratic ideal" (p. 186). The Millennial persona, identity, or frame heavily influences this generation's viewpoint on political issues and the political system. Millennials, on average, are very liberal, having a strong commitment to social issues including poverty, racism, and immigration. They tend to favor non-traditional forms of political and civic participation more so than older adults. They are also detached from and distrustful of traditional political institutions (Pew 2014a). While this generation sees current politics, politicians, and institutions as out of touch with their values and norms, they do believe government can be a vehicle for good in the world.

In comparison to older adults, Millennials are more likely to describe themselves as liberal: 29% of Millennials compared to 20% of adults aged 35–50 years, 18% of adults aged 51–69 years, and 15% of adults 70 years and older (Pew Research Center 2010a). Pew Research Center studies have shown that Millennials are considerably more liberal than older generations in their views on the role of government, poverty, racial discrimination, immigration, international affairs, the environment, and homosexuality (Kiley and Dimock 2014; Pew 2016a). Using data from the Pew Political Polarization Survey 2014, Figure 1.3 shows that Millennials are more liberal than Generation X, Baby Boomers, and the Silent Generation.

Clearly Millennials are more liberal than older adults today, but are they more liberal than generations before them when they were young? Some say that young adults are *always* more liberal than older adults. Young people tend to be more idealistic, they have less experience, and they are burdened with fewer responsibilities. While this seems logical, statistical tests show that Millennials are distinctively liberal. Consider this snapshot of generational differences for Generation X in 1990 and the Millennial Generation in 2010—the point in time when each group was 18 to 30 years old. The American National Election Study in each of these years asked questions to gauge tolerance for immigration, homosexuality, and liberal identification. As shown in Table 1.1, Millennials are more tolerant of immigration and homosexuals than older adults at a young age. It appears then, that the liberalness of Millennials is not simply or solely a life-cycle effect, but rather, a phenomenon tied to generational factors.

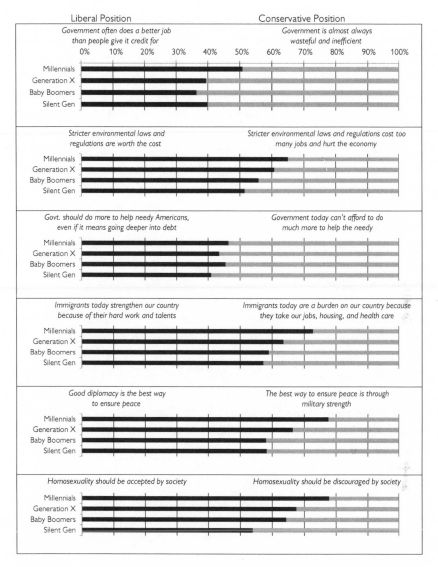

FIGURE 1.3. Millennials More Liberal in Their Political Ideology than Older Generations

Note: Data taken from Pew Research Center Political Polarization Survey 2014; dark gray bars represent percentage of respondents that support the liberal position while the light gray bars represent the percentage of respondents that agree with the conservative position.

In line with their liberal ideology, the majority of Millennials align with the Democratic Party. Approximately 51% of Millennials identify with or lean toward the Democratic Party; the Democratic advantage narrows with older generations to 40% of Generation Xers, 35% of Baby Boomers, and 33% of members of the Silent Generation (Pew Research Center 2015c). In fact, 17% more Millennials identify with the Democratic Party than their Generation X counterparts at the same age (see Table 1.1). This party identification is evident in the fact that Millennials have voted at higher rates for the Democratic party than older adults in the past three elections (2008, 2012, and 2016) (Keeter, Horowitz, and Tyson 2008; Robillard 2012; Pew Research Center 2015c; Richmond, Zinshteyn, and Gross 2016).

Despite their left-leaning tendencies, Millennials are more likely than older adults to identify as political independents (Drake 2014). Among a choice of "Republican, Democrat, or Independent"—48% of Millennials chose "Independent," according to Pew Research Center polls (Pew Research Center 2015c). In comparison to older adults, Millennials are the only generation to see a rise in political independents—6% since the year 2000 (Pew Research Center 2015c). Only 31% of Millennials say "there is a difference in what the Republican and Democratic Parties stand for," compared to 43% of Generation Xers, 49% of Baby Boomers, and 58% of members of the Silent Generation (Pew Research Center 2014a). While Millennials are clearly liberal in their ideology, they view themselves

TABLE 1.1.   Snapshot of Generational Differences

	Generation Xers in 1990	Millennials in 2010	Difference
Immigration Tolerance	–1.89%	6.65%	**8.54% increase**

Should the United States increase levels of immigration? Difference between percent 18–30 year olds and 31 year olds and older that respond "Yes" (ANES 1992 and 2008)

Homosexual Tolerance	0.30%	2.50%	**2.20% increase**

Gay feeling thermometer: Difference between percent 18–30 year olds and 31 year olds and older responding with a rating of 50 and above, indicating positive feelings (ANES 1992 and 2008)

Democratic Party Affiliation	44.67%	62.08%	**17.41% increase**

Percent of 18–30 year olds that associate with the Democratic Party (ANES 1992 and 2008)

Note: In 1990, Generation Xers aged 18–30 years had birth years of 1960–1972. In 2010, Millennials aged 18–30 years had birth years of 1980–1992.

as largely outside of the two-party system. Many have argued that the Democratic and Republican Parties have not done a good job of mobilizing support among Millennials, leaving them out of the political system (Dalton 2016). Not only are Millennials out of the mainstream with political party identification but their political participation also diverges from traditional politics.

In the book, *The Good Citizen*, Russell Dalton (2016) asks a critical question: What does it mean to be a good citizen in today's society? He approaches this question in response to the grim picture painted in recent literature on the lack of good citizenship among Millennials: ". . . political experts seemingly agree that young Americans are dropping out of politics, losing faith in government, and becoming disenchanted with their personal lives" (p. 3). Using data from the 2004 and 2014 General Social Surveys, Dalton argues that norms of citizenship among young adults today, while different, are perhaps no less effective than with past generations. He finds that young adults, on average, follow a model of "engaged citizenship" while older adults tend to adhere to a model of "duty-based citizenship." Engaged citizenship stresses direct participation and influence of government and policy; engaged citizens are "more active on referendums than elections and more active in direct action than campaign work; volunteering is preferred to party activity" (Dalton 2016: 86). Moreover, the engaged citizen is "one who is aware of others, is willing to act on his or her principles, and is willing to challenge political elites" (Dalton 2016: 29). This includes supporting values of social justice and tolerance and participating in activities such as boycotts and protests. Duty-based citizenship, on the other hand, focuses on "reinforcing the existing political order and existing authority patterns" (Dalton 2016: 33) and emphasizes voting, respect for authority, and rule of law (Dalton 2016: 30).

Dalton's findings support the idea that Millennials prescribe to an "engaged citizenship" model, which certainly makes it easier to understand their draw to and support for a candidate like Bernie Sanders. While Millennials generally have lower voter turnout than older adults, which is common of young adults in general, they are voting at higher rates in presidential elections than the previous generation—Generation X—at the same age (Robillard 2012).[7] Millennials are proving to be active in other ways as well; they match and, in some cases, exceed older age cohorts in their political interest and civic engagement, particularly in volunteering, signing petitions, and consumer activism (National Conference on Citizenship 2008; Pew Research Center 2010c; Center for Information & Research on Civic Learning and Engagement 2011).

Millennials have experienced politics in an age where, as Dalton (2016:17) describes it, "structured forms of organization, such as political parties run by backroom 'bosses' and tightly run political machines, have given way to voluntary associations and ad hoc advocacy groups, which in turn becomes less formal and more spontaneous in organization." All of this contributes to a fluid institutional environment, one where we would not expect particularly strong ties. This detachment is borne out when we compare Millennials to non-Millennials. Millennials are less likely to affiliate with one of the two major political parties (Drake 2014; Pew Research Center 2015c), they attend religious services less frequently (Alper 2015), and they have much lower tenure rates with employers (US Bureau of Labor Statistics 2014).

Beyond detachment, Millennials are more distrustful of traditional institutions, particularly political institutions. For many Millennials' lifetime, Congress has been locked in partisan gridlock. They have seen little progress on critical issues, including immigration (despite an influx of newcomers at levels not experienced by their parents and grandparents) and gun control (despite traumatic violence epitomized by the Columbine shooting and subsequent mass shootings). At the same time, some Millennials lived through the impeachment of President Clinton; many observed the massive government failures (on all levels) with the response to Hurricane Katrina; and most have witnessed the government wage a protracted war on terrorism in response to 9/11. Given the political turmoil and ineffective governance of the past two decades, it is not surprising that levels of trust in political institutions have declined among Millennials (Harvard Public Opinion Project 2014), matching the general trend among all American adults that has been present since the 1960s (Pew Research Center 2015b; Dalton 2016). When asked which institutions "can be trusted to do the right thing all or most of the time," young adults, aged 18–29 years, polled by the Harvard Institute of Politics, expressed the lowest levels of trust with Wall Street (9%), the media (11%), and the US Congress (18%). The Reason-Rupe 2014 Millennial Survey indicated widespread distrust among respondents of the major two political parties to handle issues, ranging from privacy to education, to immigration. Moreover, Millennials perceive government institutions to be hijacked by special interests (Greenberg and Weber 2008) and politicians to be captured; a recent poll indicates 58% of 18–29 year olds agree that "elected officials don't seem to have the same priorities I have" (Harvard Public Opinion Project 2014). Only 32% of Millennials think the election process is working as it should (Norman 2016).

Millennial institutional disenchantment and distrust should not be mistaken for a lack of belief in democracy or the positive role of the federal government (as previously noted). It does, however, underscore that Millennials are unhappy with the current political system; they are detached from traditional institutions and they do not feel their views and values are fully represented by current political parties and politicians. Millennials see our political institutions as rigid, outdated, and largely unaccommodating to their norms of participation. They want change to the politics of our democracy and the institutions of the political system. This is a more nuanced issue that we explore further in Chapter 9; using the 2016 election as a case study, we link traits of the Millennial Generation persona to their political engagement and attitudes.

Millennial Resiliency: Optimism and Social Justice amid Economic Crisis and Increasing Inequality

> It's getting harder and harder to be middle class in this country, especially with things like student loans and prices getting higher. I think that the rich are getting richer and the middle class are becoming less and less so. I don't think that is good because I think we should have a strong middle class.

The statement above was made by Chloe, a Millennial focus group participant in Washington, D.C., in response to a question about her biggest economic concern. Another Millennial focus group participant from the same group, Tara, said the following in response to the same question:

> I guess the Baby Boomer Generation, they don't really get it. They came from an era where they could graduate high school and still get a government job . . . I'm in the midst of trying to find a new job because what I am currently doing is not paying . . . I'm looking

for postings for jobs saying, "You must have five years of experience. You must have a bachelor's degree. Starting pay is $12.50." You can't live off of $12.50 . . . That's not middle class, that's poor.

These quotes capture the sentiments and struggles of many Millennials. This cohort has faced a number of challenges in their young lives, which often discourages their outlook about job security, wages, cost of education, debt, and their overall opportunity to pursue the "American Dream."

Millennials have been launched into the workplace in the midst and aftermath of the Great Recession. Despite being the most educated generation in US history (White House 2014), they have higher rates of unemployment—an average of 9.9% since 2000, compared to a combined average of 4.6% for other age groups (Mislinkski 2015). Disparities are even greater for Millennial racial minorities. At the peak of unemployment in 2010, the rate for young African Americans was 30%—more than twice as high as the peak unemployment rate for young whites at 14% (Carnevale, Hanson, and Gulish 2013). This disparity across racial groups is unfortunately not new in the United States; however, it has deeper implications given the racial and ethnic diversity of the Millennial Generation (Allison 2017). Even though many African American and Latino Millennials do not come from low-income families, they continue to face systemic discrimination that limits their economic opportunity (Allison 2017). We explore economic disparities *among* Millennials further in the book.

Beyond unemployment, Millennials are also more underemployed than the greater adult population (Fottrell 2014b) with rates on the rise— 51% in 2016, compared to 41% in 2013 (Stahl 2016). Millennial median earnings in comparison to older generations when they were young have remained flat, by some accounts, and decreased, by others. Studies of Millennial income levels in comparison to other generations shows that "young adult workers today earn $10,000 less than young adults in 1989, a decline of 20 percent" (Allison 2017: 6). As a result of lack of growth in median incomes, poverty is on the rise: 16% of Millennials were in poverty in 2013, compared to 13% of Generation Xers in 1995, 12% of late Baby Bloomers in 1986, and 8% of early Baby Boomers in 1979 (Pew Research Center 2014c). In addition to downward trends in earnings and wealth, Millennials hold about one-third of the growing $1.2 trillion student loan debt of the nation (Federal Reserve Bank of New York). Nearly seven in ten college seniors in 2014 had student loan debt, averaging $28,950 (The Institute for College Access and Success 2014a). This debt considerably limits many Millennials' abilities to meet their basic needs, make big purchases like cars and homes, and save for retirement (American Student Assistance 2013). We do not need to look much further than the quotes from "Chloe" and "Tara" above to observe the reality of employment, wage, and debt statistics on Millennials.

The economic conditions Millennials are facing have consequences for years to come. Many Millennials have delayed their adulthood (Thompson 2012) or slipped into protracted development period which some term "emerging adulthood" (Arnett 2000). More Millennials are living with their parents, putting off marriage, and delaying having children (Grose 2014; Pew Research Center 2014a; P. Taylor 2014; White House 2014; Matthews 2015). Moreover, research shows that adverse economic conditions experienced during early adulthood are important determinants of future career success and lifetime earnings (Oreopoulos, Wachter, and Heisz 2012). For new college graduates entering the labor force in an economic downturn, losses can persist as workers settle for less than ideal career options that, in turn, affect their earnings and ability to climb up the occupational ladder (Carnevale, Hanson, and Gulish 2013: 25).

In the face of economic crisis, Millennials have exhibited resilient optimism and have called for expansion of equality and opportunity. Despite current economic hardships, they are optimistic about their financial futures, saying that they feel they can move up the socioeconomic ladder (Pew Research Center 2014a; White House 2014). According to a USA TODAY/Rock the Vote Poll of 18–34 year olds, 30% of white Millennials strongly agree that they will be more successful professionally than the previous generation (Page and Ung 2016). This optimism is even higher among minority groups; 34% of African Americans and 32% of Hispanics believe the same. While adults of all ages are lamenting the supposed death of the American dream, Millennials are more upbeat and are reinventing what the American dream means for their generation (Kadlec 2014; Baer and Penn 2015). This is precisely the message of hope for the future touted by presidential candidate Bernie Sanders on the campaign trail that resonated so well with this cohort (The Nation 2016).

Millennials see economic issues coupled with marked inequalities (the unemployment rates for minorities mentioned above are one example).

In response, they are helping shape political and community responses to socioeconomic inequalities. As this generation's diversity demonstrates, Millennials are more aware of the need for policies to address and prevent discrimination (Joint Economic Committee 2014); members of this cohort are more likely to experience discrimination, or know someone who experiences discrimination, first hand. Their education, liberalness, and worldview also makes it more likely that they will support government intervention to fight discrimination. The same rationale holds true for other types of responses to inequalities and social justice issues such as poverty, healthcare, minimum wage, equal pay, and the environment (Joint Economic Committee 2014; The Opportunity Agenda 2014; Thompson 2015). Not only do these issues matter to Millennials, but this cohort is finding new ways to express their support for them (Dalton 2016). We discuss these issues throughout the book and evaluate how the Millennial Generational frame affects issue preferences and how these priorities may shape public policy.

Toward a "Political" Story of Millennials

The United States' forty-fourth president, Barack Obama, is a great symbol of a rapidly diversifying America. As Paul Taylor (2014: 89) noted, ". . . no racial label neatly fits our sitting president." This description can also apply to many Millennials. Obama is not a Millennial, but he has been described as the "Millennia president." This moniker applies, not only because he made strong efforts to connect with this group through their preferred tools of communication (e.g., he used a "selfie stick" to promote Obamacare) but also due to the high number of young people who were politically energized by his presidential campaigns in 2008 and 2012 (Winograd and Hais 2017). In part, Millennial support for candidate Obama was not surprising since this cohort is at the forefront of demographic changes.

Political observer and author Ronald Brownstein says that Democrats now represent the "coalition of transformation," which includes minorities, Millennials, and liberal educated whites—those that are largely comfortable with demographic change. Conversely, he notes that Republicans "champion a competing coalition of restoration"—made up mostly of blue-collar, older, religious, and non-urban whites—who are uneasy with demographic diversity (Brownstein 2016). The dichotomy is further supported by the fact that increased partisanship along racial and ethnic cleavages have coincided with growing divisions across ideology and age (P. Taylor 2014). This political reality serves as the backdrop for our narrative about the *politics* of Millennials.

This study examines the political opinions and policy preferences of the Millennial Generation as compared to older adults. The analyses presented are contingent on age. Age marks stages of life and cohort or generational membership. Both life cycle and generational effects are important to political beliefs and behavior. Life cycle effects "refer to the social, psychological, and physical changes that take place as individuals age" (Erkulwater 2012: 200). These changes are considered to be sequential, irreversible, and mostly universal (Braungart and Braungart 1986). The progression to each stage of life is associated with a particular set of orientations, needs, and interests that are often in conflict with other age cohorts. When life cycle effects are at play, differences between age groups are for the most part due to their positions in the life cycle. Generational or cohort effects, on the other hand, arise from "shared social and historical experiences of those who were born during the same era" (Erkulwater 2012: 203). A generation is not simply a cohort of individuals born during the same set of years; rather, a generation also shares a "consciousness as a unique age group with a distinct set of attitudes and behavior" (Braungart and Braungart 1986: 213). This distinctive consciousness is "fueled by differences in the political, social, economic, and/or cultural influences that different cohorts experience in their formative or impressionable years—typically identified as the years from late adolescence through early adulthood" (Dinas and Stoker 2014: 4).

While life cycle and generational effects are at play when we consider political opinion and behavior, the two cannot be neatly separated. What forms generational identity is contingent on life cycle as well as the events that take place to shape shared beliefs and values[8] (Erkulwater 2012). The young and old "may react in different ways to the same societal event, not merely because they differ in life stage, but also because their different cohort membership conditions the ways in which life stages are experienced" (Riley 1973: 41). Age, therefore, shapes the way events are experienced by a group through stages of life *and* generational effects.

In this study, we are interested in identifying what defines the Millennial Generation's political attitudes and policy preferences. We recognize that much of the cohort effect associated with this age group is dependent on life cycle. For example, the recent economic recession had a profound impact on this age cohort because of their stage of life. Entering into the job market during the worse economic recession since the Great Depression influenced their experience associated with this event in ways that are distinct from older adults. We are interested in drawing comparisons between Millennials and older adults but not in making generalizations across all generations. This study is not a generational analysis—we do not undertake systematic analyses of Millennials in comparison to Generation X, Baby Boomers, or the Silent Generation. We occasionally use such comparisons to illustrate how beliefs on a particular issue varies across generations, but our interest centers on drawing distinctions between Millennials and older adults (of all generations). Our research design creates a foundation by which the politics of the Millennial Generation can be understood and examined overtime in future work. Millennials, as the youngest adult cohort, have only recently emerged from their formative years. It will take time, and the collection of panel data, to determine if this cohort or generational effect persists to become what some scholars call a true "political generation"—one not only bound together by a shared age-group consciousness but also mobilized to act as a force for political change (Braungart and Braungart 1986: 217).

This chapter has introduced the Millennial Generation persona and detailed the characteristics and circumstances that have contributed to its development. This discussion has highlighted how the Millennial identity shapes the political attitudes, policy preferences, and modes of participation or engagement for this age cohort. We discuss important and distinguishable traits including diversity, minority identity, political ideology, economic hardship, and cosmopolitanism and collectivist worldview to make the case for how the Millennial generational imprint is likely to transcend age-only effects on their political outlook. Here, we also define the parameters of our analyses. We discuss the fact that we do not undertake a systematic comparison of Millennials to other specific generational cohorts; rather, we consider the Millennial Generation in relation to other adults.

Chapter 2 outlines the concepts and measures of the Millennial Generation persona that we focus on throughout the remainder of the book. In this chapter, we also detail and describe the data, including original surveys and focus groups, as well as the statistical models and methods we utilize to test how this persona shapes political attitudes and policy preferences. In Chapters 3 through 8, we focus on specific issues to analyze these attitudinal differences in preferences, not only between Millennials and non-Millennials but also across Millennial subgroups. Specifically, Chapter 3 looks at issues related to the economy; Chapter 4 examines the politics of education; Chapter 5 explores foreign policy attitudes; Chapter 6 deals with the issue of immigration; Chapter 7 tackles attitudes about climate change; and Chapter 8 focuses on social issues such as gun control, legalization of marijuana, and abortion rights. In Chapter 9, we address how well Millennials are engaged in the political process, paying particular attention to the 2016 presidential election. Here we focus on participation in the contest, opinions about the candidates, and overall sentiments about the political system. Finally, in Chapter 10, we return to the overarching question of how Millennials matter politically and how their attitudes, preferences, and levels of engagement affect the current and future US political landscape. In each of these chapters, we draw on research across an array of fields in an effort to gauge, in a broad sense, what the politics of Millennials entails. We further rely on a mixed-method approach (quantitative survey data analyses, focus group text, and observational analyses) to discuss our narrative. We believe this approach allows us to present a more comprehensive story. The result, we hope, is a parsimonious picture of Millennials and their influence on the US political landscape that will appeal to both the novice and expert political (and generational) observer.

CHAPTER 2

Studying the Politics of the Millennial Generation

The Millennial Generation has a set of shared values and experiences that collectively comprise a unique persona, identity, or frame. While this identity is not the equivalent of minority group identity where a specific set of values, issue priorities, and policy preferences may be assigned based on shared group interests, it is as real and relevant as race and gender in understanding group differences (Campbell et al. 2015). This chapter outlines how we approach measuring and studying the Millennial Generation identity or persona (we use these terms interchangeably), detailing the basic model we use throughout the book to test differences in attitudes between Millennials and non-Millennials, as well as among subgroups of Millennials. We present this chapter as the blueprint for exploring Millennial political beliefs and behavior throughout the book. This chapter, unlike the others, provides technical, rather than substantive, information; it describes the details on which the statistical analyses are built. We treat it as reference in the other chapters so that we are not redundant in the discussion of our model, data, or methods. To overview its contents, we begin with a discussion of the model we adopt to trace the influence of the Millennial Generation persona on political beliefs and attitudes. We then turn to detailing the data and methods, including surveys and focus groups, we use throughout the book to explore these beliefs and attitudes. This dovetails into an overview of how we measure the variables identified in the model, which we carefully outline. We also briefly present descriptive statistics on these variables. Finally, we discuss the analyses undertaken in this book. We provide an overview of the methods (quantitative and qualitative) and conclude with the topic areas of the chapters, which were driven by Millennial, and non-Millennial rank importance of political issues. Before getting into these discussions, we take a step back to provide a brief note on terminology.

A Brief Note on Millennial Terminology

In this book, we refer to members of the Millennial Generation as Millennials. This indicates that these individuals were born around 1980 through the late 1990s. The ambiguity of "around 1980" reflects, as we will detail later in this chapter, that some of our measures capture the start of the Millennial Generation as birth year 1980, while other data consider 1982 to be the start date. In our case, this is a product of data availability, but it also illustrates the general fluidity of generational assignments (Lyons and Kuron 2014). We will detail the specific year we assign to the measurement of the Millennial Generation in the variable coding section of this chapter, but it suffices to say that throughout this book, the term "Millennial" refers to an individual born around 1980 through 1997 or 1998. The end of the year range varies because survey respondents must be 18 years old to participate, and the surveys we use were collected across two years: 2015 and 2016.

"Non-Millennials" is the term we use to designate older adults, born before the 1980s. This term encompasses Generation X, Baby Boomers, and the Silent Generation. As we explain in Chapter 1, this project does not engage in a systematic inter-generational analysis. Instead, we are interested in tracing how Millennials are distinct from older adults in general; therefore, we combine all older adults into one category.[1] Note also that we routinely use the term "non" to refer to any individuals not within the specified group; you can consider it to mean "all others." We also frequently use the term "Millennial subgroup" to designate groups of individuals among Millennials distinguished typically by race/ethnicity but also other characteristics such as economic hardship.

Modeling the Millennial Generation Persona

As illustrated in Figure 2.1, Millennials have shared several formative events and trends. Chief among these are the 9/11 terrorist attacks, protracted war in the Middle East, and the Great Recession. Governance

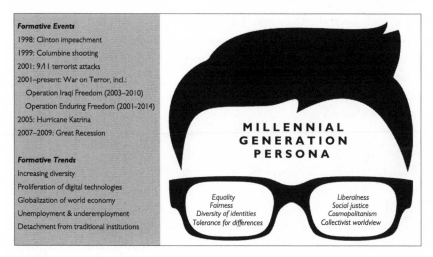

Formative Events

1998: Clinton impeachment

1999: Columbine shooting

2001: 9/11 terrorist attacks

2001–present: War on Terror, incl.:

   Operation Iraqi Freedom (2003–2010)

   Operation Enduring Freedom (2001–2014)

2005: Hurricane Katrina

2007–2009: Great Recession

Formative Trends

Increasing diversity

Proliferation of digital technologies

Globalization of world economy

Unemployment & underemployment

Detachment from traditional institutions

MILLENNIAL GENERATION PERSONA

Equality
Fairness
Diversity of identities
Tolerance for differences

Liberalness
Social justice
Cosmopolitanism
Collectivist worldview

FIGURE 2.1.   The Millennial Generation Persona

failures, including the Clinton impeachment and Hurricane Katrina, have also riddled the landscape of their formative years. In their lifetimes, Millennials have been part of increasing racial and ethnic diversity. As the most diverse adult population in US history, one in three Millennials identify as a race/ethnic minority (Pew Research Center 2015e). Millennials are also "digital natives" and have grown up in an era that has witnessed the global proliferation of technology, thereby making their world a much more connected and smaller place. This is coupled with the globalization of trade and economics. On the economic front, Millennials experienced (and are continuing to feel) the effects of the Great Recession. Many Millennials were entering the labor force at the onset of the economic recession, and many have entered in its aftermath. This has been directly linked to this age cohort's unemployment (particularly during the recession) and now underemployment. Beyond economic trends, Millennials have been a part of the general social and political tendency toward detachment from traditional institutions. While for older adults this has been a slow decline, it is the norm for most Millennials. This includes detachment to the traditional, mainstream political parties as well as political and religious institutions such as voting and attending church, respectively.

Collective social, economic, and political experiences have contributed, as we detailed in Chapter 1, to shared values among Millennials.

This includes values of equality and fairness as well as respect for a diversity of identities and tolerance for differences. These values are undoubtedly tied to their diversity; simply being part of the Millennial Generation means that one is exposed to an array of racial and ethnic identities as well as sexual orientations and views of the world (Kott 2014). This experience, along with Millennials' connectedness to the world, contributes to their political liberalness, sense of social justice, as well as cosmopolitanism and collectivist worldview. As Zogby and Kuhl (2013) note, Millennials' "frame of reference is so much larger than the world of other cohorts" (location 285).[2] For this age cohort, the world is at their fingertips (quite literally at the stroke of the keyboard or a swipe of the smartphone); they are more likely to feel like they are "citizens of the world." This cosmopolitanism is associated with a more open and accepting viewpoint on political issues. It also exposes them to the experiences of the less fortunate, the persecuted, the suffering in our country and across the world, which likely reinforces their political liberalness and collectivist worldview. Despite being detached from traditional political institutions and witnessing the failures of government in their lifetimes across multiple issues, they are more likely to see government as a platform or tool for positive change.

To capture these experiences and shared values, we model the Millennial Generation persona as being comprised of the following measureable attributes: diversity and minority group identity, liberal political ideology, economic hardship, cosmopolitanism, and collectivist worldview. We also include a measure of simply being in the Millennial Generation as not all enumerated attributes may fully capture the influence of being part of this age cohort. Modeling the key characteristics of the Millennial Generation persona separately from the measure of being part of this age cohort also allows us to determine if these characteristics have significant influences independent of the collective persona and how they may affect the beliefs of non-Millennials. In some cases, older adults and Millennials share a characteristic, and it drives certain beliefs or behavior. We also include in the model several control variables, including education, income, gender, and marital status, as they are known to influence political attitudes. We discuss the coding of each variable in the model in more detail later in the chapter. Now we turn to an overview of the data used to study Millennials in this book.

Data: National Surveys & Millennial Focus Groups

We rely on surveys and focus groups to explore the influence of the Millennial Generation persona on political attitudes and beliefs as well as compare Millennials to non-Millennials. We predominately use an original survey that we developed and executed in November 2015. The survey was conducted online and included a panel recruited by Qualtrics[3] with quotas to make the sample nationally representative. We matched US Census figures for gender, race/ethnicity, and region, but not age—we purposively oversampled Millennials. A total of 1,251 responses were collected; 621 (49.6%) were Millennials and 630 (50.4%) were non-Millennials. Given that we oversampled Millennials in our survey, we employ a weight to calibrate the sample so that it equals the general population distribution of age groups. This is an appropriate tool for non-probability samples (Baker et al. 2013). However, we recognize that this adjustment at best reduces, but does not eliminate, bias inherent to opt-in panels such as the Qualtrics panels we rely upon for our survey data.

We chose online quota-based sampling because it was cost-efficient, quick to implement, easy to replicate (Hays, Honghu Liu, and Arie Kapteyn 2015), and provided the sample size we needed. Moreover, the sample we created through the quotas specified produced a sample size with a sufficient number of observations to compare trends between Millennials and non-Millennials, as well as among Millennial subgroups, which is critical to our study. While this method of sampling provided such benefits, non-probabilistic sampling has limitations.

The reliance on quota sampling, rather than random sampling, means it is not possible to calculate margins of error for our data that provide a measure of precision. Therefore, we risk introducing unknown sampling biases into the survey estimates (Battaglia 2008). While the respondents may match the demographic, regional, and age quotas we specified, we recognize the survey sample may be different than the larger population on characteristics not controlled for in the quotas (Baker et al. 2013; Kennedy et al. 2016).[4]

The online survey took approximately twenty minutes to complete and included questions on the respondent's background—age, gender, marital status, education, income, employment status, religious affiliation—as well as questions on policy issues. The policy areas queried included: the economy, education, healthcare, foreign policy, the environment, immigration, gun control, abortion, and minimum wage. Beyond stances and policy preferences across these areas, respondents were asked to identify the most important issue facing their generation and indicate how important each issue is to their vote in the presidential election. They were also prompted to rank the importance of issues within a specific area (i.e., unemployment, federal government debt, income inequality, and retirement security among economic issues). Questions about political ideology, party affiliation, and political engagement were also posed. The full survey questionnaire is available in Appendix 2.A.

Given the unprecedented nature of the 2016 presidential election, we launched a second original, online survey in November 2016. Again, we relied on Qualtrics for the survey panel and specified the same demographic and regional quotas as the 2015 survey. Like the first survey, we oversampled Millennials; 667 Millennials and 583 non-Millennials completed the survey for a total of 1,250 respondents. This survey replicated questions about the respondent's background and also included a question asking respondents to identify the most important issue facing their generation. The majority of the questions in this survey were focused on the election—voter turnout, reasons for not voting, presidential candidate choice, reasons for candidate choice. Questions were also asked about the level of support for policies proposed by the Trump campaign on issues of trade, immigration, foreign policy, and climate change. The full questionnaire for this post-election survey is available in Appendix 2.B.

In addition to these two surveys, we also employ data from a survey commissioned by the University of Maryland's Center for American Politics and Citizenship in partnership with the Anwar Sadat Chair for Peace and Development. The survey, conducted in May 2016, consists of a probability-based representative sample recruited by Nielsen Scarborough. The panel was drawn from Nielsen's larger probability-based national panel, which was recruited by mail and telephone using a random sample of households provided by Survey Sampling International. A total of 1,580 panelists completed the survey including a national sample of 845 adults plus an oversample of 735 Millennials (18–34), resulting in a total Millennial sample of 863. The margins of error (MoE) for the national sample and for Millennials is: national—845 respondents, MoE 3.4%; Millennial (18–34 years of age)—863 respondents, MoE 3.3%. Responses were weighted by age, gender, income, education, race, and geographic region using benchmarks from the US Census. The survey was also weighted by partisan identification, and Millennials were down-weighted consistent with these groups' incidence rate in the US Census. The questions we use from the Nielsen survey are provided in Appendix 2.C.

To complement these surveys, we conducted focus groups of Millennials in four cities: Los Angeles, California; New Orleans, Louisiana; San Antonio, Texas; and Washington, DC. We chose these four cities for their population size (large, urban areas), variance in general ideological leanings, and geographic location—dispersed across the United States. In each city, we ran two focus groups that lasted two hours and explored the following themes: political engagement, the 2016 presidential race, the economy, education, healthcare, the environment, foreign policy, immigration, and social issues. We conducted the focus groups in a semi-structured format, asking specific questions to prompt conversation on particular topics and then guiding discussions among the participants. In general, we asked participants to describe the issues they care about and why. The questionnaire we used to guide the focus group discussions is provided in Appendix 2.D.

Participants were recruited predominately through Craigslist[5] and were compensated $50 for their travel expense and time. The focus groups took place on college campuses in each city. To qualify for participation, individuals had to be at least 18 years old and complete a screener survey that provided us with information on their background. We accepted almost every interested individual who qualified (a few were put on a "back-up" list because the group size got too big).

The focus groups varied in size, ranging from three to eleven individuals and averaging eight participants. The number of participants in each city totaled: fifteen in New Orleans, thirteen in Los Angeles, eleven in San Antonio, and twenty-one in Washington, DC. Figure 2.2 reports the percentage these subtotals comprise of the whole focus group sample, as well as the race and ethnic breakdown of each city's focus group subsample. The majority of the focus groups in Los Angeles and San Antonio were Latino, while the New Orleans groups were predominantly white. Notably, the New Orleans group had a substantial number of participants (four in total) identifying as "other race," many specifying "mixed race" as their race/ethnic identity. The majority of the Washington, DC group was African American, followed by white. In this group, there were also a few Asian

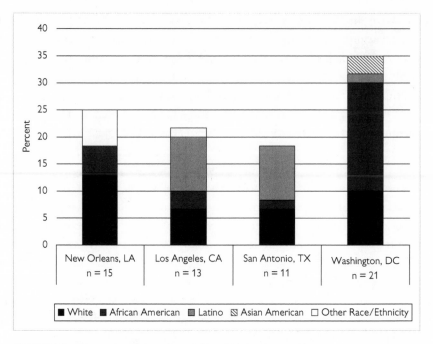

FIGURE 2.2.   Focus Group Locations & Race/Ethnic Composition

Note: The stacked bars represent the race/ethnic composition of focus groups in each location. The height of the bars indicates the number of respondents in each location.

American participants. A notable 15% of the focus group participants (across all groups) were also born outside the United States.

Beyond race and ethnicity, there were an equal number of females and males participating in the focus groups (thirty and thirty, respectively). The ages of the participants ranged from 19 (birth year of 1997) to 36 (birth year of 1980); the median age was 26 years. Twenty percent of the focus group participants reported being unemployed, while 36.7% said they worked part time (less than forty hours per week) and 43.3% worked full time (forty hours or more per week). The majority (57%) reported an annual income less than $50,000; however, it is not clear if participants were referring to a household of their own or as part of their parents. With regard to education levels, 17.8% had completed an Associate's degree, high school, or only some high school. A third had completed some college, while 40% had earned a Bachelor's degree and 8.9% had a Master's degree. The majority of the participants were also single and never married (75.6%).

With regards to political affiliation, 11.7% considered themselves to be a Republican, while 41.7% considered themselves to be Democrats. Another 23.3% said they were Independent, 20% reported not having a party affiliation, and another 3% said "other" (i.e., Libertarian Party). On the political ideology scale, 70.7% of focus group participants placed themselves on the liberal side of the scale ("extremely liberal," "liberal," or "slightly liberal"). Another 19% said they were "moderate; middle of the road," and only 10.3% identified as "slightly conservative" or "conservative." None identified as "extremely conservative." In addition to being predominantly liberal, the majority of focus group participants also reported being registered to vote.

Taken together, the surveys and focus group data we employ in this book provide us with comprehensive information to examine in depth the Millennial Generation by comparing them to older adults and evaluating subgroups within the age cohort. The surveys allow us to see trends across a large, representative sample of individuals, and the focus groups offer nuanced substance to flesh out these relationships. We use this data for mixed-method analyses, a topic we turn to after discussing variable measurement.

Measurement: Variables to Proxy the Millennial Generation Persona

As discussed at the beginning of this chapter, we model the Millennial Generation persona as comprised of multiple characteristics including: diversity and minority group identity, liberal political ideology, economic hardship, cosmopolitanism, and a collectivist worldview. We adopt multiple variables to capture this, all of which are detailed in Table 2.1. Descriptive statistics of these variables are available in Appendix 2.E; correlation matrices of the variables are available in the Online Appendices, available at https://doi.org/10.3998/mpub.9526877.fulcrum (Appendix 2.A). Our survey, conducted post-election in November 2016, is not detailed in Table 2.1 or these appendices because the variables analyzed are different from this base model. Details on variable coding of this survey will be presented in Chapter 9, where it is used to analyze Millennial political engagement. For the analysis of political engagement, we also use a variety of measures from

TABLE 2.1. Variable Coding & Source

Variable	Survey Question	Coding	Survey Source
Millennial	What year were you born?	1 = Born 1980–1997 0 = Born before 1980	Original survey, 2015
	What year were you born?	1 = Born 1980–1998 0 = Born before 1980	Original survey, 2016
	How old are you?	1 = 18–34 years 0 = 35 years and older	Nielsen survey, 2016
Latino	Are you of Hispanic or Latino background?	1 = Yes 0 = No	Original survey, 2015
	Which of the following describes your ethnic background best?	1 = Hispanic 0 = Other	Nielsen survey, 2016
African American	What is your race?	1 = African American 0 = Other	Original survey, 2015
	Which of the following describes your ethnic background best?	1 = Black or African American 0 = Other	Nielsen survey, 2016
Foreign Ties	Were you born in the United States or a US territory or in another country?	1 = Born in another country 0 = Born in US/US territory	Original survey, 2015
	Do you have relatives, including distant relatives, who reside outside of the United States?	1 = Yes 0 = No	Nielsen survey, 2016
Unemployed	Are you currently employed?	1 = No 0 = Work part- or full-time	Original survey, 2015
Negative Economic Outlook	Thinking about the national economy, do you believe our country is better or worse off than it was twenty years ago for people of your age?	1 = Worse 2 = About the same or better	Original survey, 2015

Liberal Ideology	Here is a 7-point scale on which the political views that people might hold are arranged from extremely liberal to extremely conservative. Where would you place yourself on this scale or haven't you thought much about this?	1 = Liberal (1–3: extremely liberal, liberal, and slightly liberal) 0 = Non-liberal (4–7: moderate, slightly conservative, conservative, and extremely conservative)	Original survey, 2015
	Generally speaking, do you think of yourself as a Republican, Democrat, Independent, other, or no preference? For Independent, other, and no preference – Do you think of yourself as closer to the Republican Party, Democratic Party, or neither?	1 = Republican/ Republican Party 0 = Other	Nielsen survey, 2016
Cosmopolitan Identity	In terms of what's important about you, how much do you identify with being a citizen of the world?	0 "Not at all" to 10 "very strongly"	Nielsen survey, 2016
Positive Government Worldview	For the following pair of statements, select the one that most closely aligns (agrees) with your personal opinion. 1. Cutting government spending is the only way to change our economic outlook OR more government spending is needed to alleviate the economic hardships Americans are suffering. 2. Healthcare coverage is best left up to individuals to decide OR the government should require that all individuals have healthcare. 3. The government should leave it up to the free market to determine healthcare costs OR the government should do more to reduce the costs of healthcare to individuals. 4. Individuals should have to pay back all the student loan debt they incurred OR the government should forgive all student loans.	Factor score where higher values indicate greater belief in the positive role of government	Original survey, 2015
Female	What is your gender?	1 = Female	Original survey, 2015
	Reported sex of respondent	0 = Male	Nielsen survey, 2016
Married	What is your marital status?	1 = Married or in a domestic partnership/ civil union 0 = Widowed, divorced, separated, or never married	Original survey, 2015

(continued)

TABLE 2.1. (continued)

Variable	Survey Question	Coding	Survey Source
Education	What is the highest degree or level of school that you have completed?	1 = Less than high school 2 = Some high school 3 = High school 4 = Some college 5 = Associate's degree 6 = Bachelor's degree 7 = Master's degree 8 = Professional or doctoral degree	Original survey, 2015
	Reported respondent level of education	1 = Grade school (8th grade or less) 2 = Some high school 3 = High school graduate 4 = Some college 5 = College graduate 6 = Some postgraduate 7 = Postgraduate degree	Nielsen survey, 2016
Income	Last year, that is, from January 1, 2014 to December 31, 2014, what was your total family income from all sources, before taxes?	1 = Less than $20,000 2 = $20,000 to under $30,000 3 = $30,000 to under $50,000 4 = $50,000 to under $75,000 5 = $75,000 to under $100,000 6 = $100,000+	Original survey, 2015
	Reported household income	1 = Less than $10,000 2 = $10,000–$19,999 3 = $20,000–$24,999 4 = $25,000–$29,999 5 = $30,000–$34,999 6 = $35,000–$39,999 7 = $40,000–$44,999 8 = $45,000–$49,999 9 = $50,000–$74,999 10 = $75,000–$99,999 11 = $100,000–$149,999 12 = $150,000–$249,999 13 = $250,000 or more	Nielsen survey, 2016

the 2015 survey that are not detailed here. Rather, for these as well as any other variables beyond the scope of this base model, we describe the coding in the chapter examining that particular information.

The first measure is the most basic, but fundamental, of the Millennial Generation persona—a variable that signifies if one is a member of the Millennial Generation or is a non-Millennial. This variable is created from survey respondents' birth year for our original surveys (Millennials are those born 1980–1997/1998). Age range was used for the Nielsen survey—ages 18–34 years are considered Millennials. Also central to the Millennial Generation is diversity. To measure this as it specifically relates to minority group identity, we rely on dummy variables that indicate if the respondent is Latino and/or African American. We do not include Asian American or other race/ethnic identities in our model because the number of observations were too few to make sound assumptions about statistical results that would include these variables. In addition to race and ethnicity, we include a measure of diversity that captures exposure to foreign countries (and presumably their ideas, cultures, and values). For our original surveys, this measure is a dummy variable reporting if the respondent is foreign born. The Nielsen survey variable indicates if the respondent has family that lives in a foreign country.

Beyond diversity, economic hardship is a critical part of the shared experiences of Millennials. To reflect this, we adopt one objective and one subjective measure. The objective measure is self-reported unemployment. This is a dummy variable with the positive values indicating that the respondent does not work; this includes part-time (less than forty hours per week) and full-time (at least forty hours per week) employment. The subjective measure asks respondents—*Thinking about the national economy, do you believe our country is better or worse off than it was twenty years ago for people of your age?* We code responses of "worse off" as indicative of a negative economic outlook; responses of "about the same" or "better" are combined into the other category. These questions were asked only in our original surveys (2015 and 2016); similar measures were not available in the Nielsen survey.

To measure liberal political ideology, we created a liberal dummy variable from responses to a question asking individuals to place themselves on a liberal–conservative, (7-point) scale. Responses of "extremely liberal," "liberal," and "slightly liberal," were collapsed into one category while responses of "moderate; middle of the road," "slightly conservative," "conservative," and "extremely conservative" comprised the other category. This measure was available in our original surveys but not in the Nielsen survey. In the latter, we rely on political party affiliation as a proxy for liberal ideology. Respondents were asked if they identified as a Republican, Democrat, Independent, or with another party—or if they have no preference or no party affiliation. Those who responded Independent, other, and no preference were asked a follow-up question—*Do you think of yourself as closer to the Republican Party, Democratic Party, or neither?* We created a conservative (not liberal) dummy variable based on responses to these two-party affiliation questions; individuals who responded Republican are coded into one category, while all other responses are coded into the other category. Because Millennials are more likely to be Independents and lean liberal (Pew Research Center 2016b), we deliberately chose to isolate what liberals are not—Republican. The other category is arguably comprised of a range of liberal leaning ideologies.

To measure cosmopolitanism or a feeling of being a citizen of the world, we use responses to the survey question—*In terms of what's important about you, how much do you identify with being a citizen of the world?* Respondents were instructed to select a number on a 0 to 10 point scale where 0 indicates "not at all" and 10 correspond to "very strongly." The resulting measure is an eleven-category variable with higher values indicating greater cosmopolitanism. This question was only asked in the Nielsen survey and our original 2016 survey. For our original survey conducted in 2015, we pivot to a measure of collectivist worldview.

Recall that collectivist worldview is tightly coupled with cosmopolitan identity. It places importance on the larger collective and positions society as a whole paramount to individual interest and responsible for securing shared welfare (Oyserman 1993; Tieku 2012). Those with a collectivist worldview see the government playing a pivotal role in that mission. Given the importance placed on the role of government for those with a collectivist worldview, we measure this set of values using survey questions that place responsibility on the government to provide for the collective. This is appropriate because the analyses of this book focus on policy issues—all related to government action (or inaction). Four survey questions are used to capture this. They address government spending, healthcare coverage, healthcare cost, and student loan forgiveness. Each question presents a set of statements to the respondent and instructs—*Select the one that most closely aligns (agrees) with your personal opinion.* The specific statements are listed in Table 2.1. Note that one of each pair of statements clearly indicates support of government action to solve collective problems (e.g., more spending to alleviate economic hardship, requirement for health-care, reduce costs for healthcare, and forgiven student loans). We use prin-cipal components factor analysis to estimate the degree to which these four items represent a single dimension of pro-government attitudes. All four variables load onto one dimension; therefore, we use a factor score as a measure of this concept, labeled "positive government worldview." See Appendix 2.F for more details on the factor analysis.

In addition to these measures that are specific to the Millennial Generation persona, we include a set of control variables that are likely to influence political and policy attitudes and beliefs. We include measures of education and income, as both represent key components of individual Socioeconomic Status (SES). SES is argued to be an important driver of political engagement (Rosenstone and Hanson 2002) and is also related to individual political ideology—more educated individuals tend to be liberal (Pew Research Center 2016b)—and various stances on policy issues. In our original surveys (2015 and 2016), education is measured across eight categories, ranging from less than high school education to obtainment of a professional degree or PhD. Income is measured across six categories, ranging from less than $20,000 annual income to greater than $100,000 annual income. The Nielsen survey's education variable has seven catego-ries, ranging from grade school (8th grade or less) education to completion of a postgraduate degree. Income in the Nielsen survey is measured across thirteen categories of annual income, ranging from less than $10,000 to $250,000 or more.

We also control for gender and marital status as both have been shown to influence a range of policy stances. Gender measures are available in all surveys; marital status is only measured in our original surveys (2015 and 2016). For decades public opinion polls and studies have shown that there is a gender gap in politics. Women tend to vote more Democratic than men, and they tend to support more government activism on issues to help the poor, elderly, and children as well as to protect the environment, while men tend to express more concern over economic issues (Pew Research Center 2012a). These policy preferences align with traditional roles of women as caretakers and men as breadwinners. Married individuals typically support conservative policy stances and affiliate to higher degrees with the Republican Party (Abramowitz and Saunders 2006). While we control for these characteristics, we are uncertain regarding their influence on Millennial Generation political beliefs. In many ways, gender roles—and, relatedly, marital dynamics—have been reshaped by the Millennial Generation. Millennials "neither support women's return to traditional roles nor specified male/female roles in society, and they *expect* progress toward equalization of genders to continue" (Shushok and Kidd 2015: 38). There is a general tolerance for self-expression and equality across gender lines among Millennials (Kott 2014; Paquette 2016), which may mean that the way gender has influenced policy preferences and public opinion for past generations is not the same for this one. For this reason, we do not explore gender identity in the same way we examine race/ethnic minority identity.

Mixed-Method Analysis: Studying the Millennial Generation's Political Attitudes

In order to comprehensively study the Millennial Generation's political attitudes, we utilize a mixed-method approach for our analyses. As detailed in the data section of this chapter, we draw on information from two original surveys with panels recruited by Qualtrics, as well as an additional survey conducted by Nielsen Scarborough. We complement this survey data with focus group interviews, designed to capture varied and in-depth opinions and experiences of the Millennial Generation. Therefore, we employ both quantitative and qualitative analyses throughout the book.

The quantitative analyses include correlations, tests of group differences (t-tests and Mann Whitney U test), and logistic regressions. Due to the oversample of Millennials in our original surveys, we created a weight to correct the samples and applied it to all statistical analyses. We aim in all our quantitative analyses to present the results in a manner that is easily understood, using predicted probabilities (rather than coefficients) and graphs (rather than regression output tables). For those interested in the raw regression results, we provide this information in appendices.

The qualitative data collected in the focus groups offer depth and richness to the relationships examined in the quantitative analyses. Focus group quotes are used throughout the book to provide context and tangible meaning to the concepts measured through the surveys and the dynamics identified in the regressions. Not only do we employ qualitative data as anecdotes but we also systematically analyze a set of open-ended survey questions on political engagement (in Chapter 9). Using a grounded theory approach, emergent themes were identified, refined, and integrated (Strauss and Corbin 1998).[6] This largely inductive process allows the data to "speak for itself," thereby contributing to theory building where conceptual relationships are lacking. This is certainly the case in the study of Millennials as they have not been sufficiently studied to comprise a shared understanding of their politics, policy preferences, and engagement attitudes. We use the software package QSR-NVivo for this qualitative analysis[7] and attempt to provide a conceptual analysis that may be used as a foundation of theory building in the future.

Conclusion: Where are we going? Outline of the Study of the Millennial Generation's Politics

To make this study of Millennial Generation politics salient, we focus our quantitative and qualitative analyses on the following policy areas: the economy, education, healthcare costs, foreign policy, immigration, the environment, minimum wage, abortion rights, and gun control. How relevant are these issues to Millennials and non-Millennials? To answer this, we turn to a question in our 2015 survey that asks respondents—*In your opinion, which of the following is the most important issue to your age group or generation?* Table 2.2 lists the results with the issues ordered for each group by most important to least important (based on frequency of response).

We see that for both Millennials and non-Millennials, the economy is most important. In fact, slightly more Millennials than older adults (32.85% versus 30.79% respectively) cite the economy as the most important issue facing their age group. As discussed in Chapter 1, the Great Recession has been a formative issue for this generation and continues to impact their well-being. We explore this in depth in Chapter 3. Millennials list education as their second priority, but healthcare is the issue that ranks next for non-Millennials. While over one in four (27.94%) older adults perceive healthcare as the most important issue facing their generation, only 7% of Millennials feel the same. Likewise, nearly three times as many Millennials prioritize education than non-Millennials (15.78% versus 5.71% respectively). Much of this reflects stage of life interests; Millennials are much closer to the issue of education because they have recently been or are students. Because older adults have completed their education, they are more consumed with family well-being, as well as issues of aging and retirement, which are linked to healthcare. We see convergence again between Millennials and non-Millennials on their third ranking; both groups see terrorism as fairly important. We examine one specific concern about healthcare—cost—in the chapter on the economy, and we explore attitudes about education in Chapter 4. While both rank terrorism third, the rankings are relative, and we see that only one in ten Millennials (10.95% to be precise) view this issue as most important while slightly more older adults (14.76%) deem it important. We analyze the issue of terrorism and foreign policy, more broadly, in Chapter 5.

Other noticeable trends in the issue ranks are the prominence of drug legalization and gay marriage among Millennials, while these issues sit at the bottom of non-Millennial priorities. This harkens to Millennial liberal tendencies and will be issues we unpack in Chapter 8. Further, it is surprising that only approximately 5% of both groups prioritize the issue

TABLE 2.2.   Rankings of Issue Importance

Which of the following is the most important issue to your age group or generation?

Millennials			Non-Millennials		
	Percent	*Frequency*		*Percent*	*Frequency*
Economy	32.85	204	Economy	30.79	194
Education	15.78	98	Healthcare	27.94	176
Terrorism	10.95	68	Terrorism	14.76	93
Drug legalization	7.73	48	Education	5.71	36
Gun control	7.57	47	Gun control	5.24	33
Healthcare	6.92	43	Immigration	5.08	32
Gay marriage	5.31	33	Environment	3.97	25
Environment	5.15	32	Drug legalization	2.86	18
Immigration	4.99	31	Other	2.38	15
Other	2.74	17	Gay marriage	1.27	8
Total	100	621	Total	100	630

Note: The data source is the authors' original survey conducted in 2015 with a panel recruited by Qualtrics.

of immigration. We must keep in mind, however, that these rankings are relative. When asked in the same 2015 survey how important the issue of immigration was to their 2016 presidential vote, 56.4% of Millennials and 65.2% of non-Millennials, as shown in Table 2.3, said "very important." President Trump launched his campaign on the issue of immigration and has made illegal immigration a priority of his administration (Time 2015; Nakamura 2017). This is particularly important for Millennials given the substantial diversity of the age cohort. To better understand this salient issue in connection to Millennials, we analyze immigration policy attitudes in Chapter 6.

The environment is another issue that ranks fairly low for both groups but is salient among Millennials, in particular. In fact, our survey results indicate that nearly the same percentage of Millennials say the environment is "very important" to their presidential vote as national security. Millennials, for a variety of reasons related to their generation persona (e.g., liberal ideology, cosmopolitanism, collectivist worldview, and diversity), are more concerned about environmental issues than older adults. We explore attitudes regarding one specific environmental issue that dominates our contemporary period—climate change—in Chapter 7.

Beyond these policy areas, the issue of political engagement is highly salient for the study of the Millennial Generation. They, like young members of generations before them, suffer from lower engagement with

TABLE 2.3.   Issue Salience for 2016 Presidential Vote

If you vote in the next presidential election, how important might the following issues be to your vote? Responses of "very important" reported.

	Millennials		Non-Millennials	
	Percent	*Frequency*	*Percent*	*Frequency*
Economy	84.38	524	86.98	548
Education	77.62	482	65.56	413
Healthcare	74.88	465	81.59	514
National security	68.6	426	78.41	494
Immigration	56.36	350	65.24	411
Environment	62.96	391	51.59	325
Gay marriage	34.46	214	22.38	141
Gun control	59.9	372	59.52	375

Note: The data source is the authors' original survey conducted in 2015 with a panel recruited by Qualtrics. The figures report the responses of "very important." The total number of Millennial respondents is 621; the total number of non-Millennials is 630.

traditional institutions, specifically voting. This, however, is not simply a youth trend but symptomatic of broader issues of detachment, distrust, and disengagement with traditional institutions, both political and non-political, among Millennials. In a time period where much of our political discourse is focused on the health of our democracy, it is critical that we better understand the dynamics of Millennials' (dis)engagement. We examine this in depth in Chapter 9.

Collectively our examination offers a first of its kind, in-depth analysis of the Millennial Generation's political attitudes and policy preferences. While many political studies have focused on the influence of group dynamics on political behavior, none to our knowledge has considered generational effects as the primary motivator. We make the case that while cohort effect is different than other identities such as race and ethnicity, it is no less meaningful to understanding group opinions (and for Millennials more so than any other adult generation, these identities are largely intertwined). We believe that this is an important endeavor as Millennials are the largest generation and the one poised to lead our nation and world in the near future. We are careful, however, not to generalize or speculate too much about the complete durability of Millennial political attitudes and preferences because we are unable to rely on longitudinal studies of this cohort to draw such conclusions (i.e., they have not aged yet). However, factors that comprise the Millennial persona and the influence they have had on formative Millennial attitudes give us confidence that many of our findings are cohort effects and not age-only influences. In the end, we feel that *The Politics of Millennials* captures the unique identity of this cohort and provides answers to such questions—why do Millennials matter politically, what are their political and policy choices, and why should current politicians and political leaders pay attention to their preferences? We invite you to read the subsequent chapters to share in these answers.

CHAPTER 3

"Children of the Great Recession:" Millennials and the Economy

During the 2016 presidential race, a leaked recording captured Hillary Clinton in a conversation with fundraisers, describing the young adults supporting Bernie Sanders. She said the following (Fang and Emmons 2016):

> They're children of the Great Recession. And they are living in their parents' basement. They feel they got their education and the jobs that are available to them are not at all what they envisioned for themselves. And they don't see much of a future. I met with a group of young black millennials today and you know one of the young women said, "You know, none of us feel that we have the job that we should have gotten out of college. And we don't believe the job market is going to give us much of a chance." So that is a mindset that is really affecting their politics. And so if you're feeling like you're consigned to, you know, being a barista, or you know, some other job that doesn't pay a lot, and doesn't have some other ladder of opportunity attached to it, then the idea that maybe, just maybe, you could be part of a political revolution is pretty appealing.

While many responded negatively to Clinton's remarks, her assessment of the economic situation of young adults in America, particularly the effect of the recent economic recession on their economic outlook and opportunities, was accurate. Millennials[1] were born during the longest period of

47

economic expansion in the twentieth century, yet they have entered the job market in the worst economic recession since the 1930s (Thompson 2012). They are the first generation "in the modern era to have higher levels of student loan debt, poverty and unemployment, and lower levels of wealth and personal income than their two immediate predecessor generations (Gen Xers and Boomers) had at the same stage of their life cycles" (Pew Research Center 2014a: 8). Even though they are the best educated generation in history, they are financially worse off than their parents were at their age (Allison 2017).[2] They are carrying unprecedented amounts of student loan debt (The Institute for College Access & Success 2014a), increasingly choosing to live at home with their parents (Fry 2016a), and putting off marriage, homeownership, and having babies (Pew Research Center 2014a; Fleming 2016).

Certainly, these factors have shaped their political perspective. Millennials see the rising economic inequalities in our country, the income and employment disparities between racial groups, as well as the crippling cost of higher education and healthcare, and they want change. This call for change was evident in their support for Bernie Sanders in the 2016 presidential race. Polls showed that more young adults favored Sanders' political and economic "revolution" (55%), centered on policies of free college and healthcare, to Hillary Clinton's incremental, traditional Democratic Party stances (38%) (Norman 2016). While Sanders' candidacy and the Democratic Party's economic agenda was not victorious in the election, the issues driving the call for change persist. Unemployment remains high among Millennials and is highest among young African Americans (US Bureau of Labor Statistics 2017). Even though they are generally optimistic about their financial futures (Pew Research Center 2012b), experts believe that the effects of the Great Recession will continue to impact this generation's earnings into the near future and will likely influence their financial capacity in the long term (Carnevale, Hanson, and Gulish 2013; Glinski 2015). This not only affects the well-being of young adults but also influences the strength of our national economy. It is important, therefore, to understand how Millennials view economic problems and the solutions they support.

As we detail in this chapter, Millennials are most concerned about unemployment and increasing economic inequality. While they are known for their liberal political leanings (Pew Research Center 2014a) and the majority championed Sanders' "revolution" (Blake 2016), we find in our analyses that Millennials are generally moderate in their economic stances. Millennials favor a middle-of-the-road approach and are a moderating voice among polarized ideological groups in the face of pressing economic problems. We believe that this is due, in part, to the formative economic experiences of this age cohort in the midst of the Great Recession. We also conjecture that this is simply part of what makes Millennials a unique and distinctive cohort. Undoubtedly, their economic decisions will shape our national economy, perhaps in ways we would not expect. To explore this more thoroughly, we begin with a discussion of the Great Recession and its effect on young adults and then pivot to examine the economic priorities among Millennials and non-Millennials. To explore these priorities further, we assess support for four specific economic policies—government spending to alleviate economic hardship, increasing the minimum wage, Social Security reform, and government action on healthcare costs. We pay particular attention to how Millennials and non-Millennials attitudes are distinct on these issues and also trace differences among Millennial subgroups.

Millennials and the Great Recession

The Great Recession, the economic downturn of the United States economy from 2007–2009,[3] was the deepest on record in terms of job losses (Rampbell 2010). Its effects were felt by adults of all ages; however, Millennials were hardest hit in terms of pay and employment rates (Thompson 2012). Unemployment peaked in 2010 for all adults but was highest for young adults (DeSilver 2015). According to our calculations of Bureau of Labor Statistics monthly data, the average unemployment rate in 2010[4] was 14.2% for Millennials, then aged 18–29 years, while older adults, 30 years and older, had an unemployment rate of 7.9%.[5] While young adults in general "have faced tough employment markets as they entered adulthood, as some Boomers did during the 1981–1982 recession, the labor market recovery for Millennials has been much less robust following the Great Recession" (Patten and Fry 2015). Although economists recognize that young adults' employment prospects are more sensitive to business cycle fluctuations (Carnevale, Hanson,

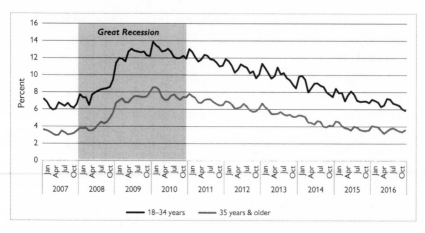

FIGURE 3.1.   Unemployment Rates for Millennials & Non-Millennials, 2007–2016

Note: Authors' calculations based on quarterly data, not seasonally adjusted, from the Bureau of Labor Statistics. Unemployment rate calculated by taking the percentage of the labor force that is unemployed as a proportion of the total civilian labor force (employed plus unemployed).

and Gulish 2013), lagging unemployment has been persistent among Millennials and is directly tied to the Great Recession.

Figure 3.1 illustrates the unemployment trends of young adults, aged 18–34 years[6] and older adults, aged 35 years and older, for the years 2007–2016. We see a steep rise in unemployment for both groups during the Great Recession and a spike at the official end of the recession period. Across the past decade, younger adults have consistently experienced higher unemployment rates than older adults. The biggest gap between the two groups occurred in May 2009 and June 2010. During these months, Millennial unemployment was nearly 6% higher than that of older adults. This gap has dwindled in the past few years, with the smallest difference between Millennials and older adults reported in December 2016.

Although Millennial unemployment rates have nearly returned to pre-recession levels, young adults remain concerned about unemployment, job competition, and the long-term effects of the Great Recession. Katie, a participant in one of the focus groups of Millennials that we conducted in San Antonio, Texas, said her biggest economic concern was jobs and the return on her educational investment. She echoes the concerns of many Millennials that have entered the job market during and in the wake of the Great Recession:

I have a degree. And how much did that degree cost and how much am I going to make now? That is a huge problem in this country. A huge problem. And what's happening is a job that, let's say, 30-40 years ago required maybe a Bachelor's [degree] now requires a Master's, and someday it will require a PhD. And you know I'm going to be graduating in May with a higher level degree, and I may not get a job because there are thousands of people that have the same exact degree that I do and we're all looking for the same job. That, in my mind, is terrifying.

For new college graduates entering the labor force in an economic down-turn, initial losses are significant and persist for 8–10 years (Glinski 2015). There are long-term effects as well, known as "cyclical downgrading," which occurs when workers settle for less than ideal career options that, in turn, affect their earnings, ability to climb up the occupational ladder, and lifetime unemployment rates (Carnevale, Hanson, and Gulish 2013). Studies of Millennial income levels in comparison to other generations show that "young adult workers today earn $10,000 less than young adults in 1989, a decline of 20 percent" (Allison 2017: 6). This is not just because they are beginning their careers but is also attributed to an inter-generational decline in wages. The catch is that to be competitive in the job market, a college degree or degrees are needed, but the payoff is less. Millennials, highly educated but strapped with unprecedented student loan debt, "earn roughly the same as young workers with no degree in the late 1980s" (Allison 2017: 7). For racial minorities, the disadvantage is even greater.

At the peak of unemployment in 2010, the rate for young whites was 14%; for young Hispanics, 20%; and for young African Americans, 30%—more than twice that of their white counterparts (Carnevale, Hanson, and Gulish 2013). This gap in incomes across racial groups is unfortunately not new in the United States. However, it has a larger impact given the considerable racial and ethnic diversity among the Millennial Generation. Moreover, the discrimination limiting young minority adults' economic opportunity persists, even for the millions of young African American and Latinos that do not come from low-income households (Allison 2017).

The Great Recession not only limited young adult earnings and employ-ment prospects but has also resulted in constraining "the ability and the inclination to take on debt among households headed by Millennials" (Buckley, Viechnicki, and Barua 2015: 9). This includes vehicle loans, home mortgages, and credit card debt. Until 2009, student loan debt had been the smallest form of household debt (excluding mortgages); since then, student loan debt has tripled (Brown et al. 2015). In 2015, about seven in ten (68%) college graduates had student loan debt, averaging $30,100—up from $17,550 in 2000 (The Institute for College Access & Success 2014b and 2016). Paying back student loan debt, in a climate where unemployment is high and incomes are low, is "the 800-pound gorilla on young adults' backs;" as a result, "young people will probably need to work for so much longer than previous generations" (Glinski 2015). In all, these income and debt patterns are shaping a generation not characterized by big spending or risk-taking when it comes to economic matters (Lee 2016). Rather, Millennials are taking the cautious route with their personal finances, and this shapes how they are living and developing into adulthood.

Saddled with student loan debt and less than ideal career opportunities, many Millennials have retreated home. They are moving back in with their parents, and a considerable portion are delaying marriage and putting off having children. According to a Pew Research Center study, 2016 marked the year when a greater percentage of young adults reported living with their parents for the first time on record (dating back to 1880) (Fry 2016a). Certainly economic conditions, particularly persistent unemployment and low wages, have contributed to this trend, as returning to the nest is a social safety net of sorts. But there are other factors influencing this behavior, including postponement of marriage (and perhaps eschewing of the institution) and general preferences by young women to live in the family home and delay having children (Fry 2016a; Steverman 2016). These evolving social norms are entangled with the economic hardships Millennials have faced. As one commentator put it (Thompson 2012): "Are they scared of adulthood? Maybe. Culture is complicated, and there are plenty of factors outside of the Great Recession that are shaping Millennials' conception of adulthood and family life. But it certainly seems like the story begins with economics." To begin unpacking how the Great Recession has affected Millennials' economic outlook, we first explore the most important economic issues among Millennials and older adults.

A Generation Gap in Economic Priorities?

Classic economic theories tell us that economic choices (and preferences) are guided by self-interest and competition (Smith 1982). Life cycle influences self-interest as the stage of life one is in determines the most salient economic issues. In many ways, the Great Recession put into sharper focus the economic needs and interests of adults in different stages of life. Young adults experienced and are continuing to deal with high rates of unemployment and low incomes, while middle-aged adults are moving forward with redefined employment, healthcare, and retirement plans (Morin 2009). These specific effects of the economic recession, as well as general stage of life influences, are likely to shape economic perceptions of both Millennials and non-Millennials.

To assess this, we turn to data collected as part of our original survey, conducted in 2015.[7] The survey asked: "Considering our country's economy, which of the following is the most important issue to your generation or age group?" Respondents were presented with six economic issues to choose from: 1) unemployment and job scarcity; 2) federal government debt; 3) cost of entitlement programs (Social Security and Medicare); 4) rising cost of education; 5) increasing gap between the wealthy, the middle class, and the poor; and 6) lack of long-term job and retirement security. The responses among Millennials and non-Millennials are shown in Figure 3.2. The group of bars to the left, shown in light gray, report non-Millennial responses, while the group of bars to the rights, shown in dark gray, indicate Millennial opinions.

As clearly shown in Figure 3.2, the top economic concern of Millennials is unemployment (31.2%). This undoubtedly reflects the unique, and somewhat unfortunate, place Millennials have in the labor market. As previously discussed, many of this age cohort entered into the job market during the height of the economic recession and have dealt with persistently higher unemployment rates than older adults. It is understandable, therefore, that nearly one in three Millennials say unemployment is the most important economic issue facing our country. Following the issue of unemployment, Millennials cite the increasing gap between the wealthy, middle class, and poor (21.7%) and then the rising cost of education (17.7%). Again, these concerns fit with the economic experiences of young adults, significantly shaped by the Great Recession. The foremost priority

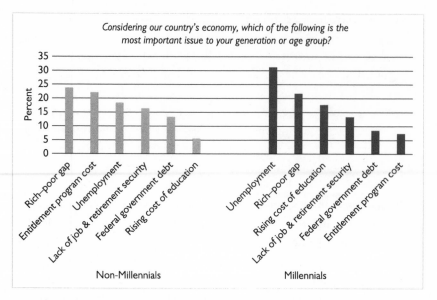

FIGURE 3.2.   Most Important Economic Issue among Millennials & Non-Millennials

of non-Millennials is this rich–poor gap (23.8%), followed very closely behind by cost of entitlement programs (22.2%), and then concern for unemployment (18.4%).

In some regard, these economic priorities signal stage of life. The higher concern for entitlement programs is likely driven by older adults' proximity to retirement and benefit from the Social Security program. Millennials' concern for education reflects young adults' focus on higher education as current or recently graduated students. Millennials, to a greater degree than the generations before them, are carrying considerable student loan debt and are experiencing a lower value returned on their educational investments (The Institute for College Access & Success 2014a; Allison 2017). This, along with other related education issues, is discussed in detail in Chapter 4.

While a focus on the cost of education among Millennials and entitlement programs among non-Millennials is understandable given the stages of life of each group, all American adults, according to our survey results, share a concern for the increasing gap between the wealthy, middle class, and the poor in our country. The concern undoubtedly reflects the fact that economic inequality in the United States is higher than other developed democracies (OECD 2014) and that rates of income and wealth inequalities in the United States are at all-time highs (Stone 2016). Income inequality is acutely felt by Millennials, Latinos, and African Americans; even individuals among these groups with college degrees have median incomes and wealth that significantly lag behind that of older, white adults in our country (Pew Research Center 2014c; Pew Research Center 2016c; Vega 2016a). Chloe, a Millennial participant in our focus group held in the Washington, DC area, echoed this reality when asked what her biggest economic concern is:

> I would say the shrinking or the disappearance of the middle class, because I think it's getting harder and harder to be middle-class in this country, especially with things like student loans and prices getting higher. I think that the rich are getting richer, and the middle class are becoming less and less so. I don't think that's good, because I think we should have a strong middle-class.

Studies have shown that a strong middle class is needed for a healthy democracy. Economic inequality translates to lower levels of political engagement and interest as well as democratic participation (Uslaner and Brown 2005; Anderson and Beramendi 2008; Solt 2008). It also limits social mobility and equal opportunity (OECD 2014) and may constrain intergenerational income mobility—a trend already manifested in Millennials' worse financial well-being than their parents' (Corak 2013; Sommeiller et al. 2016).

The policy tools available to governments to reduce economic inequality through redistributing wealth include taxes and transfers, programs such as Social Security, food stamps, and unemployment payments. These have been largely successful at softening the blow of the market on the poorest of Americans, but the problem is that the tide of the increasing inequality is so "powerful that redistribution efforts can only slow the trend" (Porter 2014). Other policy tools that may address the issue include an increased minimum wage as it directly addresses the issue of greater dispersion of wages and salaries (OECD 2014; Porter 2014). Investing in human capital is also a policy tool to address rising economic inequalities; this includes making education more affordable and ensuring the population is healthy through accessible high-quality public services (Powell n.d.; OECD 2014). To explore support for these policy tools, the remainder of this chapter examines attitudes among Millennials and non-Millennials about the minimum wage and health-care costs, as well as government spending to alleviate economic hardships and Social Security reform.

The Economic Policy Preferences of Millennials and Non-Millennials

To explore the economic issues that address, directly and indirectly, the economic priorities of Millennials and non-Millennials, we focus on four specific policies: 1) government spending to address economic hardships, 2) increased minimum wage, 3) Social Security reform, and 4) healthcare costs. We use data from two surveys—our original survey conducted in 2015 and the Nielsen survey conducted in 2016. Because the surveys are distinct in the questions they ask, both surveys are used to capture more comprehensive preferences on specific economic policies.[8] Each survey is nationally representative and oversamples the Millennial age cohort, thereby allowing for robust statistical analysis.

We focus our analyses on the factors that we believe reflect the Millennial Generation persona, identity, or frame comprised of the unique characteristics that are shared by members of this group. To capture this, we include in our statistical model a variable to designate Millennials from older adults, born before 1980.[9] We also include in the model a set of variables we believe reflects the Millennial Generation identity.[10] A central part of this identity, critical for this chapter, is the economic experiences Millennials have shared. As discussed in detail at the beginning of this chapter, Millennials have been and continue to be largely disadvantaged by the timing of their entrance into the job market during the Great Recession. This has affected their employment rates, earnings—now and into the future—as well as their choices about student loans and household spending. These experiences, shared by members of this age cohort, should shape their attitudes about economic policies. To capture this, we include measures in our model that report individual employment status and negative economic outlook. The economic outlook variable is constructed from a question in our original survey that asks: "Thinking about the national economy, do you believe our country is better or worse off than it was twenty years ago for people of your age?" Those who respond "worse" are considered to have a negative economic outlook. These factors are included only in analyses using our original survey as comparable variables were not measured in the Nielsen survey.

In addition to economic hardship, the Millennial Generation identity is characterized by this cohort's diversity, liberal political ideology, cosmopolitanism, and a collectivist worldview. We measure these independently in order to trace the effects of specific attributes on economic attitudes. We also expect some of these dynamics, specifically diversity and ideology, to work across generations and look to examine how Millennials among these subgroups are distinct from older adults. Diversity is measured by being a member of a racial or ethnic minority group, specifically African American or Latino, as well as being foreign born or having a foreign relative. Because minority groups have and continue to experience disproportionate economic hardships, we expect, in line with past studies and polls, that African Americans and Latinos will favor policies that allow for greater government economic intervention and spending (e.g., Hasenfeld and Rafferty 1989; Jones 2016). We expect the same for individuals who are foreign born or have foreign familial ties, given that the majority of developed nations outside the United States have larger social safety nets (Jusko 2016) and developing countries must manage high rates of poverty with government programs (World Bank 2015).

Political ideology should have a considerable influence on support for economic policies to address government spending, minimum wage, Social Security reform, and healthcare costs as these issues are central divisions among liberals and conservatives. Liberals and those affiliated with the Democratic Party tend to favor more government spending and an expanded role of the government in the economy, while conservatives and those of the Republican Party support limited government intervention into economic matters (Goren 2005). These ideological influences should affect Millennials and non-Millennials alike; however, it will be interesting to examine how Millennials, given their unique economic experiences, will translate these traditional economic stances into their support for economic solutions.

Cosmopolitanism or seeing oneself as a "citizen of the world" is also likely to shape economic attitudes as it is linked to a sense of civic responsibility and charity (Zogby and Kuhl 2013) as well as a general sensitivity to the plight of people from other parts of the world. We expect this to be associated with economic stances that favor collectivist approaches, namely government intervention in the economy to create safety nets. Government worldview, too, should influence economic policy opinions as belief that the government has a positive role to play in solving problems is likely to increase support for government action across the issues examined: government spending to ease economic hardship, a federal mandate for an increased minimum wage, Social Security reform, and making healthcare costs more affordable. We measure cosmopolitanism with a question in the Nielsen survey that asks respondents how strongly they identify with being "a citizen of the world." Positive government worldview is a factor variable constructed from multiple survey questions in our original survey. Beyond these characteristics central to the Millennial Generation identity, we also control for levels of education, income, gender, and marital status as these may also influence perceptions of economic issues.[11]

Government Spending

To examine attitudes about government spending, we utilize a question from the Nielsen survey that asked respondents to indicate their preference on a scale, ranging from "cutting government spending is the only way to improve our economic outlook" to "more government spending is needed to alleviate economic hardships Americans are suffering." The original scale ranges from 1 to 5. We collapsed the scale so that opinions in the middle are grouped together. The resulting variable designates the preference for cutting government spending as "1," the preference for more government spending as "3," and opinions in the middle as "2." Attitudes about government spending across Millennial and non-Millennial groups are shown in Figure 3.3.

A large percentage of both groups prefer cutting government spending. Nearly 50% of Millennials and 53.7% of non-Millennials favor this policy stance. Slightly more Millennials prefer a middle-of-the-road policy, between cutting and more spending, than non-Millennials—31.4% compared to 24.5%, respectively. About 20% of both groups see government

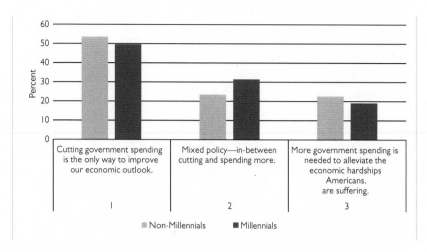

FIGURE 3.3. Government Spending Opinions among Millennials & Non-Millennials

spending as the solution to economic problems. Given the congruence in these policy beliefs, the statistical insignificance of a means test of group differences is not surprising.[12] An ordered logistic regression estimating Millennial Generation on opinions about government spending, while controlling for—ethnicity and diversity (Latino, African American, having foreign relatives[13]), political ideology (Republican party affiliation), cosmopolitan identity, as well as education, income, and gender—confirms that Millennials are not statistically different in their opinions about government spending than non-Millennials.[14] However, there may be significant differences between Millennials and non-Millennials among specific groups of the population. For example, Millennials may be distinct from older adults among ethnic minorities or the native-born population; political ideology and cosmopolitan identity may also influence Millennial and non-Millennial attitudes differently.

To test differences across specific measures, we estimate a regression model that interacts Millennials with the following variables: Latino, African American, foreign relatives, Republican affiliation, and cosmopolitan identity. We also control for education, income, and gender. Because the coefficients are difficult to interpret directly, the results of the interaction model are presented in Figure 3.4 as marginal effect contrasts between the groups.[15] The marginal effect contrast—the difference between Millennials

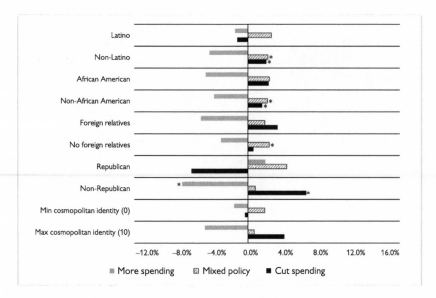

FIGURE 3.4.   Marginal Effect Contrasts between Millennials and Non-Millennials across Influences on Opinions regarding Government Spending

Notes: Results of pairwise comparisons of marginal effects shown based on estimates of ordered logistic regression analysis that interacted each independent variable with the variable Millennial. The difference in Millennial versus Non-Millennial marginal effect shown by the bars. Negative values indicate that, for that dependent variable outcome, Millennials are less likely than Non-Millennials; positive values indicate that Millennials are more likely than Non-Millennials. Statistically significant differences (p<0.05) between Millennials and Non-Millennials are marked with an asterisk at the end of the bar.

and non-Millennials in their opinion on government spending—is shown for each independent variable value and each dependent variable outcome (cutting government spending, middle-of-the-road policy, and more government spending). The bars indicate the size of the difference, and the asterisk at the end of the bars indicate the difference between Millennials and non-Millennials is statistically significant (p<0.05). Negative values (bars to the left) indicate that Millennials are less likely than non-Millennials to be associated with the dependent variable outcome; positive values (bars to the right) indicate that Millennials are more likely, in comparison to non-Millennials, to be associated with the outcome.

The first trend evident in the results is that Millennials are distinct from non-Millennials among the non-ethnic minority population. The pairwise comparisons of marginal effects indicate that among non-Latinos and non-African Americans, Millennials are more likely to favor middle-of-the-road spending policy and less likely to favor more government spending. Specifically, among non-Latinos and non-African Americans, Millennials are 2.1% more likely (for both groups) to favor a middle-of-the-road policy and 4.1% and 3.6%, respectively, are less likely to support more government spending than non-Millennials (p<0.05). Despite the lack of statistical significance across race and ethnic groups, we do observe descriptive differences.[16] African Americans have the greatest support for more government spending to solve economic problems—28.2% of African Americans say the government should spend more, compared to 20.1% of whites and 16.5% of Latinos. However, African American opinion is nearly equally divided between preferences for cutting spending, more spending, and a policy in-between the two. In contrast, the majority of whites favor cutting government spending (53.4%). Many Latinos favor cutting government spending (47.6%) as well, but more Latinos than white adults support a middle-of-the-road policy (36% compared to 26.5%, respectively). Returning to the marginal effect contrasts, we see the preference among Millennials for a middle-of-the-road government spending policy emerges, again, in statistically significant differences among the adult population without foreign relatives. Taken together, these results indicate a strong preference among Millennials who are not measurable diverse (a race/ethnic minority member or have foreign ties) for a middle-of-the-road policy on government spending to alleviate economic hardship.

The second notable trend in the results centers on political ideology. The pairwise comparisons of marginal effects report that among non-Republicans, Millennials, in comparison to non-Millennials, are 6.2% more likely to favor cutting government spending (p<0.05) and 7% less likely to support more spending (p<0.01). Among Republicans, Millennials are 4.1% more likely to favor a middle-of-the-road policy, although this difference only approaches statistical significance at conventional levels (p=0.09). These findings suggest that among moderates and liberals, Millennials favor a traditionally conservative approach to the economy and that they serve as a moderating voice among conservatives.

The moderate economic stance of Millennials is also manifested in cosmopolitan identity. Among those with a high cosmopolitan identity—a 7 on a scale of 0 ("not at all") to 10 ("very strongly") in identification with being "a citizen of the world"—Millennials are 16.4% less likely than non-Millennials to support increased government spending to solve economic problems. This finding demonstrates that the Millennial identity is shaping domestic economic attitudes, even among those who have a strong sense of being a global citizen. This indicates a streak of caution among young adults, a sentiment we found in the focus groups we conducted. Vincent, a Millennial focus group participant from San Antonio, Texas, expresses it this way:

> I just feel that the American debt, I think the way that Americans think is that we put everything on credit cards and debt and we spend more money than what we have. And so that has a lot of, a pretty big factor in it. And that's also you know the government itself spending more money than what it should. They should just, everyone should just be more careful with that.

It is clear from this analysis that despite the economic hardships that Millennials have endured in the wake of the Great Recession, they do not look to broad government spending as the answer. Rather, the experience of the recession has shaped them to be careful not only with their personal spending patterns but also with the price tag associated with the economic policies they support.

Minimum Wage

To explore the differences among Millennials and non-Millennials in their attitudes about increasing the minimum wage, we employ the following questions from our original survey conducted in 2015: "How much do you support or are likely to support the following federal government policy? Mandate for increased minimum wage." Response options included "none," "a little," "some," and "a lot." We collapsed the middle categories of "a little" and "some" to create three categories of support for an increased minimum wage. The majority—51.2%—of Millennials support an increased minimum wage, as do 45.1% of non-Millennials. A difference of means test indicates that this difference is statistically significant ($p<0.05$).[17]

The greater level of support for an increased minimum wage among Millennials is understandable considering that about half of the population working minimum wage jobs (paying $7.25 per hour) in 2015 were 25 years old and younger (US Bureau of Labor Statistics 2016). Not only do Millennials hold a disproportionate percentage of minimum wage jobs in comparison to older adults but they are also contending with higher rates of poverty than previous generations (Pew Research Center 2014a). The US Census Bureau reported in 2014 that one in five young adults, aged 18 to 34 years, lives in poverty, up from one in seven in 1980 (US Census Bureau 2014). Millennial support for an increased minimum wage is likely not just driven by economic self-interest. The Millennial Generation persona largely espouses equality, which in the economic domain translates to equality of economic opportunity (Finnie and Jagtiani 2016). Despite these motivations, the Millennial identity may not be the only driver of support for an increased minimum wage and its effect may be altered when accounting for other factors, including race/ethnicity, political ideology, economic hardship, worldview, education, income, gender, and marital status. To test this, we estimate an ordered logistic regression incorporating these measures.

The results of the regression analysis examining minimum wage beliefs indicate that Millennial identity is not statistically significant when controlling for the other factors in the model.[18] Rather, the following variables emerge as significant: African American, liberal ideology, negative economic outlook, positive government worldview, education, income, and being female. Because the ordered logit coefficients are difficult to interpret directly, we will rely on predicted probabilities to explore the results.

African Americans have a 65% predicted probability of supporting a policy to increase the minimum wage in comparison to 42.8% among non-African Americans.[19] Similarly, there is a 55.7% likelihood of supporting increases to the minimum wage among liberals, compared to a 40.6% likelihood among moderates and conservatives. Support for an increased minimum wage is also evident among those with a strong belief in the positive role of government. An average respondent with the maximum value of positive government worldview has a 78.1% likelihood of favoring increases to the minimum wage, compared to an 18.3% likelihood of the same with a respondent who has a minimum value of positive government worldview. Females are also slightly more likely to support an increase in the minimum wage. The average female respondent has a 49.8% likelihood of favoring this policy, while her male counterpart has a 42.7% likelihood of the same.

On the other hand, having a negative economic outlook—saying the economy, in comparison to twenty years ago, is worse for people of your age—is associated with less support for an increase minimum wage. The average respondent with a negative economic outlook has a 41.1% likelihood of favoring a higher minimum wage, while those that say the economy is the same or better today (than twenty years ago) had a 54% likelihood of the same. Those with higher education and income levels are also less likely to support an increase minimum wage. At first blush, these findings may seem counterintuitive, as one would expect those with a poor economic outlook to support mitigating policies that may improve the economy. Similarly, those with higher education and income are often associated with support for progressive policies. However, there may be an element of self-interest tied to attitudes about minimum wage policy (Brainard and Perry 2004), as well as a lack of confidence that raising the minimum wage will actually result in the positive economic outcome that its supporters often claim (Harvey 2014). Those with poor economic outlooks may perceive a policy for an increased minimum wage as a strain on an already-limited economy. Those with greater education and income levels are likely to be less concerned about the minimum wage because they hold jobs that pay at higher rates. Moreover, they may regard an increased minimum wage as a drain on their pocketbooks as the expense of the increase trickles down through the cost for goods and services and may have little impact on improving the economy overall.

Additional analyses, including a regression that interacts Millennials with the variable examined in the current model, revealed that there are no statistically significant differences between Millennials and non-Millennials in their attitudes about minimum wage, even among different segments of the population.[20] Analysis restricted to the Millennial respondent pool generated the same results as the regression of respondents of all ages. This tells us that the influences on preferences for the specific economic policy are felt equally among Millennials and older adults. The biggest driver of support for an increased minimum wage is the belief that government has a positive role in solving social problems. Being African American is also a strong influence on favoring an increased minimum wage. This preference undoubtedly reflects the income disparities among race and ethnic groups that have historically existed and persist today, even among young adults and those that are highly educated (Bloome 2014; Kochhar 2014; Shin 2015; Vega 2016a). In fact, the racial gap in wealth is steeper than it has ever has been on record (Kochhar 2014), and the gap is large— "the median wealth for white families in 2013 was around $141,900, compared to Hispanics at about $13,700 and blacks at about $11,000" (Vega 2016b). This is critical to address for the Millennial Generation given that one in three Millennials are African American or Latino (Pew Research Center 2015e) and that minority young adults continue to face discrimination and disproportionate economic outcomes (Carnevale, Hanson, and Gulish 2013; Allison 2017).

Social Security

To examine how Millennials and non-Millennials differ in their opinions about Social Security, we use the following question from our original 2015 survey: "For the following pair of statements, select the one that most closely aligns (agrees) with your personal opinion. Making some changes to Social Security will ensure retirement for everyone. Overhaul of our Social Security program is needed." Figure 3.7 illustrates Millennial and non-Millennial attitudes about the issue. Over 63% of non-Millennials and 60.8% of Millennials favor making some changes to the current entitlement program; 36.9% and 39.3% of non-Millennials and Millennials, respectively, believe drastic change is needed to Social Security. These figures suggest that Millennial and non-Millennial attitudes are not distinct on this issue, and a difference of means test confirms this finding.[21]

We expect, however, that there should be differences across age cohorts on this issue as non-Millennials have more at stake in the current Social Security system. Their earnings over the past decades have been poured into the program, and many have or will soon rely on that investment for retirement benefits. Millennials, on the other hand, can afford innovation of our nation's retirement plan as they have just entered the workforce and have a lifetime of savings ahead of them before retirement age. Moreover, past studies have shown that Millennials lack confidence in the

Social Security system. Half (51%) say "they do not believe there will be any money for them in the Social Security system by the time they are ready to retire, and an additional 39% say the system will only be able to provide them with retirement benefits at reduced levels" (Pew Research Center 2014a: 10).

To explore if the Millennial Generation persona has any effect on attitudes about Social Security, we run a regression analysis.[22] Employing the same set of variables used to examine minimum wage attitudes,[23] we find that the primary driver of opinions about Social Security is having the worldview that the government plays a positive role in solving social issues. Predicted probabilities indicate that those with the strongest positive government worldview have a 76% likelihood of supporting some changes to Social Security. Those with the weakest belief in the positive role of government have a 48.2% likelihood of saying the same. On the other hand, those with the strongest positive government worldview have a 24% likelihood of supporting an overhaul of the Social Security program, while those with the weakest worldview have a 51.8% likelihood of the same. The Millennial Generation variable is also positively associated with the opinion that overhaul of the Social Security system is needed. However, it only approaches conventional levels of statistical significance (p=0.06). Predicted probabilities indicate that Millennials have a 59.6% likelihood of supporting some changes to Social Security, compared to 65.5% among non-Millennials. Millennials have a 40.6% likelihood of favoring an overhaul of Social Security while non-Millennials have a 34.5% likelihood of the same.

This regression model tested for the direct effects of key explanatory factors. As in the analysis of government spending, we can also assess if the Millennial Generation persona is significant among specific segments of the population for beliefs about social security reform. We estimate a regression model that interacts Millennial with each of the following variables: Latino, African American, foreign born, liberal ideology, unemployed, negative economic outlook, and positive government worldview. We also control for education, income, gender, and marital status. Because the coefficients of this regression are difficult to interpret directly, we employ pairwise comparisons of marginal effects between Millennial and non-Millennials, as shown in Figure 3.5, and focus the discussion on those that are statistically significant (p<0.05).[24]

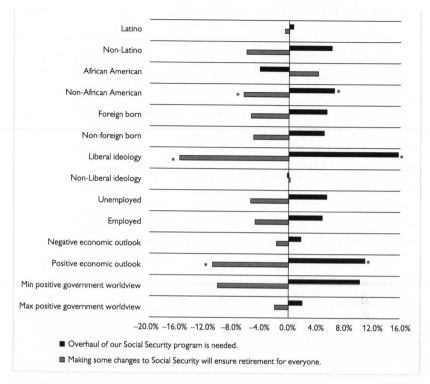

FIGURE 3.5.   Marginal Effect Contrasts between Millennials and Non-Millennials across Influences on Opinions regarding Social Security Reform

Notes: Results of pairwise comparisons of marginal effects shown based on estimates of ordered logistic regression analysis that interacted each independent variable with the variable Millennial. The difference in Millennial versus Non-Millennial marginal effect shown by the bars. Negative values indicate that, for that dependent variable outcome, Millennials are less likely than Non-Millennials; positive values indicate that Millennials are more likely than Non-Millennials. Statistically significant differences (p<0.05) between Millennials and Non-Millennials are marked with an asterisk at the end of the bar.

The marginal effects contrasts indicate that among non-African American respondents, Millennials are 6.5% more likely to favor an overhaul of Social Security. Despite the lack of statistical significance among the African American subgroup, we observe descriptive differences between young and older blacks on this issue. Overall, African American respondents have a stronger preference for some changes (not overhaul) to the Social Security system—65.4% compared to 61.3% among non-blacks. When we compare Millennial and non-Millennial African Americans on this stance, young blacks emerge as more supportive: 68% of young black adults favor small changes in comparison to 62.4% of older blacks. A preference for incremental change to Social Security by African Americans, even among African American Millennials, is understandable since this is a group that disproportionately relies on these benefits (due to lack of other income) once they reach retirement age (Hendley and Bilimoria 1999). This finding underscores that, not only are Millennials and non-Millennials distinct in their beliefs about Social Security, there are also racial differences among Millennials in their attitudes about this issue.

A preference for an overhaul of Social Security also emerged among Millennial liberals. Predicted probabilities indicate that liberal Millennials are 15.7% more likely to support a drastic change to the Social Security system than older adult liberals. This result also highlights the distinctions between liberal and non-liberal Millennials. Regression analysis restricted to the pool of Millennial respondents indicates that liberal Millennials, in comparison to their non-liberal counterparts, are 10% more likely to favor an overhaul of Social Security.[25] The same is true for those with a positive economic outlook. Among those who believe the economy today is the same or better (than twenty years ago) for people of their age, Millennials are 10.9% more likely than non-Millennials to support an overhaul of Social Security. These results indicate that while the Millennial Generation persona does not have a statistically significant direct effect on attitudes about Social Security, significant distinction emerge between Millennials and non-Millennials as well as among Millennials from various segments of society.

Healthcare Costs

To explore attitudes about healthcare costs, we utilize a survey question from the Nielsen survey that asked respondents to indicate their preference on a scale, ranging from "the government should do more to make healthcare affordable" to "the government should leave it up to the free market to determine healthcare costs." The original scale ranges from 1 to 5. We collapsed it so that opinions in the middle are grouped together. The resulting variable assigns the preference for government action to make healthcare more affordable as "1," the preference for the free market determining healthcare costs as "3," and opinions in the middle as "2."

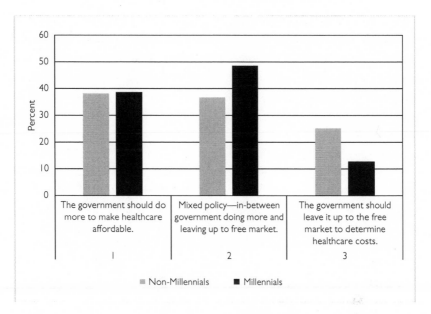

FIGURE 3.6. Healthcare Costs Opinions among Millennials & Non-Millennials

Figure 3.6 depicts the healthcare preferences Millennials and non-Millennials hold. The percentage of Millennials and non-Millennials that believe the government should do more to make healthcare more affordable is nearly equal—38.7% and 38.2%, respectively. However, there is a big gap in beliefs about leaving healthcare cost up to the free market. Only 12.8% of Millennials believe healthcare cost to be determined by the free market, while 25.1% of non-Millennials express support for the same. A means test indicates that the difference between Millennials and non-Millennials in their opinions about healthcare cost is statistically significant.[26]

This gap between Millennials and non-Millennials on opinions about healthcare costs and the free market reflects the different values and experiences each age cohort has had with healthcare. While Millennials are "as skeptical as older generations of the 2010 healthcare law" (about four in ten approve of it), the majority of Millennials believe that government should provide coverage for all (Pew Research Center 2014a: 35). Reflecting their collectivist and cosmopolitan worldview, 54% of Millennials say it is the government's responsibility to insure coverage for all, compared to 46% of Gen Xers, 42% of Baby Boomers, and 45% of the Silent Generation. Beyond worldview, Millennials have benefited from the provision in Obamacare that allows them to be covered under their parent's insurance until age 26. Cynthia, a participant in a focus group of Millennials held in Washington, DC, had this to say when asked what she would tell President Obama (then in office) about her biggest concerns:

> I would ask him if he could continue to advocate for Obamacare to the new president because I believe they're trying to maybe take it away. I would tell him that as a college student, after moving back home after graduation, it's really helpful for people like me who can't afford insurance. And it's helpful for other people. I can definitely relate to the people that can't afford insurance. I'd definitely ask him to really keep Obamacare, or advocate for Obamacare to remain.

Cynthia is one of 4.5 million young adults who gained health insurance coverage under the provisions of the Affordable Care Act, resulting in a 40% drop in the uninsured rate of Millennials (Furman and Fielder 2015). Despite these gains, Millennials, overall, do not see more government intervention in making healthcare affordable as preferable. Rather, as we saw with stances on government spending to alleviate economic hardship, the largest percentage of Millennials—48.6%—support a middle-of-the-road policy that balances government intervention and free market forces when it comes to healthcare costs.

To further explore opinions about healthcare costs, we estimate an ordered logistic regression that includes: Millennial Generation, Latino, African American, foreign relatives, Republican affiliation, and cosmopolitan identity. We also control for education, income, and gender. The regression results indicate that the Millennial Generation persona does not exert a direct influence on healthcare cost attitudes.[27] However, Republican Party affiliation, cosmopolitan identity, education, and income levels are significantly associated with opinions about healthcare cost policy.

Once again, because the logistic coefficients are difficult to interpret, we turn to predicted probabilities to explore these results. Predicted probabilities reveal that Republicans and those with higher incomes are less likely to support a policy that stipulates government action to make healthcare more affordable and more likely to support a policy that allows the free market to determine healthcare cost or a middle-of-the-road policy. The average Republican respondent has a 33.6% likelihood of supporting a policy that allows the free market to determine healthcare costs, while a non-Republican respondent has a 7% likelihood of the supporting the same. Those with higher incomes are more likely to support free market forces in healthcare. An average respondent with the highest income earnings has a 16.7% likelihood of supporting the free market, while the average respondent with the lowest level of income has a 9.7% likelihood of the same.

On the other hand, individuals with the strongest cosmopolitan identity (a score of 10 on the 0 to 10 identification as a "citizen of the world" scale) have a 40.8% likelihood of favoring government action to make healthcare affordable, while those that do not identify as a citizen of the world have a 24.2% likelihood of supporting such a policy. Individuals with higher levels of education are also more likely to support government action. Those with a postgraduate degree have a 39.2% likelihood of supporting government intervention in comparison to a 30.9% likelihood among those with a high school education. While Republican Party affiliation and income fall on the side of free market and cosmopolitan identity and higher education motivate support for government action, the greatest levels of predicted support among all groups emerge in favor of a middle-of-the-road policy.

To further explore the nuances of healthcare cost opinions, we turn to the interaction model. As discussed in the other policy sections, this model allows us to test if Millennials are distinct from non-Millennials among specific segments of the population. We estimated an ordered logistic regression that interacts the Millennial Generation with each key independent variable.[28] The results indicate that Millennials are statistically distinct from non-Millennial among particular segments of the population.[29] Figure 3.7 displays the marginal effect contrasts between Millennials and non-Millennials, estimated from the results of this regression.

The results demonstrate a strong preference among Millennials for a middle-of-the-road policy on healthcare costs. The distinction of Millennials for this policy stance is statistically significant (p<0.05) among non-Latinos, non-African Americans, the population without foreign relatives, Republicans and non-Republicans, and those without a strong

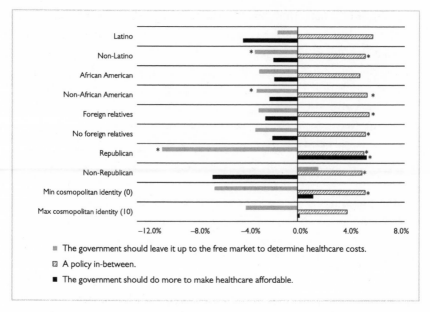

FIGURE 3.7.   Marginal Effect Contrasts between Millennials and Non-Millennials across Influences on Opinions regarding Healthcare Costs

Notes: Results of pairwise comparisons of marginal effects shown based on estimates of ordered logistic regression analysis that interacted each independent variable with the variable Millennial. The difference in Millennial versus Non-Millennial marginal effect shown by the bars. Negative values indicate that, for that dependent variable outcome, Millennials are less likely than Non-Millennials; positive values indicate that Millennials are more likely than Non-Millennials. Statistically significant differences (p<0.05) between Millennials and Non-Millennials are marked with an asterisk at the end of the bar.

feeling of being a global citizen. Across all of these groups, Millennials are about 5% more likely to favor a mixed policy to address healthcare cost than non-Millennials.[30]

The lack of significant differences between Millennials and older adults among race/ethnic minority groups on healthcare cost policy reflects congruence in beliefs on the issue, particularly on stances to allow the free market to determine healthcare costs. Non-Millennials and Millennial attitudes about the free market among African Americans and Latinos are very similar, registering only a 1% difference between the generations among African Americans and a 0.76% differences among Latinos. There is a much larger gap between white Millennials and their older adult counterparts on this issue—11.61% with non-Millennials favoring free market forces. This underscores that race/ethnicity in some ways supersedes Millennial identity in shaping economic attitudes in this specific policy domain.

Millennial opinions on healthcare cost policy stand out among Republicans. Republican Millennials, in comparison to older Republicans, are 10.1% less likely to favor allowing the free market to determine healthcare costs and 5.2% more likely to support a policy that stipulates that the government should make healthcare affordable. Furthermore, Millennials are statistically distinct from non-Millennials at low and high levels of cosmopolitan identity. We find significant differences among those with the cosmopolitan identity of 4; among this group, Millennials are 24.6% less likely to favor a policy of government action to make healthcare more affordable than non-Millennials. At a cosmopolitan identity of 8, Millennials are 8.9% less likely to favor allowing the free market to determine healthcare cost. These results align with the trend evident in the first regression analysis—as cosmopolitan identity increases, preferences for government action rise while support for the free market declines. This suggests that cosmopolitan identity has a particularly strong influence on Millennial opinions about the role of government in solving social problems.

Conclusion: Economic Attitudes of the Children of the Great Recession

The analyses in this chapter reveal patterns that are telling of the general economic attitudes of Millennials. First and perhaps foremost, Millennials are economically cautious. They are more supportive than older adults of a middle-of-the-road approach when it comes to economic policies that affect the whole society, including healthcare costs and government spending. They prefer a balanced solution, one that finds a middle ground between government action to make healthcare more affordable and allowing the free market to determine healthcare costs. They also support cutting government spending and are more likely than older adults to favor a policy in-between cutting and more government spending. Furthermore, the majority of Millennials support some change to "fix" Social Security as opposed to a complete overhaul of the system. In all, these are cautious approaches for a largely liberal group. Although most Millennials favor this middle-of-the-road approach that is less risky, there is a significant portion of young adults that want to see more drastic changes to traditional economic institutions, namely Social Security. Nearly four in ten Millennials, according to our survey, favor an overhaul of the system. This supports the findings of previous studies (Pew Research Center 2014a) and points to a need for further examination of how reform of the nation's primary financial institutions is favored by and would affect young adults. These findings also beg the question of how Millennial stances on economic issues are linked to their general distrust of traditional institutions (Harvard Public Opinion Project 2014).[31]

A second take-away point from our study is that minority Millennials share economic attitudes with older adults of their race/ethnic group. None of the analyses reported a statistically significant difference between Millennials and non-Millennials among Latinos or African Americans, but there were differences among Millennials and older adults of the white population. This was particularly evident with leaving healthcare costs up to the free market. We also observed the importance of ethnic minority identity on minimum wage policy. There were no distinctions between Millennials and non-Millennials in their attitudes on this issue, and being African American had the largest influence on supporting a federal mandate to increase the minimum wage. This reflects the persistent disadvantage of minorities in our economy, which could be more pronounced for Millennials given their considerable diversity, continued discrimination, and their unfortunate initiation into the labor market due to the Great Recession.

The final trend evident in our findings was that Millennials temper traditional liberal–conservative divides on economic issues. Among non-Republicans, Millennials are more conservative in favoring government cuts to spending. Among Republicans, Millennials are more likely to support government action to make healthcare affordable and less likely to leave costs up to the free market. We also saw these trends among those who strongly identify with being a citizen of the world. Cosmopolitan Millennials are less likely to favor government spending but are also less likely to support blind trust in free market forces (when it comes to healthcare costs).

While Millennials are sensitive to growing income inequalities and persistent disparities along racial lines in economic outcomes, they support policies that strike a balance between the classic division of liberal government intervention and conservative free market forces. They are looking for tempered, perhaps new, solutions to complex problems, and, despite the fact that past economic governance has largely failed them, they are optimistic about the future (Pew Research Center 2014a). Angelica, a Millennial focus group participant from Los Angeles, California, said that "there's so many other ways of finding your own American Dream now . . . it's just a lot more diverse than it was before." Similarly, Don, a focus group participant also from Los Angeles, sees Millennials' economic futures as benefiting from "unprecedented access to information and technologies" and feels like his generation is "empowered" by modern opportunities. As these "children of the Great Recession" mature and take a larger role in our nation's governance, we may see their optimism and economic cautiousness guide policies that abandon the traditional economic stances of the left and right. Perhaps then we will see the upward trends in economic inequality turn, and the effects of the Great Recession truly fade in the rearview mirror.

CHAPTER 4

Moving on Up? Millennials and the Politics of Education

During the 2016 presidential primary season, the issue of education garnered significant attention in campaign speeches, debate discussions, and media coverage. The reasons for a renewed focus on education by those seeking the White House were multifaceted (discussed in more detail below), but there is little doubt that the topic gained headline-level prominence by the persistent drum beating of the issue by Independent-turned-Democratic presidential candidate Bernie Sanders. On May 26, 2015, Sanders formally announced his candidacy for president in Burlington, Vermont. In his speech, Sanders pronounced the following about the importance of reforming education:

> And when we talk about education, let me be very clear. In a highly competitive global economy, we need the best educated workforce we can create. It is insane and counter-productive to the best interests of our country, that hundreds of thousands of bright young people cannot afford to go to college, and that millions of others leave school with a mountain of debt that burdens them for decades. That must end. That is why, as president, I will fight to make tuition in public colleges and universities free, as well as substantially lower interest rates on student loans.[1]

Arguably, Mr. Sanders' focus on education from the onset of his campaign helped elevate his candidacy from one thought to only symbolically challenge the front-runner, Hillary Clinton, to a serious and close bid for the Democratic nomination (Sanders won twenty-three states in the primary elections). Sanders' educational proposals were embraced by a significant portion of the population, but particularly by Millennials[2]— the cohort hardest hit by employment issues during the Great Recession, resulting in specific education-related hardships including devalued degrees and unprecedented levels of student loan debt (Fox 2014). Average cumulative borrowing for Millennials who graduated in 2011–2012 increased almost 35% (29,384), compared to the average cumulative borrowing of those that graduated in 2003–2004 ($21,990) (Miller 2014). At the same time, the median household wealth of college-graduate Millennials (age 25–32) is lower, at $26,059, than for the same age group in 1984, which was $29,521 (Kurtzleben 2014). Therefore, it is of little surprise that Bernie Sander's educational proposals were so well received among young adults.

Education has always been a central tenet of the American dream. Franklin Delano Roosevelt once said, "The real safeguard of democracy is education." With the backdrop of the need to have a more educated citizenry, the politics of education have long been a passionate and often contentious endeavor. On the one hand, most schools try to uphold an egalitarian vision for education, but on the other hand, educators often contend with and get caught up in political and bureaucratic red tape that can promote authoritarian tendencies for social control (e.g., high-stakes-test-driven-curricula) that favor some groups over others—often related to the dominant culture in society (Apple 2002; Kincheloe 2004). Thus, the competition to maximize the resource of education means that education is "inherently political" and always will be (Monchinski 2007). As Kincheloe (2004: 2) puts it, " . . . every dimension of schooling and every form of educational practice are politically contested spaces." Important examples of the politicization of education were the effects of segregation (codified with the *Plessy v. Ferguson* Supreme Court case in 1896), and then the subsequent federal orders for school desegregation (*Brown v. Board of Education* in 1954), as well as its varying and often slow implementation. Many argue that the effects of these actions are still being felt today, in terms of achieving equal educational opportunities for all (Brownstein 2014; Reece and O'Connell 2016). Modern political discourse on the issue of education also includes funding, quality, and choice (e.g., school voucher programs).

Of course, the politics of education are inextricably linked with the economy, specifically the fiscal capacity to provide education as a public good and to pay for it as a user. Take for example the Great Recession, which began in 2007.[3] This economic downturn caused significant hardship that was not only felt directly in people's pocketbooks but also indirectly in the resources available to meet educational needs. Most specifically, issues related to the increasing costs of higher education, the diminishing value of an educational degree (e.g., high level of underemployment), and the residual debt from student loans led to the issue of education being elevated to great prominence in the 2016 presidential contest. This in turn made its most staunch advocate, Bernie Sanders, a hero to many Millennials. Before we discuss the importance of education to the Millennial Generation, let's briefly take a look at how the politics surrounding the topic have developed; specifically, how the two major parties have staked out relatively distinct positions on the issue.

General Landscape of the Politics of Education

Competing educational priorities and goals lead to politicians perpetually debating the role of government in crafting education policy. Not surprisingly, the two major parties in our political system—the Republicans and the Democrats—have historically differed on their respective approaches to education. Republicans generally tend to favor a limited role for the federal government in education, opting instead for state and local governments to guide education policy (although George W. Bush's policy of "No Child Left Behind" expanded the role of the federal government in setting education policy). Republicans also favor stringent benchmarks for teacher accountability, school choice, homeschooling, and school vouchers. In particular, the Party's platform has consistently, over the years, included language that stresses the importance of education starting at home and that parents should be empowered to make the educational choices that are right for their children, rather than the government choosing for them (On the issues.

org ND, a). The Republican Party emphasized this priority with the following in their 2012 platform:

> Parents are responsible for the education of their children. We do not believe in a one size fits all approach to education and support providing broad education choices to parents and children at the State and local level . . . It recognizes the wisdom of State and local control of our schools, and it wisely sees consumer rights in educa-tion—choice—as the most important driving force for renewing our schools (*Strauss 2012*).

With respect to higher education, the Republican Party again would prefer to see a limited role for the federal government. The party plat-form has often called for the federal government to get out of the student loan business; Republicans believe there is a lack of transparency in the federal loan programs and that private loans would be much cheaper for students and their families (republicanviews.org). In the 2016 Republican Party Platform, party members once again called for ending the federal student loan program and restoring greater "private sector participa-tion in student financing" (Stratford 2016). Republicans also want to see expansion of learning opportunities that compete with four-year colleges. These opportunities include the growth of community colleges, technical schools, online schools, and work-based learning. The Republican Party believes that a four-year college degree is often overvalued and that alter-native forms of education are undervalued (Strauss 2012).

Conversely, the Democratic Party sees government, at all levels, playing a crucial role in improving and expanding education in the United States and eliminating what they call "the opportunity gap" (edu-cational disadvantages for low-income families) (Strauss 2016). Unlike Republicans, Democrats do not believe that the sole responsibility for education should be hoisted upon parents (although they believe parents play a necessary supportive role); rather the government should take the lead in offering a quality education. The Democratic Party also rejects the idea that educational opportunities should be treated like "consumer rights" or as "choices" (language used by Republicans), because this system favors the wealthy and the well-connected and disadvantages parents who cannot afford the best options. This idea is antithetical to the Democratic

Party's belief that education "is a burden to be shared by the entire population" (Education Opportunity Network 2016). In their 2016 platform, the Democratic Party states the following:

> Democrats know that every child no matter who they are, how much their families earn, or where they live, should have access to a high-quality education, from preschool to high school and beyond (*www.democrats.org*).

Overall, Democrats prefer an approach that allocates more financial resources to public education. These resources would be used to improve education by: turning around struggling or failing schools; expanding school choice for low-income families through magnet schools, charter schools, and career academies (but not through private-school vouchers that would take money out of public education); increasing resources for teachers; and revamping the way standardized testing is used in schools (tests used to advance learning and not to increase bureaucracy) (On the issues.org ND, b).

On the issue of higher education, Democrats once again see the government as playing a vital role. Similar to its goals with K-12 education, the Democratic Party aims for college to be within the reach of every student. This goal requires that cost "not be a barrier to getting a degree or credential, and debt should not hold you back after you graduate" (Education Reform Now 2016). To make this possible, the Democratic Party platform has endorsed initiatives that provide greater access to higher education and eases the burden of financing the process. These include restructuring federal financial aid programs, doubling the investment of Pell Grants, streamlining student loans to cut out the role of big banks, and facilitating the process of student loan repayment (Democratic National Committee 2017). However, unlike Bernie Sanders, the Democratic Party platform has not, to date, gone as far as to endorse free tuition at all public universities; rather, the Party platform favors free community college (Education Reform Now 2016).

In sum, Republicans emphasize the lack of accountability in public education and stress the need to use resources more efficiently, while Democrats claim that not enough priority and resources are given to education and call for equal opportunity for all students in the public education system. These two visions about education have dominated the political landscape for many years, with proposals made to achieve these goals, in one direction or another, depending on which party is in power of the national government and who controls state and local politics. These positions serve as a useful context for understanding how Millennials view the issue of education, the consequences of education policies for this cohort, and the changes they want to see enacted. We address these issues in the following sections.

Factors That Influence Millennial Attitudes about Education

The politics of education regained prominence in the 2016 election cycle. As previously mentioned, Bernie Sanders was the vehicle for this resurgence, but the issue had been simmering for many years, among the population at-large, but in particular, with Millennials. The effects of the Great Recession of 2007 produced an urgency and call for reform, especially changes related to higher education. The rising costs to attend college, the lack of job opportunities after graduation, and the debt accumulated from student loans continue to instill anxiety among this young cohort (Pew Research Center 2012b; Ayers 2013). And, while overall economic conditions have improved, Millennials remain affected by relatively higher unemployment rates, more debt, higher cost of living, and stagnant wages (Fottrell 2014a; Talty 2015). These realities impact Millennials' perceptions and attitudes about the politics of education, in particular, cost, value, and opportunities. We observed sentiments related to these issues firsthand among our Millennial focus group participants. DJ, a focus group member from San Antonio, Texas, articulated the current problems Millennials have with the higher education structure quite well when he said the following:

> I mean honestly I am going to have my bachelor's degree in February. It's worth absolutely nothing. I have spent $75,000 putting myself through school. I owe the federal government $50,000 of that $75,000 and my advisor looked me in the face and said if you don't get a masters, your bachelor's degree isn't going to do anything for you.

And Don, a focus group participant from Los Angeles, California said:

> The cost of education drives students to take out loans that could amount to the next economic collapse; it's certainly a huge bubble, its about 1.2 trillion right now . . . that's a great deal of money and that's a great deal of interest being paid on that money which is primarily owned by banks. My debt is owned by Merrill Lynch, I think, or maybe it was sold to someone else. I don't really keep track of it anymore, but that speaks to the fact that education is so expensive.

The two statements above are from Millennials living in different places, with varying political, economic, and social environments (San Antonio, Texas versus Los Angeles, California), and yet they express similar feelings about the albatross that now comes along with achieving a college education. We heard comparable thoughts from focus group participants in New Orleans and Washington, DC as well. For example, when focus group members were asked if the then President Obama was in the room with them, what they would want to discuss with him, many brought up education. Clarice, one of the focus group participants in Washington DC, said, "If he [Obama] was here, as a Millennial, I would probably speak to a specific issue which is the whole student loan thing, for me it is a big one. I would see [what happens] if it doesn't get fixed, in terms of people avoiding the effect of a Great Depression, because of the financial debt and burden of student loans . . ."

Why is education such an important issue for the Millennial Generation? We have already hit on part of the answer to this question—how education seems to be intrinsically tied to economics. However, the remaining explanation lies both in general ideas about the value of an education (also with significant economic overtones) and in the specific characteristics and circumstances of the Millennial Generation. First, with respect to general ideas about education, a significant amount of research has examined the intrinsic value of obtaining an education, exploring the link between greater educational attainment and such factors as earning potential, workforce participation, work/life satisfaction, and political participation. The literature has found fairly consistent positive effects of education on earnings (Card 1999; Pascarella and Terenzini 2005), labor force participation (Couch and Dunn 1997) and political participation (Brady, Verba, and Schlozman 1995) but less consistent findings with respect to work/ life satisfaction (Mottaz 1984; Weir 2013). Thus, historically, obtaining an education has paid off on a number of fronts, especially when it comes to increased earnings. For example, according to Pew Research Center estimates, in 1986, a full-time worker with a Bachelor's degree had 1.5 times the annual earnings of a worker with only a high school diploma. By 1995, this number had risen to 2.6 times the earning of those with only a high school education. In 2013, those with a Bachelor's degree were earning more than 2.8 times as much as those with a high school diploma (Kurtzleben 2014; Pew Research Center 2014c). While economic conditions have waxed and waned over the last several decades, and many hardships have befallen both Millennials and non-Millennials, the income gap in educational attainment has continued to widen (Pew Research Center 2014c). These figures demonstrate that an education still holds significant value, all else being equal. Of course, the advantages obtained from an education cannot be viewed in a vacuum; other factors affect the costs and benefits of educational attainment—particularly for Millennials.

Millennial-specific characteristics, as well as the circumstances this cohort has encountered, are quite important to understanding their attitudes about the politics of education. Take for example some of the factors we discussed above related to the general value of an education. Millennials are the best-educated generation in history (Thompson 2013; Pew Research Center 2014c), and yet one of the common narratives about their struggle, in the recession and during the slow economic recovery, is that although they have earned a college degree, many are serving coffee (known as "the barista with a B.A.") (Kurtzleben 2014), driving for Uber, or working behind a fast food counter. These anecdotes speak to the underemployment of Millennials, as a consequence of a poor economy, that forces them to work jobs that are far below their qualifications. Perhaps counterintuitively, though, studies show that the value of a college degree is more important than ever (Pew Research Center 2014c), but this value is relative and not absolute. There has been rising economic inequality and a widening of the income gap, and the gap is most prominent between high school-only Millennials and previous cohorts who only completed high school—Millennials fare much worse—than between Millennials with a college degree and their generational predecessors. Figure 4.1 displays this earning gap based on educational attainment (high school versus bachelor's

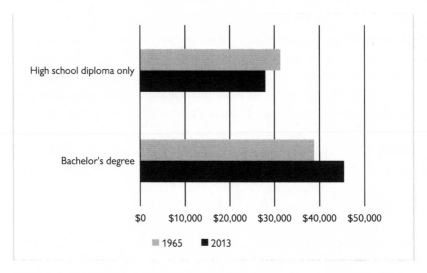

FIGURE 4.1.   Reduced Value of a High School Diploma for Millennials: Comparison of Median Annual Earnings of 25–32 Year Olds in 1965 and 2013

Note: Dollar amounts are median annual earnings for those working full-time. Data taken from Pew Research Center 2014c and Kurtzleben 2014.

degree), comparing median annual earnings for 25–32 year olds, in 1965 and 2013. It is clear why Millennials are frustrated, both by the decreased value of an education (for which they have incurred significant debt) and the lack of employment opportunities for those with and without a higher education.

Figure 4.1 drives home the point that a high school education, which used to offer some opportunities, has a much diminished value. As Paul Taylor, from the Pew Research Center, puts it, "The real story is the collapse of an economic opportunity for people who do not continue their education beyond high school" (Kurtzleben 2014). Therefore, Millennials are between a rock and a hard place—the need to obtain a college education, regardless of cost, or get caught in the morass that comes with the lack of a college degree. For the youngest adult generation, high school is no longer a viable end but rather a means to an end.

A college degree, though, is no guarantee of economic prosperity for Millennials, and this is at the heart of their frustrations. This frustration is understandable given that the poverty rate among Millennial college graduates is almost twice as high (6%) as it was for Generation X college graduates in 1995; they search longer for jobs, compared to previous generations; and they have higher rates of underemployment and unemployment, compared to other cohorts (Fottrell 2014b; Pew Research Center 2014c). Enduring ramifications of these circumstances are evident with such factors as Millennials living with their parents at higher rates than other generations (and more Millennials live with parents than any other type of living arrangement), delaying marriage longer, and having lower total wealth than other cohorts (Kurtzleben 2014; Bahrampour 2016).

The Millennial Persona and Attitudes about Education

We argue throughout this book that the Millennial persona, frame, or identity, comprised of a number of factors, helps us understand the political attitudes of this generation. As we referenced in Chapter 1, a generational cohort is defined by people who are born within the "same historical and sociocultural context, who experience the same formative experiences, and develop unifying commonalities as a result" (Lyons and Kuron 2014). This certainly describes Millennials with respect to the issue of education and explains how and why their mutual experiences are so impressionable. We know that Millennials are the most educated cohort in US history (White House 2014). This advancement has created greater knowledge and distinct opportunities for this group. However, these gains may be somewhat muted as a result of Millennials having grown up in financially difficult times (either in the midst of the Great Recession or during its gradual recovery). For this generation, the cost of education has skyrocketed and the value of education—both intrinsic and extrinsic—has been diminished.

Economic realities are set against a backdrop of transformative factors that help us better understand Millennials and their attitudes about education. Education experts have noted that each generation is different with respect to life experiences, "giving rise to different attitudes, beliefs, and sensitivities" (Oblinger 2003). These life experiences help shape the learning environment for students. Foremost in this realm of change (and consistently discussed in this book) is the importance of diversity (especially with respect to the makeup of the body of learners). Millennials are the most diverse generation in history (Pew Research Center 2014a). This serves as a prominent motivator for this cohort's views surrounding their educational policy preferences—from one that prioritizes the choices of a white majority, to one that better represents the needs of blacks, Latinos, and other minorities. We discuss in more detail factors that impact the educational attainment of minority Millennials in the section below.

Another important characteristic of Millennials in relation to education is the way this generation utilizes technology to learn. As "digital natives," Millennials have been transformed by and have transformed the way information is mined, how learning takes place (think Khan Academy and online courses for college credit, to name a few), and how knowledge is gained. The technological innovations available to Millennials are unmatched for any other generation (Experian 2014). These advances have redefined educational priorities and have made "adaptive learning" (the term describing the use of computers and technology as teaching devices) not only appealing but also crucial components of an educated society. Bill Gates, the Microsoft founder, has called the development of technology for learning "a special time in education" (The Economist 2013).

Despite technological advances, many of which have been developed domestically, the United States is not as internationally competitive as it once was when it comes to educational achievement. According to the Council on Foreign Relations, the United States ranks twelfth in educational attainment (both high school and college) for those ages 25–34. The United States also has a higher college dropout rate (47%), compared to the rest of the developed world (32%) (Alden and Strauss 2016). These statistics are in spite of the fact that the United States spends "the fifth most in the world on per-student primary and secondary education and by far the most on college education" (Alden and Strauss 2016). Thus, the benefits of technological advances in education are diminished if they are not optimally employed to maximize educational achievement.

Related to the importance of diversity and technology on Millennials' attitudes about education is this generation's proclivity to view themselves through the lens of a cosmopolitan (global) identity. As many as one-third of Millennials see themselves as "citizens of the world" (Zogby and Kuhl 2013). This perception is due in large part to their access and use of technology and their exposure to other cultures—as a result of more diversified schools. Along with a cosmopolitan identity, Millennials are also more likely to adopt a collectivist worldview in which government has a positive and important role to play in solving problems. Thus, how Millennials view the world (and their place in it) and what role they see for govern-ment likely contribute to opinions about education.

In addition to the factors already discussed, the Millennial persona, frame, or identity also includes such characteristics as tolerance, liberal and progressive policy leanings, a sense of social justice and civic responsibility, and a detachment to traditional institutions. For Millennials, their persona leads to unique learning styles that involve more emphasis on teamwork and cooperation, goal-oriented tasks, experiential learning opportunities, including volunteer work, and of course, the use of technology (Frand 2000; Oblinger 2003). In short, the Millennial identity (reflected in both experiences and personal characteristics) provides a guide for this cohort's attitudes about a number of important issues. This is a reflection of a generational imprint that has implications about education attitudes, as Millennials consider their competitive (dis)advantage, not only in the United States but also in relation to citizens around the world. These edu-cational implications are particularly important for the large minority Millennial population, a topic we discuss next.

Universal Opportunity? Minority Millennials and Education

Attitudes about important issues discussed in this book are often understood by differentiating between Millennials and non-Millennials. However, as we consistently show, Millennials are far from monolithic and their diver-sity is a crucial factor in better understanding their attitudes. In 2014 for the first time in US history, the number of African American, Latino, and Asian students in K-12 public schools surpassed the number of non-Latino whites (Krogstad and Fry 2014). This majority–minority milestone was ushered in by the youngest of the Millennial cohort and reemphasizes the need to address the challenges of a diverse student body—challenges that Millennials have experienced firsthand as 40% of their cohort is comprised of race/ethnic minorities (Pew Research Center 2015e). These challenges include more students who live in poverty,[4] more students who require English-language training, and more students who hail from backgrounds and cultures that are different from the still-majority-white teachers who instruct them (Maxwell 2014). Further, as we have already touched upon, standardized tests have been shown to disadvantage minorities and favor those with a higher socioeconomic status (Armstrong 2013). As the assistant managing editor of *Education Weekly*, Lesli Maxwell (2014:1), summarizes, "The United States must vastly improve the educational outcomes for this new and diverse majority of American students, whose success is inextricably linked to the well-being of the nation." And the president of the Southern Education Foundation, Kent McGuire, says that ". . . we are talking about the kids that we have historically served least well . . . Over the decades we have not managed to reduce the variation in performance between kids of color and white kids . . . now we have to figure out how to do something we've never done before, for the majority" (Maxwell 2014).

The challenges for addressing the needs of a diverse student population are not just limited to primary and secondary education but are present in higher education as well. These challenges are a double-edge sword. The percentage of college students who are African Americans and Latinos has increased significantly over the last several decades. According to the National Center for Education Statistics, from 1976 to 2014, the percentage of Latino college students increased, from 4% to 17%. Among African Americans, the increase in enrollment went from 10% to 14% during this same time frame (National Center for Education Statistics, ND). However, while African Americans and Latinos are attending college at higher rates than ever before, they lag significantly behind whites in graduation rates. In 2015, 47% of white students obtained at least an Associate's degree, compared to 32% of blacks and 23% of Latinos (Ryan and Bauman 2016). In addition, many minority Millennials are also "non-traditional students," students that delay enrollment, attend college part time, or work full time, among other characteristics (Oblinger 2003).[5] Both traditional and non-traditional minority students require a recognition by education leaders and politicians that they have different needs to achieve similar levels of success as their white counterparts. This extends to policies that deal with the costs and debt of going to school.

As we circle back to economic considerations, it is important to recognize that the student loan burden disproportionately affects minorities. Many minorities tend to be first-generation college students, and thus more likely to rely on student loans to finance their way through college. Minorities are also often less aware of options to finance or repay student loan debt that may ease their financial burden (Equal Justice Works 2013). Furthermore, minorities have higher rates of unemployment, which affects their ability to repay student debts (Johnson, Van Ostern, and White 2012). Even when employed, they experience more marginal earning returns (as their educational opportunities are generally more limited) (Card 1999).

The educational needs of Millennial minorities entail addressing cohort-specific issues that include depressed socioeconomic measures, different learning styles, broader goals, and more advanced learning tools, in addition to costs and benefits. All these factors likely influence attitudes about education policies among Millennials in general—as they have observed these hardships—and among Millennial subgroups who have experienced it firsthand. We test this expectation below.

Importance of Education for Millennials and Non-Millennials

We consistently make the argument in this book that a cohort's attitudes about issues or policies are influenced by both personal characteristics and shared experiences. These factors are not mutually exclusive; rather, there is a commonality among group members that help us understand why opinions may coalesce around particular issues. Is this the case for Millennials on the issue of education? In other words, *how does the Millennial persona translate to attitudes about education and do these attitudes differ from those held by older adults?*

To explore these questions, we rely on data collected in our original survey, conducted in November and December 2015. As an initial exploration of our data, we examine the importance of education, relative to other issues, among both Millennials and non-Millennials. One question in our survey asks respondents, "In your opinion, which of the following is the most important issue to your age group or generation?" The choices included: the economy, drug legalization, education, the environment, gay marriage, gun control, healthcare, immigration, terrorism, or others (respondents allowed to type in a response). Descriptive statistics on this question indicate that nearly three times more Millennial respondents (15.8%) than non-Millennials respondents (5.7%) select education as their most important issue. For Millennials, this was the second most important issue, behind the economy.[6]

The importance Millennials place on the issue of education is also evident in their vote choice. In the survey, we ask, "If you vote in the next presidential election, how important might the following issue be to your vote? Indicate if it would be important, somewhat important, or not important." More Millennials than non-Millennials view education as important to their vote for president.[7] A difference of means test confirms this, reporting that Millennials and non-Millennials are statistically distinct in the average importance they place on the issue of education when considering their presidential vote (p<0.001).[8]

It is clear that the Millennial Generation is more concerned than older adults about the issue of education. This concern is affected by their stage of life—Millennials are currently or were recently students. It is also due to the disproportionate impact of the Great Recession felt by this age cohort on issues related to education—devalued degrees, unemployment or under-employment, and higher student loan debt. How does this concern for education translate to attitudes and policy stances on specific education-related issues? Do Millennials care broadly about education or more specifically about student loan debt? And are there observable differences among Millennials and non-Millennials in their views on policy solutions to these problems?

To explore attitudes about specific issues or problems associated with education, we are first interested in identifying how respondents prioritize these problems. Our survey includes a question that asks, "Considering our country's education system, which of the following is the most important issue to your generation or age group?" The response choices included: standardized testing, overall quality of education, gap between the wealthy and those who have less in the quality of education obtained, cost of higher education/college, and college and workplace preparedness. Figure 4.2 illustrates the distribution of preferences across these issues for Millennials and non-Millennials.

Of the education-related issues, Figure 4.2 shows that Millennials overwhelmingly care most about the cost of higher education, while non-Millennials see quality of education as the most important. Both groups, though, also view the other's top choice as priorities—Millennials' second choice is quality of education, and non-Millennials' second preference is cost of higher education. Overall, respondents see quality and cost as the most pressing education-related problems.

With regards to the cost and quality of higher education, specifically, survey participants were asked to select the statement that most closely

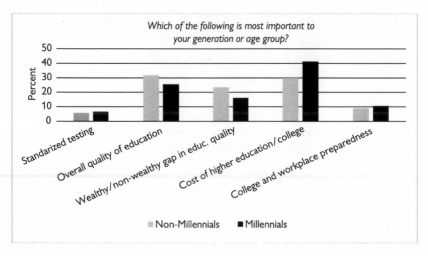

FIGURE 4.2.   Most Important Education-Related Issues among Non-Millennials and Millennials

Note: The number of observations for non-Millennials was 630; the total observations of Millennials were 621.

aligns with their personal opinion: "Higher education should be reformed to decrease costs and increase quality" or "Higher education is functioning well to keep up with economic and student demands." Responses to this question show that an overwhelming number of both Millennials and non-Millennials believe that higher education needs to be reformed to decrease cost and increase value. Only slightly more non-Millennials (79%) than Millennials (73%) hold this view.[9] While Millennials in general seem to give education and related issues more priority (and perhaps urgency), it is clear that concern about the condition of our higher education system cuts across age; those who are in the throes of obtaining a college degree (Millennials), as wells as perhaps those who are helping finance or otherwise support these endeavors (non-Millennials) recognize current deficiencies. While quality of education is, in part, related to cost (i.e., value of investment), it also relates to richness of the educational experience, which involves pedagogy, student–teacher ratio, teacher quality, satisfaction with learning outcomes, academic environment, and adequate job preparation (National Center for Education Statistics 2000). Unfortunately, we did not evaluate these individual measures in our survey, but we see the priority placed on education in terms of quality and cost as capturing many of these concerns.

Quality and Cost: Explaining Millennial Attitudes about Education

Our analyses so far show that education is more of a priority for Millennials than non-Millennials (both relative to other issues and in consideration of their presidential vote); however, both groups believe that quality and cost are the most pressing education-related problems and that reforming higher education should be a priority. Opinions about broad educational issues appear to support the narrative that, given their persona and experiences, Millennials disproportionately care about education and are quite empathetic about the struggle to obtain a quality education at a reasonable cost. What happens though when we tap into specific issues that deal with educational concerns? Do Millennial and non-Millennial opinions converge or does the young adult cohort continue to display attitudinal preferences?

Quality of Education: The Role of Standardized Testing

To more specifically examine the topic of education quality, we pivot to a contentious practice in education—standardized testing. Proponents of standardized tests believe that they provide objective and comparable measures of performance. These measures are necessary in order to hold both students and teachers/schools accountable to benchmarks that gauge student achievement and teacher/school quality (Churchill 2015). Opponents believe that pressures associated with standardized testing reduce the quality of both teaching and learning. In other words, students learn only what will be on the test and teachers teach for test outcomes rather than for broader learning outcomes. Further, opponents argue that standardized tests disadvantage minorities and favor those with a higher socioeconomic status (Armstrong 2013). This debate reflects that despite the fact standardized testing has been a feature of the US education system for more than fifty years, today standardized tests are "more pressure-packed and ubiquitous than ever before" (Fletcher 2009). Millennials know this well as they were the generation that felt the biggest impacts of "No Child Left Behind," the law in effect from 2002 to 2015 that ushered in high-stakes (for students, teachers, and school systems) standardized testing (Tooley 2015).

To explore how Millennials and non-Millennials view this specific issue related to education quality, we rely on a question from our survey that asks respondents, "For the following pair of statements, select the one that most closely aligns with your personal opinion: 1) standardized testing ensures educational outcomes or 2) standardized testing impairs teaching and learning." Results from our bivariate analysis reveal that a majority of non-Millennials (55%) and almost two-thirds of Millennials (63%) believe that standardized testing impairs teaching and learning. Broken down by race and ethnicity for Millennials—white, African American, and Latino—a majority of all three subgroups believe that standardized tests impair teaching and learning (63% of whites, 60% of African American, and 64% Latinos). Most respondents, overall, have a negative opinion about the use of standardized testing, but this opinion is stronger among Millennials than non-Millennials.

To test if the difference between Millennials and non-Millennials in negative attitudes about standardized testing are indeed a product of the Millennial Generation identity (their collective persona drawing from shared experiences), we estimate an ordered logit analysis. We include in the regression model a Millennial Generation variable that reflects if the respondent is a Millennial (born 1980–1998) or not (born before 1980. We also include measures that capture specific features of the Millennial Generation,[10] including: *diversity*—Latino, African American, and being foreign born; *liberal political ideology; economic hardship*—being unemployed and having a negative economic outlook; and a *worldview of the positive role of government* in solving problems, measured as a factor score of attitudes about government spending to reduce economic hardships, government requirement for all to have healthcare coverage, government action to reduce the cost of healthcare, and government forgiveness of student loan debt.[11] We also control for level of education, income, female, and marital status.[12]

The results of the analysis are shown in Figure 4.3. The figure represents coefficients with a dot and corresponding confidence intervals with a bar. If the bar crosses zero, we know that the variable is statistically insignificant. On the other hand, if the bar does not cross zero, the variable is statistically significant. Coefficients to the left of the zero x-line have a negative effect on the dependent variable and those to the right have a positive effect on the dependent variable. We see that the Millennial Generation variable is

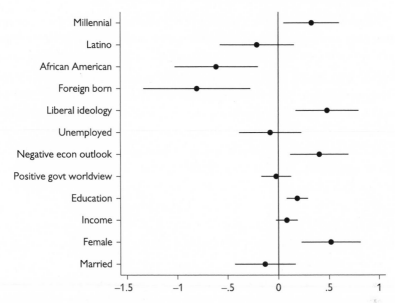

FIGURE 4.3.   The Factors That Drive Negative Attitudes about Standardized Testing

Note: Ordered logistic regression estimated. Coefficients represented by dots; 95% confidence intervals represented by lines. See Appendix 4.A for a table of the regression results.

statistically significant, as is being African American, being foreign born, having a liberal political ideology, and holding a negative economic worldview. Education, income, and being female are also significant correlates of standardized testing attitudes. Because ordered logistic coefficients are difficult to interpret, we use predicted probabilities to explore these results.[13]

Predicted probabilities indicate that Millennials have a 63.7% likelihood of believing that standardized testing impairs teaching and learning, in comparison to 55.9% of the same among non-Millennials. This confirms that Millennials (in comparison to older adults) are distinct in their attitudes about standardized testing, even when controlling for other influences. The shared experiences of Millennials, including their interaction with high-stakes standardized testing, has affected their negative attitudes about standardized testing.

In contrast, African Americans are less likely to agree that standardized testing impairs learning (46.6% likelihood), compared to non-African Americans (61.7% likelihood). Similarly, foreign-born respondents have a 41.3% likelihood of stating that standardized tests impair learning, compared to 61.2% of those who are native born. This is an interesting finding given that a central argument against standardized testing is that it disadvantages minorities (Armstrong 2013). However, the likelihood of negative attitudes about standardized testing is approximately 8% higher among Millennial African Americans and foreign-born young adults than for non-Millennials of these subgroups.

While race and foreign-born status decreases belief in the adverse effects of standardized tests, liberal political ideology and economic hardship increases it. Liberals have a 66.7% likelihood of saying standardized testing impairs learning, while conservatives have a 55.3% of saying the same. Similarly, those who think the economy was better for young people twenty years ago have a 63.2% likelihood of believing that standardized tests impair learning, in comparison to a 53.8% likelihood among those who believe the economy is the same or better today. Moreover, respondents who are more educated, have higher incomes, and are women also have a higher probability of viewing standardize tests in a negative light.[14] In all, this analysis demonstrates that there are a number of influences on negative attitudes about standardized testing, chief among them is the Millennial Generation persona or identity whose educational experiences with high-stakes testing is relevant. We examine next an issue that many Millennials continue to grapple with—student loans.

The Noose of Student Loans: Support for Education Debt Relief

The weight of a crippled higher education system, coupled with the consequences of the Great Recession that further diminished the value of a college degree, has resulted in a staggering student debt problem. In fact, 70% of bachelor degree recipients leave college with both a diploma and a bill that will soon be due, often regardless of ability to pay it (Berman 2016). The total outstanding student loan debt stands at $1.2 trillion, held by forty million borrowers, with an average balance of $29,000 (Holland 2015). In our survey, we find that 41% of Millennials and 31% of non-Millennials are currently paying or have paid student loan debt. For most Millennial respondents to our survey, their student loan debt amount totals between $11,000 and $20,000, while the debt for most non-Millennials totals less than $10,000. These numbers further drive home the disproportionate impact of student loan debt on Millennials, with far-reaching consequences. The burden of student loan debt has led to Millennials delaying marriage and starting a family, as well as putting off purchasing a home (Pew Research Center 2014c). Economists also note that this debt has contributed to a decrease in the number of entrepreneurs starting small businesses (Holland 2015). So, while student loan debt does not impact everyone directly, its effects can be felt by society as a whole.

Our Millennial focus group participants further punctuated the frustrations associated with student debt and the diminished value of their college education. Richard, a Millennial focus group participant in San Antonio, Texas, articulated the student debt problems quite well:

> I graduated and I got a job at 12 bucks an hour. That's not going to pay my student loans at all. And so yeah those are coming up next month. More likely I will start doing my masters which is kind of a good thing, but for people that didn't do so well you know they are kind of stuck and they're just getting in crippling debt.

Another Millennial, Adam, who was part of one of the focus group sessions in New Orleans, Louisiana, added the following:

> One of the main problems with going to college is the ratio for the cost of college, you know how much it's risen as opposed to income you know in the last 30 years. I don't remember what the exact percentage is but it's astronomical as far as the cost of college to the rise of income . . . But there are, you know, there's a lot of people that go to college and come out in debt with worthless degrees.

It is clear from these statements, and many other similar thoughts shared by a diverse sample of Millennials who took part in our focus groups, that the burden of student loans has saddled this cohort in a way not experienced by other generations. Pew Research Center (Fry 2014) has reported that "the typical amount of cumulative student debt for their undergraduate education increased from $12,434 for the class of 1992–1993 to $26,885 for the class of 2011–2012 (figures adjusted for inflation)."

One proposed solution to this problem (and supported by Bernie Sanders during his campaign) is for the government to forgive all student loan debt. In our final set of analyses, we examine how much support there is for such a progressive policy, whether there are differences in support among Millennials and non-Millennials and what other factors influence attitudes about student debt forgiveness.

To systematically gauge attitudes about student loan forgiveness, we asked respondents to select the statement that most closely aligns with their personal opinion: "The government should forgive all student loans" or "Individuals should have to pay back all the student loan debt they incur." More than six in ten Millennial respondents (63%) believe that the government should forgive student loan debt. Conversely, more than half of non-Millennials (56%) believe that individuals should pay back all student loans. This divergence suggests a cohort effect in attitudes about alleviating student loan burdens, and a difference of means test confirms this finding.[15]

We also expect that difference in attitudes about student loan forgiveness should extend across race and ethnicity, and in particular for Millennial subgroups. As previously discussed, minorities are often disproportionately disadvantaged by the education system in a number of ways. Specifically, though, the student loan burden is greater for minorities for a number of reasons. Many minorities tend to be first-generation college students and thus more likely to rely on student loans to finance their way through college. Minorities are also often less aware of options to finance or repay student loan debt that may ease their financial burden (Equal Justice Works 2013). Furthermore, minorities have higher rates of unemployment, which affects their ability to repay student debts (Johnson, Van Ostern, and White 2012). Descriptive analyses reveal that this is in fact the case. Figure 4.4 displays the difference between non-Millennials and Millennials in support for government forgiveness of student loans across the three subgroups. Almost six in ten (58%) white Millennials believe the government should forgive student loan debt, compared to four in ten (40%) white non-Millennials; 71% of Latino Millennials favor student loan forgiveness, in comparison to 55% of Latino non-Millennials; and 70% and 65% of African American Millennials and African American non-Millennials, respectively, believe that the government should forgive student loan debt.

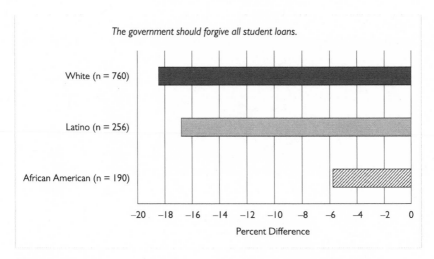

FIGURE 4.4.   Difference between Non-Millennials & Millennials in Support for Government Forgiveness of Student Loans across Race/Ethnic Groups

Note: Bars represent the difference between the percentage of respondents in the Non-Millennial and Millennial groups that say "the government should forgive all student loans" most closely aligns with their personal opinion as opposed to "individuals should have to pay back all the student loan debt they incurred."

To further explore generational effects, we consider attitudes about student loans in a regression model that interacts the variable Millennial Generation with other factors that may influence individual opinions about this policy proposal. These factors include being Latino, African American, and foreign born.[16] We also account for economic self-interest—unemployment and economic hardship, measured as thinking the economy was better for young people twenty years ago—on opinions about student debt. These variables capture the economic context in which respondents view the cost of education. Additionally, how respondents view the role of government in solving problems likely influences opinions about student loans. To account for this, we include a variable for liberal political ideology (represented by a dichotomous measure) and measures that capture opinions about the appropriate role of government in: spending to alleviate economic hardship, requiring healthcare coverage, and reducing the cost of healthcare.[17] Finally, we also control for education level, income, gender, and marital status as these characteristics may influence attitudes about student loans. Because logistic coefficients are difficult to interpret,

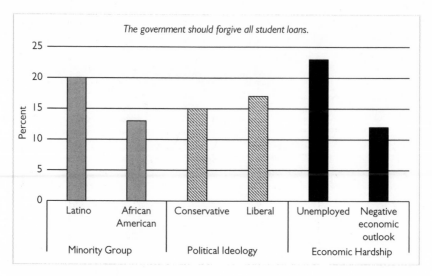

FIGURE 4.5.   The Effect of Economic Hardship, Minority Group Identity, and Political Ideology on Attitudes about Student Loan Debt

Note: Results of pairwise comparisons of marginal effects of Millennials and non-Millennials shown based on estimates of ordered logistic regression analysis that interacted each independent variable with the variable Millennial. All are statistically significant differences at $p<0.05$.

especially with interactions, we report pairwise comparisons of marginal effects between Millennials and non-Millennials to explain the regression results.[18]

The statistically significant marginal effect contrasts ($p<0.10$)—the difference between Millennials and non-Millennials on support for individuals having to pay back all the student loan debt they incurred—is shown in Figure 4.5.

The results from the interaction model highlight the effect of being Millennial across minority group status (race and ethnicity), ideology, and economic hardship on attitudes about repayment of student loans. The pairwise comparison of marginal effects show that Latino Millennials are 20% more likely to say that the government should forgive all the student loan debt, in comparison to Latino non-Millennials. The impact of race on Millennial opinions about student loans is a bit less pronounced than ethnicity but still substantively meaningful; African American Millennials are 13% more likely than African American non-Millennials to support student loan debt forgiveness. This difference approaches conventional levels of statistical significance (p<0.08). These contrasts emphasize the disproportionate appeal of a government-led student loan forgiveness program among Latino and African American youth.

We observe another example of cohort strength in the role "Millennial" plays to mitigate the effects of ideology on opinions about student loans. Liberal Millennials are 17% more likely than their non-Millennial counterparts to favor government-led relief of student loan debt. However, conservative Millennials are also similarly inclined, albeit slightly less so than their liberal counterparts—they are 15% more likely than conservative non-Millennials to favor student debt relief. The effects of economic hardship and attitudes about the economy also help distinguish Millennials and non-Millennials on the issue of student loans. Unemployed Millennials are 23% more likely to favor a student debt relief policy than their non-Millennial counterparts, while those with a negative economic outlook—expressed as belief that the economy was better for those twenty years ago—are 12% more likely to favor student debt relief, compared to non-Millennials with the same economic perspective.

The findings from these analyses reveal a consistent pattern: Millennials are remarkably steadfast in their belief that government should alleviate the burden of student debt. This belief transcends social, political, and economic factors that often produce important divisions across a number of issues, even in the face of cohort-specific influences. The Millennial Generation has endured the disproportionate burden of an overpriced and undervalued education, and regardless of whether or not they approve of government intrusion in other areas of their lives, student debt relief seems to hold a unique position in their political calculus.

Conclusion

In this chapter, we have shown that the Millennial persona, in addition to unique generational experiences, influences this cohort's attitudes about issues related to education. We emphasize two factors that are particularly useful to understanding Millennials' opinions and preferences on this topic. First is the race and ethnic diversity of this cohort and how it not only alters educational priorities but also creates new challenges for politicians and policymakers. Second is the crippling effects of the Great

Recession and the slow economic recovery—an experience that has been formative to Millennials' interaction with the education system and, thus, has contributed to their policy preferences. In this context, we find that Millennials are more likely than non-Millennials to 1) prioritize the issue of education; 2) consider education in determining their vote for president; 3) be more concerned about the impairments of standard testing; and 4) more strongly support government-led student loan debt forgiveness. The strength of opinions about student loan forgiveness is particularly powerful because the cohort ("Millennial") effect is consistent, even in the face of other factors known to exert significant explanatory value on policy preferences.

It is unclear how much, if any, educational reform will take place during the presidency of Donald Trump. Trump has spoken out in favor of policies related to school choice and education vouchers for K-12 education. He has said much less about reforms that will assist minority students and issues related to higher education. Problems related to the rising costs of obtaining a degree, the diminished value of a college education, and the lack of competitiveness of workers in a global market are not going away any time soon.

Millennials are soon to be the largest voting cohort, and their frustration and disappointment with the state of American education is palpable. We observed these sentiments throughout our Millennial focus group sessions. To articulate these sentiments, we return to Clarice, one of the Millennial focus group participants we highlighted earlier in the chapter:

> I think that there's two options nowadays, and it's either you go to college and you're going to be in debt for the rest of our life, and you'll have a good job; or, you don't, and you're going to be poor the rest of your life and work minimum-wage jobs. I think that that used to not be the case. Back in the day, they had good elementary schools and then vocational training; and I think in other countries, once you get to ninth grade, you're either taking the college route, or you're taking the vocational route. I think we should bring that back.

The education scholar, Tony Monchinski, says that our education system reflects power at work and that the politics of education is a struggle for power. We argue in this chapter that the rise in popularity of Bernie Sanders, particularly among Millennials—due in large part to the attention he placed on reforming higher education—reflected this struggle for power. His policies were so strongly embraced that Hillary Clinton was compelled to adopt some of Sander's proposals on education once she secured the Democratic Party nomination in an attempt to appeal to these young voters. If Millennials are able to exert even more political power in future presidential elections, it seems that where candidates stand on the politics of education may go a long way to determining their electoral prospects.

The 9/11 Generation: Millennials, Worldviews, and Attitudes about Foreign Policy

It is difficult to pinpoint a more defining singular moment for the Millennial Generation than the attacks of September 11, 2001. The post-9/11 world is substantially different than the pre-9/11 world, and the Millennial[1] cohort has grappled with the wide-ranging effects of that tragedy. Examples abound about how the events of that day have influenced Millennials and how it has shaped their worldviews. The media has chronicled numerous stories on both the immediate, short-term impacts of 9/11 and its longer, lingering effects. The news website, *The Morning Call*, reported one such story, titled "For millennials, 9/11 and its aftermath shaped their view of the world,"[2] highlighting several Millennials and their opinions about 9/11 and terrorism. One Millennial featured is Bret Ludlow. This is how his experience with 9/11 was conveyed in the news story:

> That Tuesday morning . . . Bret Ludlow was a seventh-grader at Orefield Middle School. Happy go-lucky and unacquainted with tragedy, he says now. After the second pixelated plane hit the World Trade Center—and then hit again, and again, and again in broadcasts throughout the day—his life changed. "It was the first time we started to see that the world was a darker place and it was the first time I realized, things can be pretty serious out there."

For Ludlow, the way he viewed the world was not only altered by 9/11, but also he recognizes that the world has indeed gotten smaller as he has grown up. Speaking of the influences on Millennial attitudes in the long run, Ludlow talks of the effects of globalization and how they are greater than the more specific incidents of September 11. On this, he says, "Young adults and teenagers in America have more alike than different with teenagers across the world because of globalization and what technology has done to connect everybody. That has impacted mindsets when it comes to international topics and viewpoints."

Ludlow's perspective is not a unique one among his peers, but there is also a diversity of opinions among Millennials in how they view terrorism in general and the 9/11 attacks, more specifically. Our own Millennial focus group participants offered some of these varying opinions. DJ, a focus group participant in San Antonio, Texas, said that the terrorist attacks of that day have to be kept in perspective. "More Americans died in the last 24 months from lone shootings reported on the news or otherwise than died in 9/11. It's ridiculous and I just read that and I was like 'Oh my god, that's a lot of people.' So yes, terrorism is a large issue but we also have other issues to deal with." And Paul, a focus group participant also in San Antonio, stated that terrorism and 9/11 have to be dealt with "in the longer scale," but expressed the need to also focus on what he calls other forms of terrorism that do not receive as much attention. To this, he said, ". . . we need to focus on what's going on here. We have terrorists, but we have a lot of gangs. We have a lot of stuff coming in from Mexico from the cartel. We need to focus on the drugs that are coming in; that's terrorism."

The events of September 11, 2001, coupled with other important forces such as the wars in Afghanistan and Iraq, have certainly had a formative impact on the Millennial cohort, not only in the way they view their own security but relatedly how they view the world around them and the United States' relationship with other countries. Issues of foreign policy for Millennials are situated within a different context than for Baby Boomers and Gen Xers. Baby Boomers were significantly influenced by the Vietnam War and the antiwar movement that was at the grassroots level a "youth crusade" (Bernstein 2007). Generation X was largely affected by the Cold War and then the thawing of relations with the Soviet Union and the fall of the Berlin Wall. To be sure, the world is a different place than it was during the time when both Baby Boomers and Gen Xers were young. First, there is not a coherent or singular enemy for Millennials to unify around (Thrall and Goepner 2015). Second, advancements in technology and communication have redefined the flow and speed of information. As a result, young people today are much less likely to think of problems (or solutions to those problems), especially foreign policy problems, as being bound by borders.

Millennials' global view for solving problems and the role of technology in this endeavor can be seen through the way this cohort is asked to engage. An example of this is *Global Citizen*, a leading non-governmental organization (NGO). This organization describes itself as "a social action platform for a global generation that wants to solve the world's biggest challenges" (www.globalcitizen.org/en/about/who-we-are/). *Global Citizen* promotes advocacy and prioritizes taking on challenges that face the world and that impact people, not only those in one's backyard but also around the world. *Global Citizen* understands the tools that Millennials use and the issues that matter to them and directly leverages them to recruit this cohort (although participation is not limited to Millennials). In short, organizations such as *Global Citizen* see the global-reaching potential of Millennials, particularly now that many are at the age of being working professionals and want to exploit their size and influence. We discuss this in much more detail in the chapter on Millennials and political engagement (Chapter 9).

The attitudes of Millennials about foreign policy therefore, may have as much, if not more, to do with the collective effects of globalization as with the narrower scope of the 9/11 attacks and the wars in the Middle East. Overall, Millennials are less likely to embrace an adversarial position (compared to other cohorts) when it comes to dealing with other countries; they believe more in diplomacy and international cooperation than resorting to military force. Of course, similar to other topics discussed in this book, Millennials are not monolithic in their preferences and attitudes about foreign policy issues. There are likely differences across factors such as partisanship and gender, as well as among Millennial race and ethnic subgroups; a diversity we explore in the analyses presented in this chapter. As the generation that will likely formulate foreign policy decisions in the not-too-distant future, these differences are important to examine and understand.

In the following sections, we briefly review the importance of the Millennial Generation and place the significance of this cohort in the context of attitudes held by the general public about how the United States should engage with the world. We then examine the factors that influence foreign policy attitudes and how these factors help differentiate preferences among Millennials. We conclude the chapter by describing the results and discussing the implications of our findings.

The Development of General Attitudes about Foreign Policy

General American foreign policy attitudes have changed over time, and as we would expect, they have been heavily dependent on the events of the time. Prior to World War II, the United States had very few formal international alliances and no American troops stationed abroad. As a result, the prevalent attitude in the United States at that time was one of isolationism (Ambrose and Brinkley 2010). Ambrose and Brinkley (2010: IX) note that during this period " . . . Americans believed in a natural harmony of interests between nations, assumed that there was a common commitment to peace, and argued that no nation or people could profit from war." Then the attack on Pearl Harbor and World War II occurred, and American foreign policy attitudes changed. The reality that we could be (and were) attacked in our own backyard was jarring. Americans were acutely faced with their own vulnerability and realized that threats needed to be dealt with elsewhere before they reached the homeland. Foreign policy attitudes, thus, shifted to one of expansionism and internationalism (Holsti 1992; Ambrose and Brinkley 2010).[3]

Fast-forward to the Cold War (post-1960), the United States and the Soviet Union were rivals, both in an economic and military sense. The rivalry was punctuated by the development of scientific and technological advancements that brought nuclear weapons (and an arms race) to the forefront of a fear of "mutually assured destruction." This time period in foreign policy significantly conflated military and political issues, and thus complicated American attitudes about foreign policy that were once thought by some to simply be marked by a bipolar classification of isolationist–interventionist or liberal–realist (Maggiotto and Wittkopf 1981; Holsti 1992).[4]

There has been far from a consensus regarding a binary division of American attitudes about foreign policy, even before the onset of the Cold War. Early work on this topic actually found no dimensions guiding these attitudes because the public held weak, uninformed, inconsistent, and intellectually unstructured opinions about foreign policy (Erskine 1963; Converse 1964; Converse and Markus 1979). This lack of uninformed and unstable opinion structure was due in part to the fact that Americans were seen by elites as indifferent to foreign policy because these sort of issues were so far removed from their everyday lives (Hurwitz and Peffley 1987; Anand and Krosnick 2003). The Vietnam War did quite a bit to challenge this notion. Public opinion and increasing skepticism about the war effort came to be viewed as an important component of what the US strategy should ultimately be in Southeast Asia. Further, a number of critics of the war believed commercial public opinion polls were too simplistic and distorted real attitudes about the war (i.e., commercial polls tended to ask whether respondents supported current US policy in Vietnam rather than probing more deeply about other policy options) (Holsti 1992).

The Vietnam War and the predicaments surrounding it provided an impetus for the development of scholarly surveys that more deeply gauged public opinion about foreign policy. Better survey techniques, coupled with greater belief about the significance of public opinion on matters related to foreign policy, resulted in the contemporary studies that have explored how these attitudes are structured (Holsti and Rosenau 1980; Maggiotto and Wittkopf 1981). While there is still debate over the coherence of mass public opinion about foreign policy, two points now find some consensus: 1) although the general public is poorly informed about international issues, attitudes about these topics do have some level of structure; 2) a binary division of isolationism–interventionism does not properly capture the multidimensions of public opinion on international matters (Hurwitz and Peffley 1987; Holsti 1992). This implies that there are factors by which public opinion on foreign policy clusters, as like-minded individuals often share political, religious, or social backgrounds. It also means that public opinion on foreign policy is more complex than scholars thought even four decades ago.

One prominent typology of opinion that attempts to get at this complexity is Eugene Wittkopf's (1990) "four faces of internationalism" framework. The framework, taking lessons from the post-Vietnam era, places people into different categories based on their willingness to engage in international affairs and the method of engagement—through diplomacy (cooperation) or through military action.[5] While other categorizations have been proposed, this is a parsimonious way to view public preferences for international intervention and serves as a powerful predictor of foreign policy preferences across numerous issues (Thrall and Goepner 2015).

Factors Impacting Millennial Foreign Policy Attitudes: Critical Periods and Cosmopolitanism

International relations scholars have long warned against the simplistic approach of trying to understand attitudes about foreign policy based solely on political ideology. This assumption was in part the motivation to develop other typologies that transcended ideology or other basic one-dimensional explanations of public opinions about foreign policy. This was especially the case because many scholars understood that the attitude structure of foreign policy may not be based on the same factors as domestic ones, especially since most of the public was so far removed from, and did not care much about, international issues. As we would expect, Millennials are impacted by similar factors that influence foreign policy attitudes of the public at large (Schuman and Corning 2012; Thrall and Goepner 2015). However, we also know that Millennials share a different set of characteristics and experiences, ranging from singular events (including 9/11) to global trends (such as the proliferation of technology), that have shaped their formative years in ways that depart from the influences on non-Millennials when they were young adults.

According to Thrall and Goepner (2015: 1), Millennials "have distinct attitudes toward a range of important foreign policy issues." The authors note that the main motivators of Millennial's foreign policy attitudes can be placed into two categories. The first category involves events that were put in motion before Millennials came of age. These events include the end of the Cold War, the development of the internet, and the spread of globalization. The second category refers to events that occurred during Millennials' formative years, or what the authors refer to as a "critical period"—the time between the ages of 14 to 24 when a person is most vulnerable to the effects of socialization. The attacks of September 11, 2001 are not only front and center here, but also include the broader wars in the Middle East. Past research has noted the importance of national and world events that are experienced during a "critical period" of childhood, adolescence, and early adulthood as a way to make generational distinctions and to understand factors that help shape political attitudes (Kinder and Sears 1985; Schuman and Corning 2012), especially those related to foreign policy (Holsti and Rosenau 1980).[6] As Schuman and Corning (2012:2) state, generations are a product of "unique events [that] affect people of the same birth cohorts at an early age, shaping them in distinctive ways." "Critical periods" are also important in that the way they affect a cohort may be conditioned by other factors. Ideology is one such example; liberal and conservative Millennials process their critical period events differently (Zaller 1992; Thrall and Goepner 2015). So, while ideology has not been the primary or even sole basis by which foreign policy attitudes are determined, it can play a meaningful role when examined in the presence of other detrimental factors.

As we have discussed previously, the Millennial generational persona, frame, or identity helps us understand this cohort's political beliefs, attitudes, and policy preferences. The Millennial persona includes demographic diversity, tolerance, liberal and progressive policy leanings, a cosmopolitan worldview, and detachment to traditional institutions. We expect these characteristics will influence opinions about foreign policy. In fact, several disparities between Millennials' views on foreign policy and those of non-Millennials have been previously observed. Thrall and Goepner (2015), highlight three differences in particular. First, Millennials see the world as less threatening than non-Millennials. Second, Millennials are more likely to support foreign policies aimed at cooperation with other nations. Finally, Millennials are less supportive of military action, compared to older generations. The authors argue that this sentiment is due in large part to fatigue over the wars in Iraq and Afghanistan, which they have labeled as the "Iraq Aversion."

And so the story of 9/11 specifically, and the events surrounding the conflicts more broadly, continue to be prominent in understanding how Millennial formulate foreign policy choices. This is especially important because one major debate about the formation of, and interest in, foreign policy is how distant international affairs were perceived to be to most Americans at one point in time. While World War II and the attack on

Pearl Harbor were an initial introduction into the United States's inability to isolate itself from the world (and its efforts post-war to be a world leader), the events of 9/11 and the rapid advancements in communication technology have almost entirely removed barriers to interaction and made the United States, for better or for worse, a vital part of the global community. The consequence, for our purposes here, is the increasing prominence of a worldview and a Cosmopolitan identity, primarily among Millennials.

The Importance of Cosmopolitan Identity on the Foreign Policy Attitudes of Millennials

The events of September 11, 2001 and the subsequent wars in Iraq and Afghanistan brought the world into our backyard, something that had not occurred that suddenly since the attacks on Pearl Harbor in 1941. However, the world was already "arriving," and Millennials, more so than any previous generation, are easily and instantly exposed to life outside US borders on a regular basis. Whether it is through cell phones, the internet, social media, or 24-hour news services, it is much harder today to isolate oneself from the world than to actually be an active part of it. Millennials have largely lived their entire lives in this context and, thus, these circumstances inform their worldview. Relatedly, and as previously emphasized, Millennials are the most diverse generation in US history. This diversity is, in large part, due to immigration, which has exposed Millennials to many cultures and, as a result, has made their world a much more integrated place.

Millennials are the first digital natives and the generation most steeped in the international environment. Millennials are known as the "first globals" (Zogby and Kuhl 2013) and are more likely than other generations to espouse a sense of being a global citizen, which has also led to the identity of cosmopolitanism, or seeing oneself as a "citizen of the world" above other identities (Nussbaum 1996; Telhami 2015). As many as one-third of Millennials are likely to see themselves through the lens of cosmopolitanism, more so than other identities (Zogby and Kuhl 2013; Telhami 2015). The feeling of connectedness brought forth by a cosmopolitan identity offers the opportunity for a sense of empathy of cultures, traditions, and ideas, which is likely to influence Millennials' views about US foreign policy. The question, though, remains whether and how a Millennial cosmopolitan identity and worldview translate into foreign policy opinions held by this cohort.

How does the Millennial Generation persona manifest itself into tangible and observable foreign policy preferences? Do differences of foreign policy opinions exist between Millennials and non-Millennials? And are there differences among Millennial subgroups in their foreign policy choices? We now turn to a recent survey to explore these questions.

Differences in Global Priorities between Millennials and Non-Millennials

To examine how Millennial foreign policy opinions differ from older adults and how these preferences also vary among Millennials, we utilize a survey comprised of 1,580 panelists from across the United States. The data include a sample of 845 adults, age 35 years and older and 863 Millennials adults, age 18–34 years. The survey was conducted by Nielsen Scarborough on May 20–31, 2016 with a panel consisting of a probability-based representative sample. Millennials were oversampled in order to gather additional responses from this age cohort that allow for deeper analyses. Further information about the survey and the methodology used can be found in Chapter 2.

To probe the differences among Millennials and non-Millennials in their foreign policy preferences, let us look first at the top global priorities of respondents. The survey asked respondents to identify two issues they considered to be a top global priority for the United States. The following issues were included as response options: 1) the rise of China, 2) the assertiveness of Russia, 3) North Korea, 4) Iran, 5) trade deficit, 6) the Israeli–Palestinian conflict, 7) the war on ISIS, 8) the war on al-Qaeda, 9) the civil war in Libya, 10) the civil war in Yemen, 11) US immigration policy, and 12) the tense relations with Egypt and Saudi Arabia. Figure 5.1 displays the percentage of Millennials and non-Millennials responding that each issue is a top global priority. For purposes of examination of this survey and to be consistent with the analyses in this book, Millennials are considered to be those respondents aged 18–34 years.

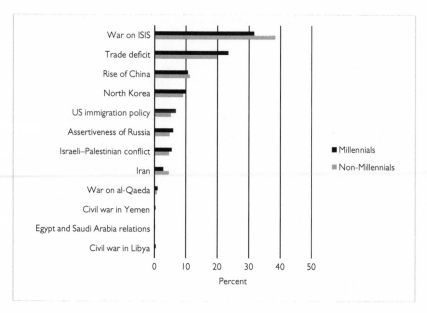

FIGURE 5.1.   Global Priorities among Millennials and Non-Millennials

With close examination of the results shown in Figure 5.1, we gain some interesting insights into the global issues Millennials and non-Millennials prioritize. One, the rank of the priorities of both groups are the same. This implies that the pressures facing our nation in relation to the rest of the world are felt by adults of all ages and that there are clear foreign policy priorities across the American population. This is tempered, however, by the second observation we can make—a lower percentage of Millennials place importance on terrorism, specifically *The War with ISIS*. As discussed in the introduction to this chapter, we observed this lesser emphasis given to terrorism in the focus groups we conducted.

Across the board, Millennial focus group participants expressed some concern with Islamic terrorism; however, they pointed to violence within our country as important as well, and the rhetoric of fear surrounding terrorism as inciting a false sense of alarm. Many voiced the opinion that the term "terrorism" should not be reserved solely for violence perpetrated by radical Islamic groups. As Simone from New Orleans put it: "There are crazy people that have easy access to guns in our country that kill us, ourselves, our own countrymen. They're real terrorists, and we don't even call them that." Others voiced the concern that terrorism is linked to a fear campaign in our country, one that inspires an unfounded sense of risk. On this, Tara, a focus group participant from the Washington, DC area, asserts:

> You should be more scared of what you're ordering at McDonald's than a terrorist from another country attacking us. You should be more scared of the homegrown terrorists that are here, because there's more terrorists in this country that are from this country than the chances of ISIS attacking us; because it's not going to happen anytime soon. They love to throw it in our faces. "Oh, be scared," "Be scared, America"; but it's not [true] . . . It's an isolated affair.

These are important insights into what Millennials are thinking with regards to terrorism. However, we do not know whether the importance placed on terrorism or the other global issues identified as priorities by Millennials is significantly different from the importance placed by non-Millennials. In other words, we cannot say with certainty that there are significant differences between Millennials and non-Millennials. In order to establish this, let us examine more closely the importance each group places on global issues. While we have already seen the issues that Millennials and non-Millennials rank as top priorities, we can gain further understanding by looking at the survey question that asks respondents to rate the importance of each issue on a scale of 1–10 (where 1 is "not important" and 10 is "very important). The mean, variations, and maximum and minimum values of the ratings given by Millennials and non-Millennials of the five issues deemed most important—*The War on ISIS, Trade Deficit, The Rise of China, North Korea,* and *US Immigration Policy,* are depicted in Figure 5.2.[7]

Figure 5.2 highlights yet again that Millennials and non-Millennials are thinking similarly about foreign policy priorities. Each group rated the same five issues as higher on the importance scale. Also, both Millennial and non-Millennial perceptions of the importance of each issue trend together, although Millennials place less importance on all issues, in comparison to non-Millennials. Given these trends, are Millennial foreign policy priorities actually different than older adults? Using responses to this question about the importance of each global issue, we conducted a statistical test

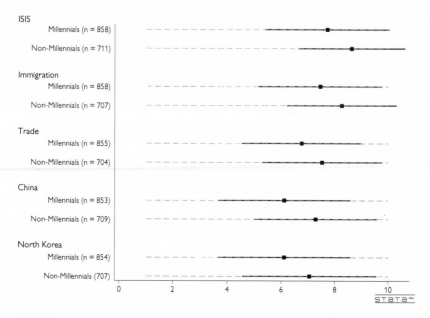

FIGURE 5.2. Non-Millennials' and Millennials' Opinions about the Importance of Global Issues

Notes: Dots represent the means of each variable, the solid lines extend from the mean minus one standard deviation to the mean plus one standard deviation, and the dashed lines extend from the minimum to maximum values. The number of millennial respondents is in parenthesis next to each variable. Variables are listed from highest to lowest mean values.

of means to compare the response averages between Millennials and non-Millennials in the importance they place on each of the top five global issues. The tests indicate that there is a statistically significant difference between Millennials and non-Millennials in the average importance placed on all five of these issues.[8] And for all five issues, the average importance placed on the issue by Millennials is lower than by non-Millennials.

Non-Millennials, in comparison to Millennials, perceive the issue of *the War on ISIS* and the issue of *Immigration Policy* to be of greater importance. These same patterns hold true for the other three top global priority issues—*Trade Deficit, The Rise of China,* and *North Korea*. Millennials rate all five issues, on average, less important than non-Millennials (at least in relative terms). The lower average of importance placed on each issue reflects that among Millennials, there are more individuals rating the issue as lower in importance than their non-Millennial counterparts. In other words, there is more diversity of opinion on the importance of these issues among the Millennial Generation than among older adults.

Differences in Global Policy Priorities among Millennial Subgroups

We have asserted throughout this book that Millennials are not mono-lithic in their attitudes, and we expect this to be no different when it comes to opinions about foreign policy. Specifically, we explore whether political ideology, gender, and race and ethnicity have a mediating effect on how Millennials prioritize issues of foreign policy as these are typical influences on policy preferences. Continuing with the survey question that asks respondents to rate the importance of each global issue, we test for differences of mean importance between Republicans and non-Republicans, females and males, and white, African American, and Latino Millennials.[9] Figure 5.3 displays the mean values for policy priorities among these groups.

As shown in Figure 5.3, there are some differences across the subgroups of Millennials in the priorities they place on the five top global issues. We test whether these differences are statistically significant between specific groups.[10] First, we find that Millennial females are slightly less likely than male Millennials to rate two of the five issues as important (p<0.01). For the issues of *The Rise of China* and *Trade Deficit*, Millennial females, on average, rate this 0.42 points and 0.64 points, respectively, below their male counterparts. We also see significant differences among Millennial Republicans and their non-Republican peers on the issues of *The War with ISIS, Trade Deficit,* and *Immigration Policy* (p<0.01). The biggest difference is evident with the issue of immigration: Republican Millennials, on average, rate the issue nearly 1 point higher in importance than non-Republican Millennials.

Turning to differences among race and ethnic groups, we see a pattern emerge across all five global issues: Latinos prioritize each issue the most, while African Americans prioritize four of the five global issues the least. Immigration is the exception to this pattern; whites, on average, give less priority to immigration than African Americans.[11] However, only on the issue of *The Rise of China* do we observe statistically significant differences across the race and ethnic subgroups. There is a statistically distinct

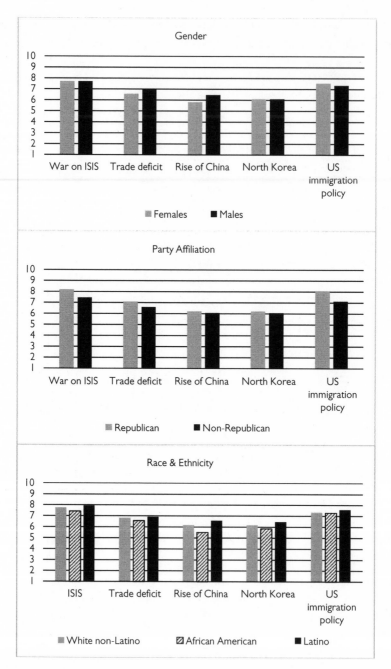

FIGURE 5.3. Opinions about Global Priorities among Millennial Subgroups

Note: Bars represent mean value of importance, ranging from 1 (not important) to 10 (very important). Number of respondents for each subgroup is as follows: Females = 469, Males = 394, Republicans = 298, Non-Republicans = 565, Whites = 343, African Americans = 83, Latinos = 107.

difference in means between Latino Millennials and African American Millennials in the importance they place on China (p< 0.01); Latinos are more likely than African Americans to prioritize this issue. Also, there is a statistically distinct difference in means between Latinos and white Millennials (p<0.05.); whites are less likely to prioritize the issue of China than their Latino peers.

So far, we have seen that there are clear differences between Millennials and non-Millennials and among Millennial subgroups. Based on the general literature on foreign policy attitudes and the specific literature about Millennials, we suspect that these differences are a product of how Millennials view these issues or priorities, relative to non-Millennials. These differences suggest that foreign policy preferences are a product of Millennial views that the world is not as threatening as non-Millennials view it—or as the previous analyses have shown as white Millennials, compared to minority Millennials; female Millennials, compared to male Millennials; and non-Republican Millennials, compared to Republican Millennials see it. Even accounting for the differences among young adults, Millennials seem to think that a more productive international strategy is one based on cooperation rather than conflict (Thrall and Goepner 2015). To this point, though, these differences are relative and not absolute; it is important to remember that both non-Millennials and Millennials similarly ranked the top five global issues. However, the relative differences serve as an important illustration that variations in opinion across and within cohorts can be missed without more nuanced examinations. Below we delve further into this exploration to test how other individual-level factors influence the foreign policy attitudes of Millennials, compared to non-Millennials.

Solving International Issues: Explaining Millennial Foreign Policy Attitudes

Our initial analyses on global policy priorities revealed that while both Millennials and non-Millennials rank global issues in the same order of importance, Millennial intensity for these issues is not as strong as those of non-Millennials. We also saw that there are statistically distinct differences among Millennials across gender, party affiliation, and race and ethnic lines. However, this examination tells us little about the approach to foreign policy that these groups support and what factors influence these attitudes. To account for this, we conduct more extensive analyses that include other likely influences on foreign policy attitudes among and between Millennials and non-Millennials.

We again utilize our survey conducted by Nielsen Scarborough in May 2016 to explore distinctions in foreign policy attitudes. We focus on the survey question that asks respondents to indicate their preferred *method for solving international conflicts*. Respondents were given a scale of choices, ranging from 1–5, where 1 is "diplomatic methods of negotiations or sanctions is the best way to solve international conflict" and 5 is "armed/militarized action or force is the best way to solve international conflict." We collapsed responses of 1 and 2 as well as 4 and 5 to create a three-category scale where on one end there are those who prefer or lean toward diplomatic methods and on the other end are those who support or lean toward military action; those in the middle support a mix of the two methods. Therefore, this three-category scale runs from "dove" preferences for diplomatic methods to "hawk" preferences supportive of military action with "mixed" preferences falling in the middle.

First, we examine responses to this question about *solving international conflict* across a number of individual factors, including generation (Millennials/non-Millennials); exposure to diverse cultures, proxied by ethnicity and race (Latinos/non-Latinos and African American/non-African American) and foreign country connections (have relatives residing in foreign countries); political ideology (Republicans/non-Republicans); and cosmopolitan identity (the strength of identifying as a "global citizen"). The variable that captures cosmopolitan identity is created from a question in the survey that asks, "in terms of what is important to you, how much do you identify with being a citizen of the world?" Respondents are provided choices from a scale of 1–10, where 1 equals "not at all" important and 10 represents "very strongly" important. The higher the value, the more strongly a respondent embraces a cosmopolitan identity.

Figure 5.4 displays preferences for solving international conflict, "dove," "mixed," and "hawk," for each group. The bars indicate the percentage of respondents that chose each foreign policy approach. Looking first at Millennials versus non-Millennials, we see the most frequently chosen approach for both groups is "dove" or diplomatic methods. Fifty-one

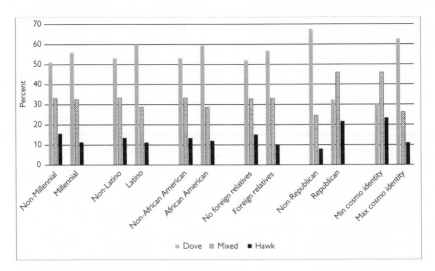

FIGURE 5.4. Doves or Hawks? Opinions about Methods for Solving International Conflict (Diplomatic, Mixed, or Military Force)

Note: Percentage of respondents in each group shown across preferences for solving international conflict (dove, mixed, hawk). Number of respondents for each subgroup is as follows: Non-Millennial = 717; Millennial = 863; Non-Latino = 1,407; Latino = 173; Non-African Americans = 1,449; African Americans = 173; No foreign relatives = 995; Foreign relative = 581; Non-Republicans = 971; Republicans = 609; No Cosmopolitan identity = 137; Max Cosmopolitan identity = 380.

percent of non-Millennials and 56% of Millennials support this approach, compared to 15.64% and 11.30%, non-Millennials and Millennials respectively, support for "hawk" methods. Approximately one-third of both groups prefer "mixed" methods of solving international conflicts. At first glance, there seems to be little difference among Millennials and non-Millennials in their preferences for foreign policy solutions, but a statistical test of means demonstrates there are distinct differences ($p<0.05$) with Millennials leaning toward diplomatic solutions to international conflict.[12]

Figure 5.4 also shows that Latinos are more likely to be "doves" in their approach to foreign policy than non-Latinos. Sixty percent of Latinos support diplomatic methods of solving international conflict, compared to 53.12% of non-Latinos. A greater percentage of African Americans and those with relatives in foreign countries also prefer diplomatic methods in comparison to their counterparts. The biggest gap in preferences for diplomacy over military action occurs with Republicans and non-Republicans: 67.44% of non-Republicans prefer "dove" methods, while only 32.27% of their Republican counterparts support the same. Most Republicans, 46.05%, support "mixed" methods.

We also find that a cosmopolitan identity influences respondents' preferences for dealing with international conflicts. Respondents who hold a high cosmopolitan identity are more likely to hold a "dove" perspective toward international issues, compared to those who have a lower cosmopolitan identity. Slightly less than 31% of those who have no cosmopolitan identity (respond that they do "not at all" identify with being "a citizen of the world"—a rating of "0" on the identity scale) support "dove" methods of solving international conflict. In comparison, 62.63% of those who have the most cosmopolitan identity (respond that they "very strongly" identify with being "a citizen of the world"—a rating of "10" on the identity scale) prefer diplomatic solutions.

We now know that upon initial inspection, there are differences in attitudes about foreign policy across a number of measures: Millennials are very slightly more likely to be "doves," Latinos are more likely to be "doves" as are African Americans and those with relatives in foreign countries, Republicans are more likely to prefer "mixed" methods, and respondents with a greater cosmopolitan identity are also more likely to be "doves" in their approach to foreign policy. This indicates that preferences for solving international conflict vary across ethnicity, exposure to different cultures, partisanship, and worldview. The generational effect is small and may likely disappear when controlling for these other influences. It is probable, however, that generational effects may be present within these groups. That is, we may see the effect of these individual-level characteristics translated differently for Millennials and non-Millennials in their foreign policy preferences.

To examine this closer, we run a statistical analysis that regresses an interaction of the variable Millennial Generation with each of the other explanatory factors, including ethnicity, having foreign relatives, party affiliation, and cosmopolitan identity, on *method for solving international conflict*. Given that the dependent variable is coded 1 through 3 (1 = "dove" or diplomatic methods, 2 = "mixed" methods, and 3 = "hawk" or military action), an ordered logit analysis is estimated. We also control for being female, education levels, and income, as these characteristics may represent experiences or interests that influence foreign policy beliefs. Because logistic coefficients are difficult to interpret, particularly for interactions,

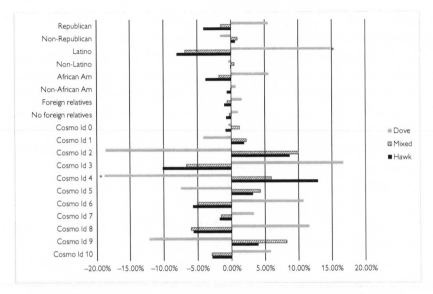

FIGURE 5.5. Marginal Effect Contrasts between Millennials and Non-Millennials across Influences on Support for Method of Solving International Conflict

Notes: Results of pairwise comparisons of marginal effects shown based on estimates of ordered logistic regression analysis that interacted each independent variable with the variable Millennial. Difference in Millennial versus Non-Millennial marginal effect shown by the bars. Negative values indicate that, for that dependent variable outcome, Millennials are less likely than Non-Millennials; positive values indicate that Millennials are more likely than Non-Millennials. Statistically significant differences (p<0.10) between Millennials and Non-Millennials are marked with an asterisk at the end of the bar.

we rely on pairwise comparisons of marginal effects to explore the regression results.[13]

Figure 5.5 displays the marginal effect contrast—the difference between Millennials and non-Millennials in their likelihood of preference for solving international conflict—for each independent variable value and each dependent variable outcome (dove, mixed, and hawk). The bars indicate the size of the difference, and asterisks at the end of the bars indicate if the difference between Millennials and non-Millennials is statistically significant (p<0.10). Bars to the left of the zero line indicate that Millennials among that group are less likely to prefer the method for solving international conflict in comparison to non-Millennials, while bars to the right indicate Millennials are more likely than older adults to express support for the method. The results indicate that there are statistically significant differences between Millennials and non-Millennials among Latinos and across various values of the cosmopolitan identity variable.

Among Latinos, Millennials are more likely to be doves and less likely to support mixed and hawk methods of solving international conflict. Millennial Latinos are 14.81% more likely to support diplomatic methods and 8.01% less likely to prefer military action than older adults of their ethnic group. They are 6.79% less likely to support mixed methods than non-Millennial Latinos. Given that we have already seen that Latinos as a group are more likely to be doves than non-Latinos, this finding suggests that Millennial Latinos are especially liberal and progressive in their stances on foreign policy.

We also find that cosmopolitan identity influences foreign policy attitudes. Among those that are less inclined to identify with being "a citizen of the world," Millennials, when compared to non-Millennials, are less likely to support dove solutions and more likely to support mixed methods for solving international conflict. Specifically, we see a statistically significant effect for those who self-identify as a "4" on the 0 ("not at all") to 10 ("very strongly") cosmopolitan identity scale; among this group, Millennials are 18.86% less likely to support diplomatic methods and 5.94% more likely to prefer mixed methods. Millennials are also more likely to prefer mixed methods—10% more likely than non-Millennials—at the cosmopolitan identity value of "2," which leans even closer to no cosmopolitan identity. On the other hand, among those who more strongly identify as a global citizen at a value of "8," Millennials are 11.62% more likely than non-Millennials to be doves and 5.65% less likely to be hawks. These significant differences indicate that Millennials' feelings of being connected to the rest of the world strongly influence their foreign policy attitudes.

The remaining influences on foreign policy that we tested, specifically Republican Party affiliation, African American ethnicity, and having foreign relatives, were not statistically significant when controlling for the other factors in the model. However, it is notable that the control variable education emerged as significant. The results indicate that lower levels of education are associated with a higher likelihood of support for hawk solutions, while higher levels of education are associated with a greater likelihood for dove solutions.

These analyses have shown that Millennials are distinct in their foreign policy attitudes and approaches in comparison to non-Millennials. While at first glance their preferences for solutions to international conflict do not seem much different than older adults, a closer examination reveals that their generational persona is clearly translated through cosmopolitan identity into preferences for being doves over hawks. This support for diplomatic methods is particularly strong among Latino Millennials when compared to older Latino adults. Overall, we see important, albeit subtle, differences between Millennials and the rest of the adult population in their stances on international conflict.

Conclusion: Millennial Worldview on Foreign Policy

It's [terrorism] definitely a fear campaign. I'm afraid of terrorism in the respect just for global mankind. If you check the news, every day there is some tragic things that are . . . it seems like, somewhere around the world. Here in America, I live one mile from the White House. I actually don't feel any personal safety issues with that. There's a chance for anything, but my concern is more just about humans, in general, that are getting targeted around the world; but here in the U.S., I think the risk level is actually really low.

As we have discussed in this chapter, and throughout the book, Millennials are more easily and more regularly exposed to the world than any other previous generation. Further, Millennials are the most diverse generation in US history. This diversity and exposure present a different view of the world for this cohort—one that is based on, among other things, liberal and progressive policy leanings and a cosmopolitan worldview.

The quote above, from Michael, a Millennial focus group participant in Washington, DC, is illustrative of this generation's frame for viewing international relations and conflict. In his statement, Michael reveals the persistent role that terrorism has played in his young life. However, he also emphasizes the importance of considering its effects from a global perspective and how it impacts other human beings, rather than simply how it affects the United States. Chloe, another Millennial focus group participant from Washington, DC, echoed similar sentiments: "I don't think that terrorism is really a big problem at home; but I think terrorism, and more specifically, ISIS is a growing problem in countries in the Middle East, where radical Islamists are killing all the non-radical Muslims." Non-Millennials may view this perspective as naïve and idealistic, but Millennial foreign policy attitudes are shaped by characteristics and issues that affect this cohort differently than other generations.

Millennial attitudes are shaped by events that occurred before Millennials came of age and those that occurred during their formative years. One seminal event in this "critical period" was the terrorist attacks on September 11, 2001. By all accounts, this day, and the events that followed it, has been instrumental in the attitudes of this cohort and how they formulate foreign policy choices. Our findings support this, but not in ways that comport with the opinions of other segments of the population. As we see based on the quotes from our Millennial focus group participants, this cohort is worried about issues of terrorism and other foreign threats, but their concerns are largely framed in terms of how these threats impact the world at large, how we can cooperate with other nations to combat the problem, or how the fear of terrorism (both real and imagined) distracts from other more immediate problems.

The quantitative results presented throughout this chapter punctuate this understanding of the Millennial Generation identity and foreign policy attitudes. We found that although there is consistency among Millennials and non-Millennials in perceptions of the nation's policy priorities, including—*the War on ISIS, Trade Deficit, The Rise of China, North Korea*, and *US Immigration Policy*—Millennials rate the importance of these lower than older adults. We also found that Millennials' level of concern for these issues, reflected in their rating of importance, varied across gender, political ideology, and race and ethnicity. Specifically, Millennial females rate two of the five issues (*The Rise of China* and *Trade Deficit*) as less important than Millennial males, Millennial Republicans rate three of the five foreign policy issues (*The War with ISIS, Trade Deficit,* and *Immigration Policy*) as more important than non-Republican Millennials, and Latinos prioritize all five issues the most while African Americans are the least likely racial/ethnic group to prioritize most of the foreign policy issues, except for immigration. These results show the diversity that exists among Millennials and the importance of not only exploring distinctions across groups, but within groups, as well.

Turning to preferences for solving international conflict, we found that the most frequently chosen approach by both non-Millennials and Millennials is diplomatic methods. However, Millennials are more likely to choose diplomatic solutions, compared to non-Millennials. Exploring deeper, we also found that Latino Millennials, Cosmopolitan Millennials, and better-educated Millennials are more likely to prefer diplomatic solutions for solving international conflicts over military action. The findings support our arguments that Millennials are distinct in their foreign policy attitudes; this cohort prefers to approach international conflicts in a cooperative, rather than a combative manner. Millennials' foreign policy attitudes are reflected in their unique persona, most strongly influenced by their liberal and progressive policy preferences, their diversity, and their connection to the world.

It is not terribly surprising that Millennials view the world differently than other generational cohorts. Each generation reacts to events and other factors that are present during their "critical period." The Vietnam War and the Cold War were important influences on Baby Boomers and Gen Xers, respectively. However, those US foreign policy objectives were still viewed with a considerable amount of remoteness. This is in contrast to the Millennial outlook of the world. This cohort's sense of interconnectedness and global belonging, coupled with their unique persona, informs their foreign policy priorities and strategy choices. We have a decent grasp of the short-term effects of 9/11 and the "war on terror" on Millennials' opinions about how to deal with the world, but the long-term consequences of these events are less assured. As this generation ages, it will be interesting to see if their attitudes about foreign policy will continue to be guided by seeing the "Twin Towers" fall, or if other factors will emerge that dilute the impact of this critical event. Only time will bring greater clarity to these questions and to our full understanding of the foreign policy politics of the Millennial Generation.

CHAPTER 6

The Melted Pot: Millennials and Immigration

On June 16, 2015 President Donald Trump announced that he would seek the Republican presidential nomination. At the time, most thought he would sell himself primarily as an entrepreneur and political outsider (and to a large extent he did) in a crowded field of candidates. However, equally as popular and perhaps more enduring was the position he took that day on immigration. In his presidential announcement speech, Trump declared the United States is "a dumping ground" for the world's problems, including immigrants from Mexico. Trump asserted (Time 2015):

> When Mexico sends its people, they're not sending their best . . . They're sending people that have lots of problems, and they're bringing those problems with us. They're bringing drugs. They're bringing crime. They're rapists.

Later in the speech, he also announced that his solution to the problem is to build a wall along the southern border and to have Mexico pay for it (Gamboa 2015). Further into his campaign and following a mass shooting in San Bernardino, California in December 2015, Donald Trump called for a "total and complete shutdown" of the country's borders to Muslims "until we are able to understand this problem [Islamic terrorism]" (Pilkington 2015). Short on evidence supporting his claims about the criminal element flow of immigration and brief on details about how to implement his proposed policies, the anti-immigrant messages established throughout his campaign, nonetheless, resonated with a large segment of Republican voters and arguably helped catapult Donald Trump to the top of the Republican presidential contender field. A robust three-quarters of Republicans (76%) favor building a wall along the Mexico border (Moore 2016). And according to a poll conducted soon after the San Bernardino shootings, almost six in ten Republicans (59%) agreed with Mr. Trump on his proposed temporary Muslim ban (ABC News/Washington Post 2015).

The popularity of Trump's stringent immigration positions and his strong rhetoric—as well as the ensuing backlash to his proposals, evident in the outcries at his campaign rallies that sometimes resulted in violence—emphasize the divisiveness of the immigration issue and the heated discussions surrounding policy solutions. Debates about immigration have a long contentious history in the US. Political conflicts surrounding immigration date back to anti-Asian immigrant sentiment with the Chinese Exclusion Act of 1882 and the Immigration Act of 1924, to Mexican animus displayed with Eisenhower's "Operation Wetback" in 1954, California Governor Pete Wilson's support of Proposition 187 ("Save our State") designed to prohibit undocumented immigrants from using state services, and the introduction of House Bill 4437 in 2006, which proposed to classify illegal immigrants and those assisting them as felons (among other provisions). However, one key difference highlighting the present controversy is the increased (and increasing) diversity of the American population, led by the Millennial Generation. The issue of immigration became front and center in the 2016 presidential election cycle due to the palpable and undeniable reality of a rapidly changing America.

As we will elaborate in this chapter, Millennials[1] and immigration are complementary topics of discussion for two main reasons. First, the makeup of the Millennial Generation accounts for much of the significant demographic shift occurring in the United States. Second, and relatedly, this cohort's attitudes about immigration are influenced by the increased diversity of the population and their exposure to and interaction with immigrants. The attitudes of the Millennial Generation toward immigrants and immigration have both short-term and long-term implications for policy formulation in the United States. Their opinions on the issue are distinct from older adults; while there are some subpopulations of the Millennial age cohort that are less accepting of immigrants, by and large Millennials are more open and supportive of immigrants in our country.

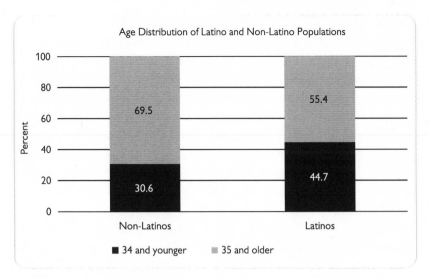

FIGURE 6.1.   Latinos Are Younger than Non-Latinos

Source: US Census Bureau, Current Population Survey, 2012 Civic Engagement Supplement.

Millennials Are Minorities; Minorities Are Millennials

As the largest cohort in American history, Millennials make up 83.1 million of the US population, surpassing Baby Boomers who number 75.4 million (US Census Bureau 2015a). In a random interaction with someone on the street, there is a greater than one in four chance that the person you encounter will be a Millennial. Further, Millennials are also the most diverse generation ever in the United States. Racial and ethnic minorities comprise 44.2% of all Millennials. So, not only does one have a decent opportunity of interacting with a Millennial on the street, but the chances are also pretty good that the interaction will involve a Millennial minority. The diversity of the Millennial Generation has been primarily driven by the large waves of Latinos and Asians that have been emigrating to the United States for the last fifty years (Pew Research Center 2014a). Together, Latinos and Asians make up almost a quarter (24%) of all Millennials (Nielsen 2014).

Specifically, to emphasize the numerical influence of Latinos within the Millennial cohort, Figure 6.1 illustrates the youth of Latinos, compared to non-Latinos. Latinos who are 34 years of age or younger account for 44.7% of the entire Latino population, contrasted with just 30.6% of non-Latinos that comprise this same age group.

These demographic figures are telling in terms of the significant immigrant footprint among Millennials. Therefore, demographic factors should shape, to some degree, Millennial attitudes about immigration. The diversity of this generation, as well as the fact that non-Hispanic Millennial whites have grown up within the "melted pot" makes the atmosphere ripe for more tolerant attitudes about immigrants among this cohort. However, do these tolerant attitudes really bare out or are they more an artifact of demographic expectations? In recent times (as in other periods in US history), we have seen a rise in anti-immigrant attitudes, especially among disillusioned voters. According to Pew Research Center (2016d), 46% of registered voters believe life in America today is worse than it was fifty years ago. Republican voters are more than twice as likely as Democratic voters to hold this sentiment (66% to 28%). And among Republican voters, 56% say that immigrants are a burden on the country. This anti-immigrant sentiment is more than three times as likely among Republican voters as among Democratic voters (17%). Perhaps even more revealing, close to seven in ten (69%) Republicans who support Donald Trump believe this is the case. Clearly, sentiments about economic unfairness, at least in part related to the impact of immigration and diversity, is present among the more general populace.

The Millennial Persona and Attitudes about Immigration

A group's attitudes about many issues are affected by both personal and shared experiences, which are not mutually exclusive. The Millennial Generation's persona is described in this manner—as a set of attitudes that are influenced by experiences having to do with family life, relationships with friends and peers, and exposure to and interaction with social and political institutions (Howe and Strauss 2000). This "persona" affects Millennials' opinions about many political, social, and economic issues, including the issue of immigration.

As highlighted above and discussed in detail in Chapter 1, a principal feature of the Millennial persona is their incredible ethnic and racial diversity. The Millennial Generation is the most diverse adult generation in American history (Pew Research Center 2014a). To emphasize this point, note the following: Baby Boomers (those born between 1946 and 1964) are 32% of the US population (76 million) with 72% being non-Hispanic white; Millennials are 27% of the population (86 million) but are only 56% white (US Census Bureau 2015a). Further, while no new Millennials are being born, the population continues to grow because of immigration. About 14% of Millennials are foreign born, and 11% have at least one parent that was born outside the United States. (Reason-Rupe 2014). This diversity has exposed young adults to a variety of cultures and experiences, as well as heightened their concern for the plight of immigrants, since many are immigrants themselves or have immigrant family members.

In addition to diversity, the Millennial Generation persona is defined by this cohort's liberalness. Although Millennials are less likely to identify with a political party, they have overwhelmingly voted Democratic (60% voted for Obama in 2012) and are more likely to describe themselves as liberal and independent (Pew Research Center 2014a). Not only are Millennials more liberal relative to other generations in current time but they also appear to be more liberal when comparing them at similar ages (Ross and Rouse 2015). Therefore, it seems that the liberalness that defines, in part, the Millennial Generation persona is not just a "youth effect" (although this remains to be seen as this cohort ages).

Beyond their liberal leanings, Millennials are also connected to the world by a largely cosmopolitan identity or view of being a "citizen of the world" that likely contributes to how they perceive immigrants and immigration. Millennials have grown up in the age of technology; the advent of the internet, smartphones, and social media has produced a significantly more interconnected world. These technological advances have allowed people (particularly young people) to easily link up with people around the world in a way that underscores the fact that country and continent barriers are no longer an impediment to communication and collaboration. This connectedness has led to the rise of cosmopolitanism, particularly among Millennials (Spence 2001; Telhami and Kishi 2015).

Millennials, more so than any other cohort (as many as one-third), are likely to view themselves through the lens of a cosmopolitan identity (Zogby and Kuhl 2013). Telhami (2015) finds that the cosmopolitan identity for Millennials is only second to identifying as "citizen of the United States." In contrast, older generations are more likely to identify with their religious group after identifying as US citizens. Not only do Millennials view themselves as cosmopolitans because of their prolific and constant use of technology and the internet but also because of their greater personal exposure to and interest in other parts of the world. Millennials also espouse a worldview that the government has a positive role to play in solving problems. This, too, may shape their attitudes about immigration, specifically policy action taken by the government to address the issue.

Differences in Immigrant Tolerance among Millennials and Non-Millennials

The Millennial Generation persona is largely defined by this cohort's considerable ethnic and racial diversity as well as its cosmopolitan identity or feeling of being "a citizen of the world." These two features that Millennials largely share are distinct from the experiences and sentiments of the older American adult population. It is unclear, however, if this generation persona is reflected in attitudes toward immigration. *Does the Millennial Generation persona—this age cohort's diversity, liberalness, cosmopolitan identity, and worldview of a positive government role—translate to attitudes held among the Millennial population? And how do these compare to older adults' opinions about immigrants and immigration?*

To explore these questions, we turn to data collected in our original survey, conducted in November and December 2015. We asked a series of questions that capture attitudes of tolerance toward immigrants. Respondents were asked to select the statement that most closely aligned with their personal opinion on three immigration issues:

1. *Values*: "Immigrants strengthen the diversity of our country." Or—"The growing number of immigrants from other countries threatens traditional American customs and values."
2. *Jobs*: "Immigrants only take jobs Americans do not want to do." Or—"Immigrants take jobs away from Americans."
3. *Security*: "Illegal immigrants do not threaten our safety." Or— "Illegal immigrants threaten our nation's security."

Responses to these three items were combined to generate a factor score representing the latent tolerance each individual has for immigrants. The resulting factor score variable has a range of values, running from –1.348 to 1.157, with higher values indicating greater intolerance. This *immigrant intolerance* factor score allows us to explore group differences between Millennials and non-Millennials to determine if the Millennial Generation persona translates to more tolerant immigration attitudes.

The results of a difference of means test indicate that there is a statistically significant difference between Millennials and non-Millennials in their immigrant tolerance.[2] This confirms our expectation that given their diversity, liberalness, and connectedness to the rest of the world, Millennials are more tolerant of immigrants than older adults.

While Millennial immigrant intolerance is indeed lower, on average, and distinct from the non-Millennial group, the Millennial factor scores demonstrate widespread variance across the range of values. There is a group of Millennials that display strong intolerance toward immigrants, but there is also a slightly greater percentage that are strongly tolerant of immigrants. This begs the question—*What explains differences among Millennials in their immigration attitudes?* We will explore this question later in the chapter, but now we turn to a further investigation of the immigration attitude differences between non-Millennials and Millennials.

Support for Immigration Policies among Millennials and Non-Millennials

Differences in immigrant tolerance are only one component of understanding attitudes about immigration; it is equally important to explore the support given for policies to address the issue. This is not because immigration ranks as the top policy concern among either group but because it is a salient issue for politics involving both groups. In fact, immigration is a chief priority for very few American adults. As highlighted in Chapter 2, our 2015 survey indicated that only about 5% of Millennial and non-Millennial respondents ranked it as the *most* important issue facing our country. Immigration policy is consistently subordinated to other national issues, including the economy, security, healthcare, and education. Yet, immigration policy is deeply connected to all of these issues and remains a highly salient issue in its own right. This was quite evident during the 2016 presidential campaign and in the first days of the Trump administration when the President signed executive orders to build a wall along the Mexican border, to deport undocumented immigrants who have been convicted of a crime, and to cut federal funding from cities that protect undocumented immigrants (known as sanctuary cities). Our survey reflected its importance for the majority of all adults in the election; 56% of Millennials and 65% of non-Millennials said it was an "important" issue for their 2016 presidential vote.

To explore immigration policy, we examine whether differences exist between Millennials and non-Millennials in their views on solutions to key immigration problems. Our survey asked respondents to indicate *how much they support or are likely to support* the following federal government immigration policies:[3]

1) *E-Verify*: Require that all companies verify the legal status of workers before employing them.
2) *Border Security*: Strengthen border security and extend wall or fence along the US–Mexican border.
3) *Undocumented Childhood Arrivals*: Allow undocumented children and childhood arrivals under the age of 30 years to stay in the United States.
4) *Undocumented Immigrant Tuition*: Allow in-state tuition and fees at state universities for undocumented immigrants who arrived in the United States as children.

Figure 6.2 illustrates levels of support for these immigration policies among Millennials and non-Millennials, respectively.

The figure depicts the mean, standard deviation, and minimum and maximum values for responses to each of the four immigration policy questions. The dots represent the mean of each variable, the solid lines extend left from the mean minus one standard deviation and right from the mean plus one standard deviation, and the dashed lines extend from the minimum to maximum values. The distribution of each individual variable allows for comparisons, since the scale of the variables are the same. We can discern from the mean values shown in the figure that E-Verify is the most supported policy among both Millennials and non-Millennials. However, non-Millennials are more likely to support the policy compared to Millennials. Almost two-thirds of non-Millennials (73%) say they

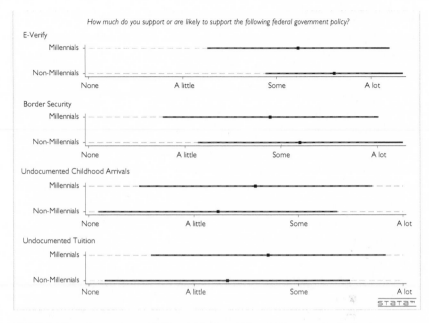

FIGURE 6.2.   Comparison of Millennial & Non-Millennial Support for Federal Immigration Policies

Note: The dots represent the mean values of each variable, the solid lines extend from the mean minus one standard deviation to the mean plus one standard deviation, and the dashed lines extend from the minimum to maximum of observed values. The number of Millennial observations totaled 621, and the number of non-Millennial observations totaled 630.

support this policy "a lot." By contrast, about half of Millennials (52%) offered the same response.

The level of support given for the remaining three federal immigration policies is consistent across both groups. More support is expressed for strengthening border security, followed by in-state tuition for undocumented immigrants. Allowing undocumented children under the age of 30 years to stay in the United States trails with the lowest level of support among Millennials and non-Millennials alike. Again, though, the strength of support for each of these three policies varies between non-Millennials and Millennials. Similar to E-verify, the majority of non-Millennials are more likely to support increasing border security "a lot" (57% of respondents), compared to only 41% of Millennial respondents. Conversely, Millennials are more supportive of in-state tuition for undocumented immigrants (31% of respondents support it "a lot") and allowing undocumented children to stay in the United States (28% of respondents support it "a lot"). In comparison, 21% of non-Millennials support the in-state tuition policy "a lot," and only 19% give the same level of support to allowing undocumented children to stay in the country.

It appears that more non-Millennials than Millennials favor tougher immigration policies, while more Millennials than non-Millennials support policies that expand immigrant rights. These preliminary findings on Millennials' opinions about immigration are well in line with what we know about the Millennial Generation persona, which is grounded in greater liberalism, more exposure to and contact with minorities and immigrants, and a stronger cosmopolitan identity. While neither group particularly prioritizes immigration as the most important issue (discussed in detail in Chapter 2), there are conditions under which immigration policies receive greater support.

Immigration attitudes are likely to vary within the Millennial cohort. A glimpse of these in-group differences was revealed earlier in the chapter with the distribution of immigration intolerance factor scores; a sizeable group of intolerant Millennials emerged. Given that immigration is an issue fundamentally tied to race and ethnic identity, we turn to an examination of the immigration attitudes across Millennial race/ethnic subgroups.

Differences in Support for Immigration Policies across Millennial Race/Ethnic Subgroups

As we have previously discussed, one major factor that distinguishes Millennials from other generations is their racial and ethnic diversity. The issue of immigration is innately connected to this diversity, given both the composition of this cohort and their social milieu. While we assert that this diversity is coupled with a higher level of tolerance, not just for immigration but for social issues more broadly, there is reason to expect differences across race and ethnic lines in immigration attitudes, even among the largely tolerant Millennial cohort. Past studies have shown that among the general population, factors such as economic hardship and feelings of cultural threat lead to greater intolerance of immigrants and immigration (Espenshade and Hempstead 1996; Burns and Gimpel 2000; Tichenor 2002; Harell et al. 2012). Across different minority groups, African

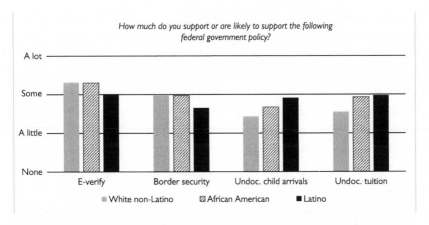

FIGURE 6.3. Opinions about Federal Immigration Policies among Millennial Race/Ethnic Subgroups

Note: Bars represent the mean value of responses for each subgroup. Number of respondents for each subgroup are as follows: Whites = 335, African Americans = 106, Latinos = 158.

Americans are more likely than Latinos to say that immigrants take jobs away from Americans and that immigration increases both economic and political competition (McClain and Tauber 1998; Pew Research Center 2008). This leads us to ask—*do Latino Millennials and African American Millennials display similar levels of support for immigration policies as white Millennials?*

To answer this question, we examine differences among Millennial race/ethnic subgroups in support for the same four immigration policies explored in the previous section—E-Verify, border security, undocumented childhood arrivals, and undocumented immigrant tuition. Figure 6.3 displays the mean values for Millennial subgroups'—whites, African Americans, and Latinos—average support for the four federal immigration policies discussed above.

The figure illustrates that there are some distinctions across the three subgroups related to immigration policies. White and African American Millennials hold similar levels of average support for E-Verify and border security, but Latino Millennials are less likely to support either of these policies. In fact, there is a statistically distinct difference in means between Latino Millennials and white Millennials and Latino Millennials and African American Millennials for both E-Verify and border security.[4] We also see distinctions in average support for in-state tuition for undocumented immigrants and for allowing undocumented children to stay in the United States. African American and Latino Millennials display similar levels of average support for in-state tuition for undocumented immigrants, but white Millennials are less likely to support this policy. There is a statistically distinct difference in means between African American Millennials and white Millennials and between Latino Millennials and white Millennials on opinions about in-state tuition. Finally, Latino Millennials are more likely than white and African American Millennials to support allowing undocumented children to stay in the country. However, African American Millennials are more supportive of this policy than white Millennials. On this policy, we also observe statistically distinct difference in means between African American Millennials and white Millennials and between Latinos Millennials and white Millennials.

It appears that even though Millennials (compared to non-Millennials) are less likely to support stringent immigration policies and seem to favor more progressive immigration solutions, distinct differences in opinions do exist *among* Millennials, across race/ethnic subgroups. Enforcement-related policies (E-Verify and border security) receive greater average support from white and African American Millennials, while policies to expand the rights of immigrants (in-state tuition for undocumented immigrants and allowing undocumented children to stay in the United States) receive the highest average support from Latino Millennials, followed by African American Millennials. These findings reveal that the Millennial persona is not equally translated across this cohort's subgroups, at least with respect to attitudes about immigration. While Millennials, in general, are more liberal and progressive than non-Millennials, there are clear distinctions across Millennial race/ethnic subgroups as demonstrated by variance in their attitudes about specific immigration policies.

Explaining Millennial Immigration Attitudes

Our analyses thus far indicate that while Millennials are more tolerant than non-Millennials about immigrants and exhibit greater support for policies to expand rights of immigrants, there is variation within the Millennial cohort on both immigration tolerance (see Figure 6.1) and support for immigration policies (see Figure 6.3). We know from past studies that immigration attitudes can be affected by factors that impact a person's self-interests (Passel and Fix 1994; Alvarez and Butterfield 2000; Scheve and Slaughter 2001; Hainmueller and Hiscox 2010). Indeed we observed fears about immigrant threats to national security and jobs propelling the hostility evident in the 2016 campaign (and helping to secure President Trump's victory) (Gramlich 2016; Morin 2016). According to a nationally representative poll we conducted in the weeks following the presidential election,[5] nearly 61% of those who voted for President Trump said that "immigrants take jobs away from Americans" (as opposed to "immigrants only take jobs Americans do not want to do"). *What happens when seemingly tolerant attitudes about immigration among Millennials conflict with factors that may affect issues of self-interest?*

A very useful test of this scenario occurred during the Great Recession. Drawing on data from that time period, specifically responses from the 2008 American National Election Study, we demonstrated in a published paper (Ross and Rouse 2015) that Millennials were more tolerant of immigration than older adults in that they were less likely to support decreasing the number of immigrants from foreign countries permitted to come and live in the United States. This finding holds up even under conditions of economic self-interest; while heightened perceptions of job threat by immigrants and a sense of worsening future finances are associated with increases in intolerance, Millennials maintained lower levels of intolerance compared to non-Millennials. Our current data still capture a time where economic self-interest is highly relevant, particularly for young adults who have not seen the same gains in employment as older adults in the workforce (Gandel 2016). Moreover, there appears to be significant animus toward immigrants, as evidenced by populace support for a politician like Donald Trump, whose initial, persistent, and most vocal policy position is one that clamps down on immigration.[6] To explore what drives Millennial immigration attitudes in this context, we now turn to a more comprehensive analysis of tolerance among this age cohort that accounts for other variables that may influence opinions on this topic.

Again, using our survey conducted in November and December 2015, we are interested in identifying the characteristics and experiences that are associated with immigrant intolerance among Millennials. To measure this, we employ the *immigrant intolerance* factor score described earlier in the chapter which is constructed from survey responses to questions that ask individuals to choose the statement that most closely aligns with their personal opinion. The survey responses include choices among three statements: 1) "immigrants strengthen the diversity of our country" or "the growing number of immigrants from other countries threatens traditional American customs and values;" 2) "immigrants only take jobs Americans do not want to do" or "immigrants take jobs away from Americans;" and 3) "illegal immigrants do not threaten our safety" or "illegal immigrants threaten our nation's security." Higher values of the factor score indicate greater intolerance for immigrants, both legal and illegal.

We also adopt a measure of tolerance focused on public policy— agreement with the statement that "the federal government should reform immigration policy to reduce the number of newcomers coming into our country." The alternative choice is "the federal government should keep immigration policy the way it is now." This is a measure that has been commonly used in past studies on the issue (Espenshade and Hempstead 1996; Hopkins 2010; Ross and Rouse 2015) as supporting immigration reform to reduce the number of immigrants coming into our country is indicative of intolerance for immigrants. We are confident that these two operationalizations of immigrant intolerance are measuring similar sentiments because the two measures are highly and significantly correlated with one another (p-value = 0.0546).

We examine a number of factors that may influence individual sentiments of immigration intolerance, including being Latino, African American, and foreign born.[7] As established in the previous section, minority Millennials exhibit different support for immigration policies than their white peers; they tend to be more supportive of policies that expand immigrant rights. Given this, we expect minority Millennials to exhibit greater tolerance for immigrants, even when controlling for other factors. Relatedly, we expect foreign-born Millennials to be tolerant as they are immigrants themselves and likely have family members and friends who have been subject to immigration policy.

We also investigate if economic self-interest, measured by being unemployed and thinking that the economy was better twenty years ago for young people, explains immigration tolerance. This is particularly important given the economic context in which Millennials have come of age. As a result of the economic recession, the scarcity of jobs, and the trickle-down effects of these financial situations—including but not limited to living at home with parents, delaying marriage, and putting off big purchases such as homes (see Pew Research Center 2014a)—there may be some within the Millennial cohort that see immigrants as an economic threat. These individuals may be less tolerant of immigrants given their own economic self-interest.

Additionally, we examine how liberal political ideology, represented by a dichotomous measure, influences immigration attitudes. Conservative and moderate Millennials may be more likely to exhibit less tolerance for immigrants, given the harsh stance Republicans and conservatives have taken on the issue—particularly in the Trump era. Liberals, on the other hand, have been bolstered by President Obama's executive actions to defer deportation of undocumented immigrant children and young adults and continue to support more lenient immigration policies.

Political ideology is not the only viewpoint that shapes attitudes; we recognize that perceptions about the role of government in solving problems should also influence immigration tolerance.[8] We address this by including a factor score of responses to multiple survey questions that should capture this viewpoint, including the appropriate role of government in: 1) spending to alleviate economic hardships, 2) requiring healthcare coverage, 3) reducing the cost of healthcare, and 4) forgiving student loans. Higher values of the factor score represent more support for government intervention in solving economic, health, and education problems. We expect those who have greater support for this worldview to have more tolerance for immigrants.

We also account for education level, income, gender, and marital status in exploring immigrant tolerance as these experiences may shape individual attitudes. Education, specifically, may be an important explanatory factor as individuals gain exposure to diverse peoples, cultures, and ideas in higher education settings. This exposure may, in turn, increase tolerance and support for immigration.

Results of the linear regression examining the *immigrant intolerance* factor score are shown in Figure 6.4.[9] The dots in the figure represent each variable's coefficient or the change in the dependent variable associated with a one-unit increase in the explanatory factor, while the lines indicate the range of the 95% confidence interval. The results show that being Latino and foreign born is associated with lower levels of intolerance. Among Millennials, being Latino is associated with a 0.36 lower intolerance score than a non-Latino Millennial. Similarly, foreign-born Millennials

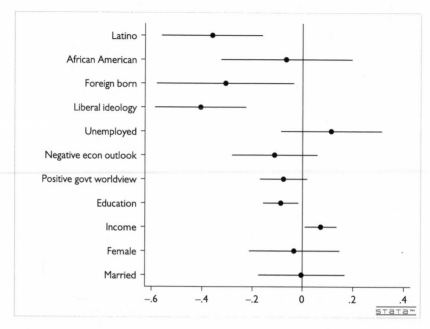

FIGURE 6.4.   Factors Influencing Millennial Generation Immigration Intolerance

Note: Linear regression estimated with robust standard errors. The dots represent the coefficient, and the lines indicate the range of the 95% confidence interval, two-tailed tests.

have a 0.31 lower intolerance factor score than their counterparts born in the United States.

Liberal political outlook and higher levels of education are also related to more tolerant immigrant attitudes. The regression results indicate that liberal Millennials have a 0.41 lower intolerance factor score than their moderate and conservative peers. Millennials with higher education, too, have lower levels of intolerance. A Millennial with a high school education is predicted to have a 0.06 intolerance factor score, while a young adult with a professional or doctoral degree is predicted to have a –0.37 score.[10]

While being Latino and foreign born, having liberal political ideology, and being more educated are related to less immigrant intolerance, higher levels of income are associated with heightened intolerance. Predicted probabilities indicate that an average Millennial making less than $20,000 has a –0.25 intolerance factor score while their counterparts with an annual income of $30,000–$50,000 have a –0.11 score and those with an income greater than $100,000 have a 0.11 score. This is an interesting finding given

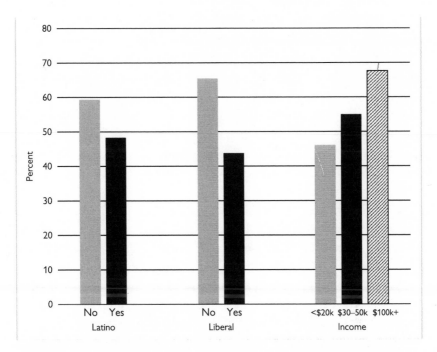

FIGURE 6.5. Predicted Probability of Support to Reduce the Number of Immigrants among Millennials

Note: Predicted probabilities shown based on estimates of logistic regression. All variables were held at their means to calculate the predicted probability.

that individuals with greater education typically have higher incomes; yet, we see income having an independent and opposite effect on tolerance than education.

The results of the logistic analysis examining *support for immigration reform that reduces the number of newcomers* coming into the country largely confirm these findings.[11] The variables "Latino," political ideology, and income again emerge as significant explanatory factors of immigration tolerance. Because logistic coefficients are difficult to interpret directly, we turn to predicted probabilities to explore the results. Figure 6.5 illustrates the predicted probability of these variables; the bar height represents the probability of supporting a reduction in the number of immigrants coming into our country (as opposed to keeping the policy as is it now).

As shown in Figure 6.5, a Millennial Latino has a 48.3% likelihood of supporting a reduction in immigrants in comparison to a 59.3% likelihood of the same among non-Latino Millennials. Liberal Millennials, too, have a lower likelihood of support for this policy; a liberal Millennial has a 43.7% likelihood compared to a 65.4% likelihood among non-liberal (moderate and conservative) Millennials. While being Latino and liberal *decreases* support for a reduction in newcomers coming into our country, income increases it. A Millennial with an annual income of $20,000 or less has a 46.1% likelihood of supporting a reduction in newcomers. This increases to a 55% likelihood of support with an increase in income to the $30,000–$50,000 range and 67.6% likelihood with an income of $100,000 and more.

Collectively, these findings support that greater exposure to immigrants (through the Latino population or by being an immigrant oneself) and to diverse peoples and ideas (presumably through higher education) positively influences tolerance for immigrants. On the other hand, the findings support that conservative, non-Latino (predominantly white), native born, and lower educated Millennials are one of the subgroups most likely to express immigrant intolerance. Not surprisingly, it is precisely this group that has been most supportive of Trump's anti-immigrant rhetoric (Morin 2016) and propelled him to win the presidency in the 2016 presidential race (Tyson and Maniam 2016).

While liberal political ideology, education, being Latino, and being foreign born are all significantly associated with immigrant intolerance among Millennials, a positive government worldview and economic self-interest, measured through unemployment and a negative economic outlook, is not. Furthermore, although the worldview that the government has a greater role to play in solving problems is fundamental to the Millennial Generation's persona, it does not influence immigration attitudes when tested against the other factors included in the regression model (although it approaches statistical significance with the immigrant intolerance factor score). The same is true for the economic self-interest measures; while these measures represent important experiences of Millennials, they do not exert a significant influence on immigrant intolerance. However, the positive and significant relationship of income with intolerance demonstrates that there is some economic component to immigration attitudes. It is not clear why intolerance rises with increased income among Millennials or what mechanism is driving a perception that immigrants threaten wealth. Past research on immigration attitudes among the general public has found that higher income marginally increases support for decreased immigration levels (Burns and Gimpel 2000). These scholars emphasize the fact that education and income do not capture the same thing and that concerns about immigration and ethnic diversity may diverge on these two measures based on feelings of prejudice.

In our own past work (Ross and Rouse 2015), we have found a more consistent message that Millennials do not feel they compete with immigrants for jobs. This is further reinforced by the focus groups conducted for this project. As one focus group participant from New Orleans, Christian, put it: "I think whoever is more qualified will get the job, and if I am I'll get it." Quanisha from Los Angeles agreed, saying, "I feel like they [immigrants] do a lot of jobs that other people might not want to do, but also if they're good at something, if they take a job away from a Millennial, then they're good at what they do . . . everybody deserves a fair chance." Cynthia from the Washington, DC area echoed this, saying immigration makes her more competitive and that she endeavors "to work harder because I know I'm competing with people from different countries." The regression findings discussed above underscore a similar sentiment, given the lack of statistical significance of unemployed and negative economic outlook. This suggests that job threat is not motivating higher income Millennials to be more intolerant of immigrants. Clearly, the influence of economic factors can be nuanced and complex, and more data and analysis are needed to fully understand their impact.

In all these, statistical tests demonstrate that not all Millennials share the same preferences and beliefs when it comes to the issue of immigration. In particular, conservative Millennials and those with higher incomes are likely to support greater restrictions on immigration and are associated with higher levels of negative immigrant sentiment or intolerance (believing that immigrants take jobs, threaten traditional American values, and threaten national security). On the other hand, there are subgroups of Millennials that exhibit greater than average support for immigrants and immigration, including Latinos, those who are foreign born, and those with higher levels of education. This underscores that while the Millennial persona shapes generational beliefs, there remains variance within this cohort that has meaningful implications for how immigration policy will develop in our country.

Conclusion—Millennials and Immigration: The Threads that Bind

The rise of the Millennial Generation as the most diverse adult cohort in history has redefined what it means to live in a "melting pot" society. For all intents and purposes, the "melting" or fusing of multiculturalism has occurred. As a result, Millennials will help guide us into a new political, social, and economic reality based on a country soon to be comprised of a majority–minority population. Immigration, therefore, is a thread that binds the fabric of this generation, embodied in high levels of tolerance for immigrants and openness to immigration. The findings in this chapter have demonstrated that Millennials, in comparison to older adults, have more tolerance for immigrants (in terms of threats to culture, security, and jobs) and are more supportive of policies that expand, rather than limit, immigrant rights (specifically allowing childhood arrivals to stay in the country and permitting illegal immigrants in-state tuition). This tolerance and support is even higher among minorities, namely Latino Millennials, as well as liberal and highly educated young adults. How this generation's immigration attitudes affect immigration policy in the future is unclear as the durability of their opinions remains to be seen.[12] Nonetheless, we are optimistic that Millennials' attitudes will be a positive current in the present political landscape riddled with immigrant hostility and the fear of a changing society. While President Trump moved swiftly in his first days in office—via executive orders—to fulfill his campaign promises of building a wall along the US–Mexico border and banning immigrants from certain Muslim countries, Millennials, like Tim from the Washington, DC area, are promoting alternative immigration solutions: "Instead of making a bigger border, you could build a bigger table so everybody can come and bring their culture."

Millennials to the Rescue? Climate Change (Dis)Belief in the United States and the Future of Environmental Policy

In the final weeks of her 2016 presidential election campaign, Democratic candidate Hillary Clinton enlisted the help of former Vice President Al Gore Jr. to woo Millennial[1] voters, the majority of whom supported Bernie Sanders in the primary elections and were gravitating toward third-party candidates (Wagner 2016). Why Gore? As an environmental activist and Nobel Peace prize winner, he was uniquely qualified to connect to Millennials on an issue that they demonstrate deep concern for: climate change (Eilperin 2016). Speaking at Miami Dade College on October 11, 2016, Gore had this to say (CSPAN 2016):

> When it comes to the most urgent issue facing our country and the world, the choice in this election is extremely clear. Hillary Clinton will make solving the climate crisis a top national priority. Her opponent, based on the ideas that he has presented, would take us toward a climate catastrophe.

The "catastrophe" Gore asserts alludes to the stance President Donald Trump has taken on the issue—one that denies climate change. Trump's position on climate change was established well before his presidential run. In 2012 Trump tweeted, "The concept of global warming was created by and for the Chinese in order to make US manufacturing non-competitive" (Kreutz and Haskell 2016). Trump later claimed this tweet was a joke, but

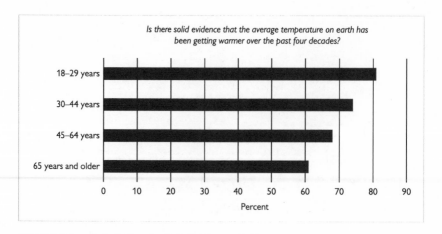

FIGURE 7.1.   Global Warming Belief Highest with Young Adults

Note: Authors' calculation using information taken from the National Surveys on Energy and Environment, public use dataset, Spring 2015.

his stance as a businessman and politician has consistently been that climate change is a "hoax" and that US climate policies are "draconian" and harmful to businesses (Jacobson 2016). This stance has guided his choice of Scott Pruitt, a known climate change denialist, to head the Environmental Protection Agency and will likely influence his executive actions in the years to come on national and international initiatives aimed at mitigating climate change (Davenport and Lipton 2016).

President Trump's views on climate change are shared by a significant portion of the American adult population. In the spring of 2015, nearly one in four adults reported that they do not believe in climate change (National Surveys on Energy and the Environment 2015). However, this denial is not equal across all American adults. Not surprisingly, Millennials have the highest belief in global warming, as shown in Figure 7.1, while older adults' denial is more prevalent. This pattern fits with the Millennial Generation's frame, largely defined by their liberal ideological leanings that champion protection and good stewardship of the environment, their cosmopolitan identity that connects them to problems global in scope, and their sensitivity to issues of tolerance that calls their attention to problems that disproportionately affect minorities and the poor. What we will see in this chapter is that this Millennial identity shapes young adults' beliefs in and concern for the issue of climate change.

This chapter examines in-depth climate change belief among American adults and briefly explores policy preferences to address the issue. Using original public opinion poll data, we focus on the distinctions among Millennial and non-Millennials as well as differences among Millennial adults, across political ideology, economic conditions, and religious affiliation to determine how the Millennial Generation persona affects climate change belief and how Millennials will shape our environmental future. Before looking at these analyses in detail, we review the state of climate change public opinion in the United States.

Climate Change (Dis)Belief in the United States

While it is widely accepted among scientific experts that climate change is occurring and human activity is contributing to it (Anderegg et al. 2010; Liu et al. 2015), public opinion on climate change in the United States in the past decade has demonstrated patterns akin to a rollercoaster—ups and downs in belief and concern. At the turn of the century, the Gallup Poll reported that 72% of Americans expressed a great deal or fair amount of concern for climate change. Since then concern has dipped, dived, and most recently rebounded. This wavering concern has been coupled with declines in global warming belief, as illustrated in Figure 7.2.

The decline in climate change concern and belief among the American public since the turn of the century was in part due to the impacts of the Great Recession. In times of economic crisis, the public has, as Weber (2006) puts it, a "finite pool of worry" and, therefore, has limited attention for issues, like climate change, that seem abstract and too far in the future. In the face of the housing crisis, rising unemployment, and stagnating family incomes, climate change took a backseat for most Americans. Compounding this was the "Climategate" scandal—a controversy over the leaked personal emails of prominent scientists that fueled skeptics' claims that there is scientific dishonesty regarding climate change (Whitemarsh 2011). Conflict over scientific evidence was further bolstered by media framing and coverage of the issue, which exaggerated the degree of valid skepticism about climate science (Dispensa and Brulle 2003; Boykoff 2007). Against this backdrop of controversy, Republican and Democratic Party stances on the issue became more polarized. In less than a decade,

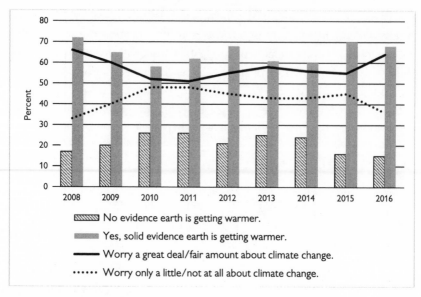

FIGURE 7.2.   American Climate Change Belief and Concern: 2008–2016

Notes: Global warming belief data taken from National Surveys on Energy and the Environment Fall surveys for years 2008–2015 and Spring survey for 2016. Gallup Poll data used for concern about climate change (Saad and Jones 2016).

the Republican Party has moved from an approach that would facilitate bipartisan action to one that denies climate science, rejects international climate agreements, and criticized the priority given to climate change by the Obama administration.[2]

The confluence of these factors—economic recession, scientific scandal, media exaggeration of climate change science unreliability, and a sharp right-turn of the Republican Party stance on the issue—has resulted in skepticism among the American public that was not evident at the turn of the century. While outright denial of global warming is presently the lowest it has been in nearly a decade (15%), the percentage of Americans (19%) that say they are not sure whether climate change is occurring is higher than ever (National Surveys on Energy and Environment 2015). The Yale Program on Climate Change Communication estimates that a quarter of the US population is disengaged, doubtful, or dismissive of the issue. This, however, is not evenly spread among all Americans. As noted in the introduction to this chapter, there are big gaps among age groups in their climate change beliefs and concern. Individual political ideology and party affiliation, too, is related to very different ideas about the environment and global warming. The next section explores these in greater detail, along with other individual influences on personal perceptions of climate change.

Influences on Climate Change Perceptions

Climate change refers to systemic, usually gradual, changes in average conditions for a region in temperature, precipitation, and extreme weather events (World Meteorological Association n.d.). Global warming refers to the earth's increasing surface temperature (Kennedy and Lindsey 2015). While some consider global warming as one symptom of climate change, others point to climate change as the side effect of global warming, and many (particularly non-scientists) use the terms interchangeably. Regardless of the term used, the issue is psychologically distant for most, both spatially (in that it is perceived as a global, not local issue) and temporally (in that it is perceived to affect the future, not present) (Spence et al. 2012). Typically, the general public is not good at detecting actual climate change and often confuses climate change with ozone depletion, pollution, and greenhouse effects (Bostrom et al. 1994; Dunlap 1998). Without the scientific and statistical tools and expertise needed to make accurate assessments about climate change, individuals rely on affect-based processing of information to form associations between events, information, and perceptions of risk. These judgments are based in a collection of decision heuristics, constituting a type of bounded rationality (Kahan et al. 2011). Personal experiences and values, as well as cues from political elites, form the foundation of these heuristic devices and, therefore, play a key role in shaping individual perceptions of climate change. We assert that the Millennial Generation persona is another lens by which young adults process information and make assessments of climate change.

Partisan Cues

In processing information, political ideology plays a chief role (Wood and Vedlitz 2007; McCright and Dunlap 2011). More often than not, individuals look to party leaders and political elites for information and cues. Because trust in scientists is not uniformly high in the United States, most people are "likely to accept and internalize messages from elites to who affiliate with his or her own party" (Malka, Krosnick, and Langer 2009: 635). Typically, these messages about climate change reinforce pre-existing political beliefs and strengthen partisan divisions on the issue (McCright and Dunlap 2011). Since the "Reagan Revolution" of the 1980s, the Republican Party has been anti-environment (Dunlap and McCright 2008), holding the position that environmental protection challenges conservative values of property rights and free market. The Democratic Party, on the other hand, has supported policies to protect the environment as it is "consistent with liberals' view that protecting collective welfare is the proper role of government" (McCright and Dunlap 2011: 160). On the issue of climate change, political elites "on the Left largely promote mainstream scientific knowledge regarding climate change . . . while those on the right regularly challenge the scientific knowledge by promoting the views of a handful of contrarian scientists" (McCright and Dunlap 2011: 161).

The division among liberals (Democrats) and conservatives (Republicans) with regards to climate change has been growing in recent decades, most noticeably with political elites, including members of Congress, but also among the public (Dunlap and McCright 2008; McCright and Dunlap 2011; Weber and Stern 2011). Gallup polls report that the gap between Democrats and Republicans in their personal concern about climate change has increased from 27% in 2001 to 35% in 2013 (Saad 2013). This ideological gap reflects mainstream ideological currents, but we must recognize that these do not resonate with all of the American adult population and that there are other factors besides partisanship that influence climate change beliefs.

Economic Assessments

Political attitudes are steeped in personal interest, particularly economic self-interest. As mentioned earlier in the chapter, most have a "finite pool of worry" and view national issues of importance, including environmental issues like climate change, as a whole package. Attention paid to one issue (and the related resources devoted to addressing it) detract from others.

Particularly in poor economic conditions, individuals place a lower priority on the environment and may see environmental action as diverting resources that could be directed to initiatives to improve employment and alleviate economic hardship. Supporting this, Kahn and Kotchen (2011) found that increases in unemployment and lower levels of income have a negative impact on public concern for the environment. Similarly, Brulle et al. (2011) concluded that concern for climate change, specifically, decreased with increases in the unemployment rate but rose with greater GDP levels. The effect of economic pressures on public opinion is not, however, equal across all segments of society. Ross and Rouse (2015) in a study of public opinion on immigration found that Millennials, despite being a group that has borne disproportionate negative impacts of the recent economic recession, are less affected by personal economic hardship. They do not translate poor economic experiences in the same way older adults do; rather, their beliefs remain liberal and progressive in the face of a poor economy.

Religious Values among the Evangelical Community

Religion has played an important role in the American climate change debate (Hulme 2009; Wardekker et al. 2009; Wilkinson 2012). On the individual level, it serves as a guide to processing the issue, forming "a lens through which many individuals read the world, the contemporary issues facing it, and proposed solutions to those problems" (Wilkinson 2012: 2). It also serves as mobilizing force to represent individual opinion, with religious groups taking an active advocacy role in our democracy. Evangelical Christian groups and leaders have, in particular, significant power and influence on our political system, particularly in partnership with the Republican Party (Hulme 2009; Wilkinson 2012).

Environmental values over many decades have developed among evangelical Christians to focus on good stewardship of natural world (Djube and Hunt 2009; Wilkinson 2012).[3] However, most evangelicals continue to reject climate change. For many, this rejection is grounded in the belief, known as pre-millennialism, that the end of the world is near with an era of direct divine rule to follow (Hulme 2009). As this era approaches, declining and turbulent environmental, social, and political conditions are expected. Studies drawing on public opinion data from the past few years have shown that the evangelical Christian public is most skeptical of climate change and global warming; they are the least likely to believe climate change is occurring and that it is caused by human activity (Funk and Alper 2015; Leiserowitz et al. 2015). A study of environmental attitudes among clergy also found that evangelical clergy are the least environmental (Guth et al. 1995).

Ethnic Minorities and the Environment

In recent years, the debate about climate change has shifted from a focus on the planet as a whole (consequences that are felt equally across-the-board) to a frame about social justice—priorities should be on those most impacted by its effects, but who are least able to cope with them. In the United States, more attention has been paid to environmental impact on minority populations, as scholars and practitioners have recognized that people of color have equal or greater concerns than whites about the environment (Jones and Carter 1994; Mohai and Bryant 1998). This concern stems largely from "greater perceived exposure to environmental health risks and environmental injustices" (Macias 2015: 3). And it is not just perception, it is reality. Many studies show that awareness about environmental risks among minorities is based on disproportionate exposure to pollution and other environmental hazards (Mohai and Bryant 1998). Known as the "climate gap," minorities incur the unequal impact of climate change which affects their health and economic well-being, as well as overall quality of life (Fischer 2009; Morello-Frosch et al. 2009; Jesdale et al. 2013). Current public opinion polls highlight that climate change is particularly salient with Latinos. Pew Research Center surveys from 2014 report that Hispanics (70%) are more likely than Whites (44%) and Blacks (56%) to believe the earth is getting warmer because of human activity and say that the country should do whatever it takes to protect the environment (76% compared to 86% and 67%, respectively) (Krogstad 2015).

The Millennial Persona and Climate Change

As we have previously discussed, the Millennial persona is comprised of characteristics and events, resulting from social, political, and economic conditions during the formative years of this generation's development. This generation is the most diverse cohort in our nation's history; 44.2% of Millennials are part of a minority race or ethnic group (US Census Bureau 2015a). This means that many of this generation are part of minority communities who are disproportionately exposed to environmental risks (Morello-Frosch, et al. 2009; Jesdale et al. 2013). This translates to a heightened awareness of the need to address racial and ethnic inequities, including those related to the environment (Joint Economic Committee 2014; The Opportunity Agenda 2014).

We also know that Millennials are more liberal and progressive than previous generations. In particular, they are more progressive on social issues than other generations at their age (Rouse and Ross 2015) and more supportive of the environment than older adults (Pew Research Center 2014a). Millennials are also more connected to the rest of the world because of the rapid pace of globalization as they have come of age. In their lifetimes, goods, services, people, information, and cultures largely flow freely across both real and virtual borders, providing opportunities to develop understanding and empathy for cultures, traditions, and ideas from around the world (Vertovec and Cohen 2002; Hopper 2007). This contributes to a larger identity known as cosmopolitanism or feeling as one is "a global citizen" (Nussbaum 1996). This is accompanied with a sense of global civic responsibility that arguably shapes their climate change beliefs and concern.

Millennials are also more trusting in science, which is important to shaping their perceptions about climate change. A poll conducted by the Harvard's Institute of Politics in 2015 reported that Millennial trust is highest for scientists; 56% of respondents said you can trust scientists to do the right thing all or most of the time—much higher than for other institutions queried, including the president, the media, federal and local government, and the military. For many Millennials, this trust in science leads them to see climate change as fact, not opinion. One focus group participant, Shelley, in the Washington, DC area summed this up:

> I don't understand why scientific fact is like a political debate issue. I think that pretty much everyone in our generation can see that this is a pretty clear issue.

And finally, Millennials are more likely to espouse a worldview that sees the government as a platform for positive change in domestic and international issues (Molyneux and Teixeria 2010). In particular, Millennials view the government's role as critical in tackling collective action problems, like the environment (Roosevelt Institute 2013). Taken together, this set of values and experiences should translate into acceptance and concern for climate change among Millennials. We contend that this effect should be discernible when comparing Millennials to older adults and when accounting for other factors, including political ideology, economic outlook, religious affiliation, and ethnic identity. The next section tests this contention using an original survey.

The Millennial Effect on Climate Change Belief

Are Millennials different than older adults in their climate change beliefs? Does their generation persona shape their beliefs in distinct ways? Analysis of our nationally representative survey, administered in November and December 2015,[4] demonstrates that Millennials are more accepting of the evidence of climate change and more likely to say human activity is the cause of global warming. When asked—*From what you've read and heard, is there solid evidence of global warming and climate change, or not?*—a greater percentage of Millennials answered "yes" or "some or mixed evidence" (92%) than their non-Millennial counterparts (85%), while a higher percentage of non-Millennials answered "no" (15% for non-Millennials compared to 8% for Millennials). An even bigger distinction between Millennials and non-Millennials is evident with responses to the follow-up question:[5] *What do you think? The earth is getting warmer mostly because of [I don't know; natural patterns in the Earth's environment; human activities such as burning fuels.]* Millennials overwhelmingly agree with the scientific consensus that global warming is attributed to human activity, while this belief is less prevalent among older adults: 62.1% of Millennials see human activity as the cause of the earth getting warmer, but only 52.9% of non-Millennials state the same. These differences are further supported by statistical tests of means that report the difference between Millennials and non-Millennials as significant with a higher mean of climate change belief and belief that global warming is caused by human activity among

Millennials.[6] This affirms that the Millennial Generation persona exerts influence on climate change perceptions. But does this continue to matter when we account for other factors that may shape climate change beliefs?

Variables and Method

Personal political ideology, economic outlook, religious beliefs, and minority identity should affect how one sees the issues surrounding global warming and climate change. To examine how the Millennial Generation persona shapes climate change beliefs, we turn to statistical analyses that test the effect of being Millennial against these other individual characteristics. Similar to previous studies and surveys (e.g., Public Religion Research Institute, Harvard Institute of Politics, Pew Research Center), we focus on two specific climate change beliefs: 1) belief in the *evidence* of global warming and climate change, and 2) belief in the *cause* of global warming.

We expect Millennials, as result of their generation persona, to be more likely than non-Millennials to believe the evidence of climate change and point to human activity as the cause of climate change as it conforms to scientific consensus. Recognizing that Millennial Generation values are not the only ones to affect climate change beliefs, we also account for *liberal political ideology*, measured as self-identification as liberal (score of 1, 2, or 3) on a 7-point scale, and *born again Christian*, measured as self-identification as a "born again Christian."[7] We expect those who are liberal in their political ideology to be more accepting of climate change, while being a born again Christian is likely to decrease belief in the evidence of climate change and anthropogenic causes of global warming as these beliefs often clash within the evangelical community.

As discussed in detail earlier in this chapter, we also acknowledge that minorities view the issue of climate change differently as they have been and are more likely to be negatively and disproportionately affected by the impacts of global warming and environmental degradation in general. We believe that individuals with ties to foreign counties, too, have environmental perspectives that should be linked to heightened belief in the evidence of climate change. Americans are more doubtful about climate change than people in other countries (Roppolo 2014). In fact, in a survey conducted by Ipsos-MORI (2014), the United States ranks last in a poll of twenty countries on agreement with the statement, "The climate change we are currently seeing is largely the result of human activity." Only 54% of American respondents agreed with this statement. To account for the potential impact of these factors, we include the following variables: *Latino*, measured as self-identification as Hispanic or Latino background; *African American*, measured as self-identification as African American; and *foreign born*, measured as identifying as being born in a country outside the United States.

To account for the effects of economic experiences on climate change beliefs, we include a variable reporting if a respondent is *unemployed*, measured as not working full time or part time, and *negative economic outlook*, measured as saying the economy today is worse (as opposed to the same or better) than twenty years ago for people of your age. We expect those that are experiencing economic hardship to be less likely to express belief in the evidence and human causes of climate change as such opinions may support action that diverts attention and resources away from economic problems.

We also expect those individuals who have a *positive government worldview*, one that perceives a positive role for the government in solving problems, to be more likely to be concerned about climate change. A positive government worldview is one manifestation of the larger collectivist culture orientation, which considers society as a whole as paramount to individual interests and responsible for securing the collective welfare (Kahan et al. 2011). Studies have shown that individuals with collectivist worldviews perceive climate change as riskier than those with individualist values (Kahan et al. 2012).[8] To capture this worldview, we employ a factor score of attitudes about the government's role in government spending to alleviate economic hardship, government provision of health insurance, government action to reduce healthcare cost, and government forgiveness of student loans.

Finally, as individual demographic characteristics may influence opinion on climate change, we control for: *education*, measured as highest degree or level of school completed; *income*, a categorical variable reporting household income; gender, measured as being *female*; and marital status, measured as being *married*, not single, divorced, separated, or widowed. We estimate a series of ordered logistic or logistic regression analyses, depending on the measurement of the dependent variable. Each regression

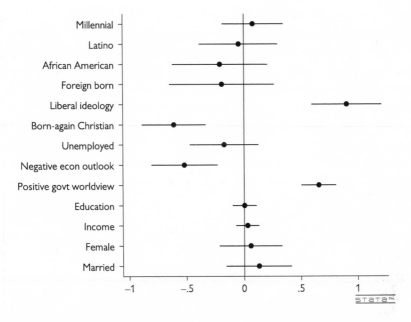

FIGURE 7.3. Factors Explaining Belief in the Evidence of Global Warming

Notes: Ordered logistic regression estimated. Coefficients represented by dots; 95% confidence intervals represented by lines. See Appendix 7.B for a table of the regression results.

analysis is weighted to adjust for the over-sample of Millennials as compared to the national population.[9]

Belief in the Evidence of Global Warming and Climate Change

Let's first examine perceptions about the evidence of global warming and climate change, specifically responses to the question: *From what you've read and heard, is there solid evidence of global warming and climate change, or not?* Due to the nature of the dependent variable, an ordered logistic regression was estimated, the results of which are depicted in Figure 7.3.[10] The figure represents coefficients with a dot and corresponding confidence intervals with a bar. If the bar crosses zero, we know that variable is statistically insignificant. On the other hand, if the bar does not cross zero, the variable is statistically significant. Coefficients to the left of the zero x-line have a negative effect on the dependent variable, and those to the right have a positive effect on the dependent variable.

The regression results indicate that being liberal and holding a positive government worldview has a positive effect on belief in the evidence of global warming while having a negative economic outlook and being a born again Christian is associated with denial of the evidence of global warming. Because logistic coefficients are difficult to interpret directly, we look to predicted probabilities to indicate the magnitude of these factors' influence on the dependent variable. An individual with liberal political ideology has a 60.4% likelihood of saying "yes, there is solid evidence" of global warming and climate change as compared to a 38.2% likelihood among those who are not liberal (moderate or conservative). On the other hand, liberals have a 5% likelihood of saying there is no evidence of global warming or climate change as compared to an 11.5% likelihood among non-liberals. Having the worldview that the government has a positive role in solving problems is also associated with a higher likelihood of belief in the evidence of global warming. Predicted probabilities indicate that at a maximum value of worldview, individuals have a 73.6% likelihood saying that "yes, there is solid evidence" of global warming compared to 22.3% likelihood at the minimum value. Those with the lowest worldview attitudes, however, are the most likely (21.8%) to say there is no evidence of global warming.

While liberal ideology and a positive government worldview increases the likelihood of belief and climate change evidence, the regression results indicate that a poor economic outlook depresses it. Individuals that say the national economy today is worse off than it was twenty years ago for people of their age have a 41.3% likelihood of saying there is solid evidence of global warming and climate change as compared to a 54.1% likelihood among those that say the economy is the same or better today. Those with this negative economic outlook also have a 10.2% likelihood of saying there is no evidence of global warming while those with a better economic outlook have a much lower chance—6.4% likelihood of the same. This suggests that those who are economically hard-pressed are translating economic pressures to their opinion on climate change. This may be motivated by a lack of concern for this issue—the "finite pool of worry" that Weber (2006) asserts—or a calculus that such belief supports actions that would divert limited resources away from addressing economic issues.

Similarly, being a born again Christian also decreases the likelihood of belief in the evidence of global warming and climate change. Born again

Christians have a 36.7% likelihood of saying there is solid evidence of global warming, as compared to 51.6% likelihood among those who do not identify as a born again Christian. On the other hand, born again Christians have a 12.1% likelihood of saying there is no evidence of global warming, but those who do not identify as a born again Christian have a 7% likelihood of the same. These findings are in line with recent surveys that report the evangelical public continues to reject climate change evidence (Funk and Alper 2015; Leiserowitz et al. 2015).

The results also indicate that the Millennial Generation identity, measured as being Millennial, does not directly affect individual beliefs about the evidence of global warming and climate change. However, it is possible that the Millennial identity shapes climate change belief indirectly by, for example, compounding the influence of liberal ideology or filtering how Millennials translate their experience with the economy. We examine this through an interaction model that allows us to test the differences among Millennials and non-Millennials for each independent variable—Latino, African American, foreign born, liberal, born again Christian, unemployment, economic outlook, and positive government worldview. Again, we use an ordered logistic regression model to test these associations.

Because the coefficients are difficult to interpret directly, the results of the interaction model are presented in Figure 7.4 as marginal effect contrasts between the groups.[11] The marginal effect contrast—the difference between Millennials and non-Millennials in their likelihood of belief in the evidence of global warming and climate change—is shown for each independent variable value and each dependent variable outcome (no evidence, some/mixed evidence, and yes evidence). The bars indicate the size of the difference, and asterisks at the end of the bars indicate if the difference between Millennials and non-Millennials is statistically significant ($p<0.05$). Negative values (bars to the left) indicate that Millennials are less likely than non-Millennials to be associated with the dependent variable outcome; positive values (bars to the right) indicate that Millennials are more likely in comparison to non-Millennials.

The results show that Millennials are distinct from non-Millennials across the following areas: exposure to different cultures, represented by the variables Latino and foreign born; economic assessments, measured by being unemployed and holding a negative outlook; and having a positive government worldview. The pairwise comparisons of marginal

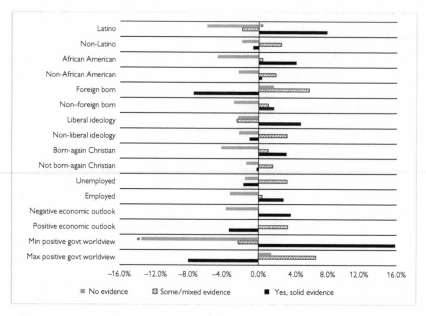

FIGURE 7.4.   Interaction Effects of Millennial Identity: Differences between Millennials and Non-Millennials in Likelihood of Belief in Evidence of Global Warming

Notes: Results of pairwise comparisons of marginal effects shown based on estimates of ordered logistic regression analysis that interacted each independent variable with the variable Millennial. Difference in Millennial versus Non-Millennial marginal effect shown by the bars. Negative values indicate that, for that dependent variable outcome, Millennials are less likely than Non-Millennials; positive values indicate that Millennials are more likely than Non-Millennials. Statistically significant differences ($p < 0.05$) between Millennials and Non-Millennials are marked with asterisk at the end of the bar.

effects indicate that there is a statistically significance difference among Latinos. Latino Millennials are 5.9% less likely to say there is no evidence of global warming in comparison to Latino non-Millennials. This underscores that Millennials are more progressive among a group that is already more accepting of global warming; according to our survey, 47.1% of Latinos, compared to 44.9% of non-Latinos, say there is evidence of global warming. We see this same trend among the employed. Employed individuals are more likely to say there is evidence of global warming (48.3% employed versus 41.1% unemployed). Among this group, the difference between Millennials and non-Millennials approaches statistical significance[12] with young adults being 3.3% less likely to say there is no evidence of global warming than older adults.

Being born in the United States (labeled "non-foreign born" in the figure) is another subgroup where differences between Millennials and non-Millennials emerge. Among this group, Millennials are 2.9% less likely than non-Millennials to say there is no evidence of global warming. Even though this difference only approaches statistical significance,[13] this is an important finding considering that the native-born population is the predominant group in the survey sample and in our nation; 91.4% of respondents to our survey and 87.1% of the country's population were born in the United States.[14] The lack of significance among those who are foreign born is equally telling. According to our survey, a greater percentage of foreign-born individuals (71% foreign born versus 56.3% native born) say there is evidence of global warming. This is in line with our expectations that climate change acceptance and concern is higher among this group.

Millennials are also more accepting of the evidence of global warming among those with a negative economic outlook. Among those who say the economy is worse today than twenty years ago for people of their age, Millennials are 3.7% less likely than non-Millennials to believe there is no evidence of global warming and climate change. Again, while this difference only approaches statistical significance,[15] the result suggests that the Millennial Generation persona is working to lessen the effect of poor economic experiences on acceptance of the evidence regarding global warming and climate change. This underscores that Millennial beliefs are more resilient to economic hardship than non-Millennials, a finding in line with past work (Ross and Rouse 2015).

The distinction among Millennials and non-Millennials is also significant when considering the context of beliefs in the role of government. Among those with the lowest value of the worldview variable—a variable that captures attitudes about the positive role government plays in solving problems—Millennials are 13.5% less likely to say there is no evidence and 15.9% more likely to say there is solid evidence of global warming. Similar to negative economic outlook, we see Millennials emerge among this group expected to have less accepting attitudes about global warming as more progressive.

These statistical analyses collectively tell us that perceptions about the evidence of global warming are driven largely by political ideology and worldview. Both non-Millennial and Millennial liberals and those who believe to a higher degree that the government plays a positive role in solving problems are much more likely to say there is solid evidence of global warming than their counterparts. These perceptions are also shaped by economic outlook and religious beliefs; those who believe the economy today is worse than for the previous generation and who are evangelical Christians are less likely to believe in the evidence of global warming. However, the Millennial Generation persona tempers the effect of a poor economy, and Millennials emerge as being more progressive on global warming among Latinos, the employed, and—most importantly—among the native-born population. This underscores that political ideology, economic experiences, religious beliefs, and the Millennial Generation persona explain the acceptance (or denial) of global warming among American adults. Do these same factors explain how individuals perceive the causes of global warming?

Belief in the Anthropogenic Causes of Global Warming

To examine the individual factors related to perceptions of the cause of global warming, we turn to a logistic analysis that regresses the same set of independent variables on responses to the survey question—*What do you think? The earth is getting warmer mostly because of . . . natural patterns in the earth's environment OR human activities such as burning fossil fuels.* Recall that this question was asked only of those respondents that believe there is solid evidence or some/mixed evidence of global warming and climate change. Multiple variables emerge as statistically significant in the regression analysis. [16] Millennial, being foreign born, liberal ideology, and positive government worldview are all significantly and positively associated with the belief that global warming is caused by human activities, as opposed to natural patterns.

Turning again to predicted probabilities to explore the magnitude of these effects, we see that Millennials have a 62.9% likelihood of saying the earth is getting warmer because of human activity as compared to a 55.2% likelihood with non-Millennials. As discussed earlier in this chapter, the Millennial Generation is liberal and open-minded in their thinking and trusts science to a high degree. This translates into a cohort accepting of the scientific consensus on global warming. For most Millennials, there is not much doubt in the science around this issue. As one focus group participant, Chloe, in the Washington, DC area put it:

> I think that it's 100 percent occurring, and I 100 percent think that the majority of the problem is man-made. Politically, I think it's ridiculous that one of the major parties of our country still denies that it might not exist, because it exists.

Similar to Millennials, foreign born and liberal respondents are more likely to attribute global warming to human activity. Predicted probability estimates indicate that foreign-born respondents have a 71% likelihood of saying global warming is caused by human activity, compared to 57.8% likelihood among native-born individuals. Liberals have a 66.5% likelihood of believing in the anthropogenic causes of global warming, while non-liberals (moderates and conservatives) have a 53.8% likelihood the same. The same trend is evident across worldview values; those with the highest value of positive government worldview have a 73.7% likelihood of belief in the human causes of global warming, while those with the lowest value of worldview have a 41.6% likelihood of the same. The underscores what we have already seen—those who are foreign born, liberal, and have greater belief in the positive role of government are more likely to accept the science around climate change.

As with the analysis of global warming evidence, we can explore the interaction effects of the Millennial Generation identity with each independent variable. The results are consistent with the findings on belief in the evidence of global warming—the effect of the Millennial Generation persona translates to statistically significant differences among the majority population and tempers the effect of negative economic experiences. Again, let's turn to pairwise comparisons of marginal effects to interpret these results.[17] As shown in Figure 7.5, among non-Latinos and native-born individuals (labeled "non-foreign born" in the figure), Millennials are more likely to say global warming is caused by human activity (7.4% and 7.5%, respectively). This finding underscores that among the larger population of American adults, Millennials are distinct from non-Millennials in this belief. Where they are not different—among Latinos and those who are foreign born—belief and concern for global warming causes are high.[18]

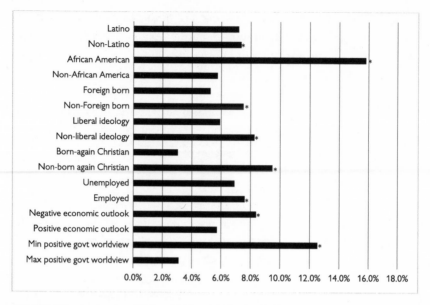

FIGURE 7.5. Interaction Effects of Millennial Identity: Differences between Millennials and Non-Millennials in the Likelihood of Attributing Global Warming to Human Activity

Notes: Results of pairwise comparisons of marginal effects shown based on estimates of logistic regression analysis that interacted each independent variable with the variable Millennial. Difference in Millennial versus Non-Millennial marginal effect shown by the bars. Negative values indicate that, for that dependent variable outcome, Millennials are less likely than Non-Millennials; positive values indicate that Millennials are more likely than Non-Millennials. Statistically significant differences (p<0.05) between Millennials and Non-Millennials are marked with asterisk at the end of the bar.

The effect of the Millennial Generation persona is also evident among those who do not identify as a born again Christian. Millennials are 9.5% more likely to say global warming is caused by humans than non-Millennials among this group. The same is not true among born again Christians, suggesting that Evangelical values shape global warming attitudes equally across age groups. However, we do see the tempering effect of the Millennial Generation persona among moderates and conservatives—groups more doubtful of the human causes of global warming. Among non-liberals (moderates and conservatives), Millennials are 8.3% more likely to believe the anthropogenic causes of global warming.

With regard to economic circumstance, we see that Millennials are 7.6% and 8.4% more likely to say human activity is the cause of global warming among the employed and those with a negative economic outlook, respectively. Among those with the lowest belief in the positive role of government, Millennials, again, are more likely to support the anthropogenic causes of global warming; among this group, they are 12.5% more likely to say human activity causes global warming. These findings highlight additional scenarios where Millennials emerge as more progressive on the issue of climate change.

This set of regression analyses demonstrate that the Millennial Generation identity affects the way young adults assess global warming. The findings show that Millennials, as a generation, are generally liberal and open-minded in their thinking about the issue of global warming and that these attitudes are resilient to political and economic factors that may constrain the thinking of older adults on the issue. How does the Millennial Generation persona guide thinking about policies to address climate change and global warming?

Conclusion: How Millennials May Shape Our Environmental Future

Employing information from our original survey, we can assess if Millennials are distinct in their policy preferences as compared to older adults through a series of climate change policy questions. These asked survey respondents to indicate how much support or likely support they have for the following federal government policies: 1) increased taxes and penalties for pollution by corporations; 2) aggressively pursue the production and use of alternative energy sources; and 3) increased regulation of carbon emissions for automobiles. Possible responses included: "none," "a little," "some," and "a lot." As shown in Figure 7.6, Millennials expressed less support than non-Millennials for these policy prescriptions. Even when taking into account factors that should boost support, including liberal ideology and positive government worldview, Millennials were less likely to prefer these policy options.[19] For example, on the issue of pursuing alternative energy, 55.8% of liberal Millennials support it "a lot;" this is far surpassed by the 70.1% of older adult liberals who express the same support for the policy.

So what gives? Why does the Millennial Generation persona influence climate change beliefs but falls short of affecting support for policies to mitigate the problem? One interpretation of this is that Millennials do not understand policy or are not savvy at translating their values to policy choices. While the latter argument is difficult to trace, the first argument is supported by

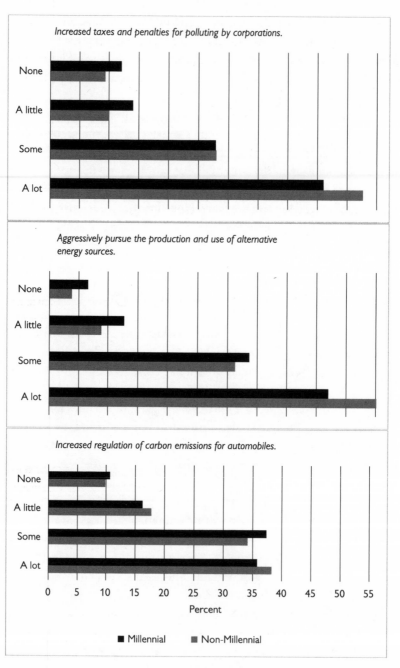

FIGURE 7.6. Policy Support among Millennials and Non-Millennials for Federal Government Action to Mitigate Global Warming and Climate Change

Note: Percentages shown for Millennial and Non-Millennial respondents.

a Pew Research Center political knowledge study conducted in 2010. This analysis found that Millennials considerably lagged behind older adults in their knowledge of key political and economic issues. Other studies (e.g., The Media Insight Project), however, have shown that Millennials are informed on political issues.

Another take is that Millennials are looking for a different set of solutions. We know that Millennials are largely disengaged from traditional institutions (in their current form) and that they do not trust those in power within our primary political institutions. A 2015 Harvard Institute of Politics poll reports that Millennial trust in Congress is the lowest of all institutions surveyed, followed by the federal government. While declining trust over the past two decades in the federal government is well documented for the American adult population,[20] this distrust has characterized Millennials' experience with government as teenagers and young adults. Moreover, Millennials have seen little movement on environmental issues in their lifetimes, instead witnessing partisan gridlock and vehement debate over climate change. Taken together, this provides little incentive for young adults to look to political leadership for solutions to the climate change problem. Rather, Millennials may be seeking solutions closer to home or those provided by non-governmental actors. While our survey unfortunately did not tap into alternative actions to address global warming (beyond federal government policies), our focus group participants offered insight into what environmental policy alternatives this generation may be considering.

The focus groups revealed that Millennials are not necessarily looking to the government for solutions but rather see climate change as a problem to be solved with local efforts and individual actions. Vincent, a San Antonio, Texas area focus group participant, put it this way:

It's [climate change] not like a big issue that the government has control over it. It starts with every individual.

The Millennials we talked to are looking to small changes they can make on a daily basis that affects positive change. For example, Quanisha from Los Angeles, California said she does not mind taking "smaller steps" and part of that for her is using reusable bags in place of plastic bags. Other daily choices include transportation—taking the bus or driving a hybrid car. But, as our focus group participants pointed out, these choices could be improved. Millennials want more flexible and connected public transportation and expanded choices—in terms of appearance, quality, and cost—of hybrid cars. Keisha in our Washington, DC focus group asserted: "All the hybrid cars I've seen, they're not attractive . . . [if] you want to promote this product, but you're going to have to give us different options." Turning to cost, Don from Los Angeles, California said he would be "willing to take on the expense of solar panels or an electric car when it becomes a little more affordable." The Millennials we talked to, like many across the United States, are leery of taking on additional expenses. They are supportive of subsidies to offset the cost but are looking for options that are relevant to them. Solar panels, while subsidized by some programs, do not affect most Millennials as the majority are not home owners. They, therefore, look to the routine consumer choices they can affect.

As we will see in the chapter on political engagement (Chapter 9), a preference for making changes on the local level fits with how Millennials perceive problems and address them. States and local governments have taken a similar approach to climate change and environmental policy, making rules and creating incentives where they have jurisdiction to affect change. For Millennials, this approach very well may be the most effective in generating results and providing a sense of efficacy. This is particularly important at a time when the federal government is controlled by Republicans and President Trump has promised to reduce environmental regulations and to withdraw the United States from the Paris Agreement on climate change.[21] We are unlikely to see federal government action that progresses mitigation of climate change in the near future, but we may see local movements, perhaps propelled by Millennials, to address environmental issues in everyday activities and consumer choices.

CHAPTER 8

Their Own Brand of Liberal—Millennials and Contemporary Social Issues

The Millennial Generation is perhaps best known for, politically speaking, liberalness and tolerance on social issues. This generation was at the forefront of the rise in public support for same-sex marriage, and they consistently maintain greater levels of support for this right. In 2016, 71% of Millennials[1] favored same-sex marriage. This is 15% higher than support among older generations (Pew Research Center 2016f). Moreover, Millennials have stood out recently for their overwhelming support for legalization of marijuana, not only for medicinal but also recreational purposes (Jones 2015). Polls show that this support has been growing over the past decade and now 68% of Millennials say they support legalization—16% more than older generations (Motel 2015). This stance gives these "hipsters" much in common with "hippies" of the Baby Boomer Generation (Margolin 2016), when both cohorts were young, and in present day, as reports indicate increased usage of marijuana among aging Boomers (Ingraham 2016).

Not only are Millennial stances on contemporary social issues liberal, but their overall political outlook also skews to the left. In fact, the report *Millennials in Adulthood* maintains that they are "the most liberal and least conservative of the four [adult] generations, and the only generation in which liberals are not significantly outnumbered by conservatives" (Pew Research Center 2014a: 22). This references a decade of political ideology data comparing the Millennial Generation (born 1980–1997) to Generation X (born 1965–1980), Baby Boomers (born 1946–1964), and members of the Silent Generation (born 1928–1945). Our original

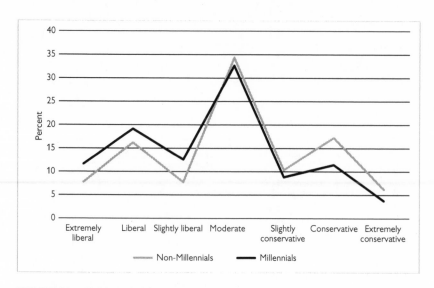

FIGURE 8.1.   Political Ideology and Party Affiliation of Non-Millennials & Millennials

Note: Average responses for non-Millennials (n = 579) and Millennials (n = 533) shown to the survey question—"We hear a lot of talk these days about liberals and conservatives. Here is a 7-point scale on which the political views that people might hold are arranged from extremely liberal to extremely conservative. Where would you place yourself on this scale?"

survey data,[2] collected in 2015, confirms this. As shown in Figure 8.1, a greater percentage of Millennials,[3] in comparison to older adults, identify as liberal rather than conservative when asked to place themselves on a 7-point ideology scale. A total of 43.3% of Millennials identify as liberal ("extremely liberal," "liberal," or "slightly liberal") compared to 31.8% of non-Millennials. In contrast, non-Millennial conservatives ("extremely conservative," "conservative," or "slightly conservative") outnumber Millennial conservatives, 33.9% to 24% respectively, while nearly the same percentage of both groups identify as "moderate" (34.4% and 32.7% respectively).

We have asserted, throughout this book, that liberalness of the Millennial Generation is a defining feature of this age group's persona, identity, or frame—even more so than for generations of the past (Ross and Rouse 2015).[4] Rather than expound on their liberalness from an ideological standpoint—an approach that has been covered by past studies (Halpin and Agne 2009; Pew Research Center 2014a; Ross and Rouse 2015)—this chapter considers the characteristic from a policy standpoint. We examine three social issues that dominate the political landscape today—gun control, legalization of marijuana, and the right to abortion—by unpacking the opinions of Millennials in comparison to older adults. We also assess the variance in attitudes that exists among Millennials, recognizing that, despite their shared identity, subgroups of this age cohort are unlikely to be uniform in their opinions on these issues. To preview our findings—Millennial social liberalness is nuanced, varying in degree across issues and dispositional characteristics such as race and ethnicity, individual political ideology, and religious beliefs. Rather than fit the traditional bounds of liberal ideology, Millennials share a set of values and policy stances that define their brand of liberalness.

Lukewarm, Passionate, and Not So Different: Millennial Attitudes Compared to Older Adults on Guns, Marijuana, and Abortions

To examine the social liberalness of Millennials, in comparison to older adults, we draw upon responses to our original survey, conducted in 2015,[5] that probe support for three contemporary social issues—gun control, legalization of marijuana, and right to an abortion. Political ideology on social issues is value driven and typically does not fall into neat categories as economic issues are more likely to do so (i.e., conservatives want less government in the economy while liberals want more government intervention). While there are certainly some variations, politically liberal individuals tend to support heightened government control and restrictions on gun ownership and use, while conservatives typically champion the interpretation of the second amendment in favor of gun rights and support limits on government gun control (Lindaman and Haider-Markel 2002; Adams 2004). Liberals are more likely to support the full (recreational) legalization of marijuana, while conservatives tend to prefer keeping the drug illegal (MacCoun and Paletz 2009). Liberals are more likely to support women's rights to choose in cases of abortion, while conservatives, adhering to "traditional family values," tend to favor restrictions on abortions to protect the rights of the unborn (Carmines and Woods 2002). To gauge attitudes on these issues, our survey asked, "How much do you support or are likely to support the following federal

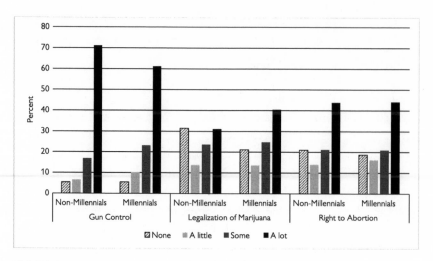

FIGURE 8.2.   Distribution of Millennial & Non-Millennial Support across Three
Social Issues

Note: Average responses for non-Millennials (n = 630) and Millennials (n = 621) shown for three
policy areas: 1) gun control, 2) legalization of marijuana, and 3) right to an abortion.

government policy?" The following three federal government policies
were posed:

1. Requirement for background checks and waiting periods before
   purchase of a gun.
2. Marijuana for recreational use by adults.
3. Women's right to an abortion.

Support for these policy propositions is shown in Figure 8.2. Possible
responses included: "none," "a little," "some," and "a lot."

The majority of both Millennials and non-Millennials support gun
control in the form of federally mandated background checks and waiting
periods before the purchase of a gun. However, there is nearly a 10% gap
between Millennials and older adults that say they have "a lot" of support
for this—61.2% versus 71.1%, respectively, highlighting that Millennials
are lukewarm on this issue. This cohort is not as liberal as we might expect
on this issue (Witkin 2016), and many support gun rights—a recent poll
reports that 49% of Millennials in 2014 said it is "more important to control gun ownership than protect the right of Americans to own guns" (Pew

Research Center 2014a: 34). Representing this split on gun control and gun rights, Eli, a Millennial focus group participant from Los Angeles, California, had this to say:

> I don't think they should be selling AK-47's. I think that's completely ridiculous. No one needs an AK-47. I could see like a shotgun, having it in their home, but I think psychological tests should be given out before issuing guns. I think that's a really big factor in issuing guns out, but I'm not completely against people having guns.

Another take on the issue is offered in a recent *Washington Times* opinion piece by Jesse Winton (2016) that asserts Millennials are data driven in their attitudes about gun control. The author claims:

> At the heart of the push for gun control is a mindset—admittedly sincere in many instances—that is rooted in the false belief that gun laws will remove guns from the hands of those who would use them to commit crimes. The obvious problem is that criminals are criminals. They are a class of people whose inherent attitudes towards laws is to disobey them, particularly those laws that would restrict their own access to firearms . . . Millennials may be a lot of things, but they are not stupid . . . For all the hysterical talk about gun violence in the United States, the truth is that our nation ranks relatively low in terms of gun murders per 100,000 people. It is impossible to reconcile that with the fact the United States leads the world in civilian firearms ownership. Millennials—to their credit—don't try to.

An Ipsos Public Affairs poll of Millennials, conducted in 2016, offers evidence of perceptions about gun ownership and violent crime. According to this poll, only 32% of respondents said that they "strongly agree" that "stricter gun laws would help to prevent gun violence." As Winton asserts, it seems that Millennials do not buy into the connection that gun restrictions prevent crime. This certainly does not imply that Millennials are turning a cold shoulder to gun violence; quite the contrary, Millennials are aware and concerned with the issue on many fronts.[6]

While Millennials are lukewarm in support for gun control, they are passionate about the legalization of marijuana for recreational use. Our survey results, shown in Figure 2, indicate that 40.4% of Millennials have "a lot" of support for the legalization of marijuana compared to only 31.1% among older adults. While there is a clear bimodal distribution among non-Millennials in support for legalization of marijuana—31.4% of older adults have no support—Millennial support skews toward favoring the policy, only one in five young adults have no support for the legalization of recreational marijuana. Pew Research Center polls (2014a) show that support among Millennials for legalization of marijuana has surged in the past decade, and even young Republicans support the policy to higher degrees than Democrats of older generations (Gao 2015).

Participants in our focus groups of Millennials had a lot to say about the issue of marijuana—it dominated the discussion of social issues in every one of the eight focus groups. For them, the legalization of marijuana is about generational values—attitudes that influence stances on other issues such as same-sex marriage and which have to do with a "live and let live" approach. Tara from Washington, DC had this to say about the generational aspect, connecting attitudes about marijuana to opinions on same-sex marriage:

> I think a lot of it being a generational thing is . . . I feel like Millennials have the attitude like, "What does it have to do with me?" If two guys are getting married, how does that affect me? It doesn't. I don't care. I'm focused on my problems, and I think a lot of Millennials, we have so many issues that we're dealing with. The last thing we care about is if two people are getting married, or if this person wants to smoke weed. It doesn't affect me.

Despite being more conservative than Tara, Ari from San Antonio, Texas echoed a similar sentiment, stating, "When I started hearing all about the marijuana and legalizing it, I was like yeah that's good. No, I'm not going to do it, but I'm not against it. I'm not going to tell people not to do it."

For Zach, also in Washington, DC, legalization of marijuana addresses "current problems like injustices with the criminal justice system." Jonathan in New Orleans shared the following thought:

> I think the benefit of legalizing it most is the money saved by not imprisoning people for something that, at least with marijuana, is

not really harming anybody. I mean, yes everything has a draw-back. Some people will smoke and drive, and somebody's going to get hurt. But the cost of imprisoning so many young people—and not only the cost to keep them in prison, but the effect of putting them in prison from their early 20s, late teens, where they should be starting their career, basically puts them behind everybody and is a much harsher sentence than just putting them in prison.

As illustrated by these focus group quotes, the legalization of marijuana connects to deeper values held by the Millennial Generation, including tolerance and ethnic and racial justice expounded upon previously and in Chapter 1.

The third social policy issue we have probed is abortion, and our survey results (shown in Figure 2) indicate that this issue, unlike gun control and the legalization of marijuana, is not driven by generational attitudes or experiences. Rather, the distribution of abortion attitudes is very similar between Millennials and older adults. Those with "a lot" of support for a federal policy that would establish a woman's right to an abortion include 44.1% of Millennials and 43.8% of non-Millennials. On the other end of the spectrum, 18.7% of Millennials and 21% of non-Millennials have no support for such a policy. Our survey results reflect slight differences in views on abortion, an observation that has been made by other polling agencies, including Pew Research Center (2014a) and Gallup (Jacoby 2015).

Despite the similarities in abortion attitudes across generations, there are some Millennial nuances to this social issue. The Public Religion Research Institute (PRRI) conducted an in-depth study of abortion attitudes with specific focus on Millennials in comparison to older genera-tions. The report highlights that Millennials are conflicted by the morality of abortion but committed to making it available as part of healthcare. The authors, Cox and Jones, state (2011: 2):

Unlike all other age groups, Millennials register different levels of support for the availability and legality of abortion. On the one hand, Millennials are strongly committed to the availability of abortion and are significantly more likely than the general public to say that at least some health care professionals in their commu-nity should provide legal abortions (68% vs. 58% respectively). But they are no more likely than the general public to say that abortion should be legal in all or most cases. These findings suggest general measures of legality may not fully capture support for legal abortion among Millennials.

These report findings underscore that young adults are committed to making legal abortions available, which has been eroded by heightened restrictions in conservative states, including Texas and Louisiana, as well as the threat of withdrawal of federal funding for Planned Parenthood. Our focus group participants addressed these current trends and confirmed the findings of the PRRI report by emphasizing women's healthcare as it relates to abortion rights. Chloe in Washington, DC asserted, "I think if a woman can't even have access to healthcare and women's healthcare, then how are they going to be equal in society?" Chelsea in San Antonio, Texas, also connected restrictions on abortions to women's healthcare, stating, "Women's healthcare, I think that at least in certain age brackets, I think it should be absolutely covered or provided. I really don't even want to live in a world where you can take that away. Like Planned Parenthood was a great place, I don't understand."[7]

These descriptive analyses of our survey responses underscore that Millennials' social liberalness does not apply equally to all issues. Young adults, in comparison to older adults, are fairly lukewarm on the issue of gun control but passionate about the full legalization of marijuana. They are not so different from older adults on opinions regarding abortion rights but are more likely to view the issue through the lens of access to women's healthcare. To examine more closely how the Millennial Generation persona, frame, or identity influences attitudes about these issues while controlling for other factors, we turn our attention to regression analyses in the next section.

Why Do They Support . . .? Understanding Attitudes about Social Issues between Millennials & Non-Millennials and among Millennial Subgroups

We have seen so far in this chapter that there are clear generational differences between Millennials and non-Millennials in their attitudes about gun control and legalization of marijuana. We have also shown that Millennials and older adults are remarkably similar in their opinions on abortion rights. This leads us to ask—*In addition to generation, what factors explain attitudes about gun control, legalization of marijuana, and right to an abortion? And do these attitudes vary among Millennials?* To explore this statistically, we pivot to the model used throughout this book that sets up individual opinions as a product of: The Millennial Generation persona—being a Millennial in terms of birth year; diversity—being Latino, African American, or foreign born; political ideology—liberal or conservative; economic experiences—specifically, employment status and economic outlook; and worldview—the perceived role of government in solving social and economic problems.[8]

Given the descriptive statistics explored in the previous section, we expect that Millennials will be more socially liberal on legalization of marijuana but not on gun control or right to abortion. We also anticipate that those individuals who prescribe to a liberal political ideology and hold a worldview that the government has a positive role to play in society will have more support for these social policy stances (Lakoff 2002). We measure liberal as self-identifying as "extremely liberal," "liberal," or "somewhat liberal" (as opposed to moderate or any of the categories of conservative) on the 7-point ideology scale discussed in the introduction to this chapter. Positive government worldview is measured as a factor score of attitudes about government spending to reduce economic hardships, government requirement for all to have healthcare coverage, government action to reduce the cost of healthcare, and government forgiveness of student loan debt. While we have expectations about the influence of the Millennial Generation persona, liberal ideology, and positive government worldview on gun control, legalization of marijuana, and abortion rights, we do not have expectations about how economic hardship may shape stances on these policies. However, we include economic hardship because it is a critical experience shared by Millennials and, thus, an important part of their collective identity. We measure being economically hard pressed as being unemployed and having a negative economic outlook—saying the economy today is worse than it was for people of your age twenty years ago.

We have mixed expectations regarding the dynamics of support for socially liberal policies among those individuals with diverse backgrounds—who are members of an ethnic/race minority group or are foreign born. On the one hand, one might expect that minorities, who are largely concentrated in urban centers and experience more gun-related crime, favor heightened gun control (Mzezewa and DiNapoli 2015). However, opinions about gun policies among African Americans have been shifting over the last several decades; while a majority of group members still favor gun control policies, this number has been steadily decreasing (Williams 2014). Latinos, on the other hand, consistently demonstrate greater support for gun control over expanded gun rights (Lopez et al. 2014). Minorities may also support the legalization of marijuana, but differences across groups also exist on this issue. A recent Pew Research Center poll showed that almost six in ten African Americans (59%) favor legalization of marijuana—a number identical to whites. By contrast, Latinos are more divided on the issue, with 49% stating that the drug should be illegal, while 45% support legalization (Geiger 2016). Finally, attitudes about abortion across minority groups are similarly diverse as with gun control and marijuana. By far, African Americans are most supportive of abortion being legal (62%), compared to whites (58%) and Latinos (48%). Out of the three groups, Latinos are more likely to oppose (49%) abortion rights than support them (Pew Research Center 2017). We regress measures of these factors as well as the control variables of education level, income level, gender, and marital status on support ("none," "a little," "some," or "a lot") for federal policies mandating gun control, legalization of marijuana, and right to an abortion.[9] All the data were taken from our original 2015 survey.[10] Given the measurement of the dependent variables, we estimate ordinal logistic regression models.[11]

The results of the regression models are reported in Table 8.1.[12] Note that variables with a negative sign have a statistically significant (p<0.05), negative relationship with the dependent variable while those with a plus sign have a statistically significant, positive relationship; variables with "ns" are not statistically significant. Overall, we find support for our expectations and observe, once again, that the Millennial Generation persona, largely built on shared social liberalness, does not equally affect support for policies on gun control, legalization of marijuana, and right to an abortion. Rather, Millennials are actually statistically less likely to support gun control but more likely to support legalization of marijuana; there are no statistical differences between Millennials and non-Millennials on attitudes

TABLE 8.1.　Regression Results Estimating the Effect of the Millennial Generation Persona on Social Issue Stances

How much do you support or are likely to support the following federal government policy?

	Gun Control	Legalization of Marijuana	Right to an Abortion
	Background checks and waiting periods before purchase of a gun.	Marijuana for recreational use.	Women's right to an abortion.
Millennial	−	+	ns
Latino	ns	ns	ns
African American	ns	ns	ns
Foreign born	ns	ns	−
Liberal ideology	+	+	+
Unemployed	+	−	ns
Negative economic outlook	ns	−	ns
Positive government worldview	+	+	+
Education	ns	−	ns
Income	ns	ns	+
Female	+	ns	+
Married	ns	ns	−

Note: Regression results shown based on ordered logistic estimations. A plus sign (+) denotes a positive, statistically significant correlate; a negative sign (−) denotes a negative, statistically significant correlate; "ns" represents that the variable is not statistically significant. Statistical significance is considered at the p<0.05 level. See appendices for regression results tables: Appendix 8.A gun control, Appendix 8.B legalization of marijuana, and Appendix 8.C right to an abortion.

about abortion rights. Because logit coefficients are difficult to interpret directly, we rely on predicted probabilities to demonstrate the direction of the relationship between the independent and dependent variables and the magnitude of the effect of the independent variable. We discuss these for each significant variable across each policy issue, in turn.

Gun Control

The regression results indicate that Millennials are less likely to support federally mandated gun control, specifically "requirement for background checks and waiting periods before purchase of a gun," than older adults. Predicted probabilities report that Millennials have a 63.4% likelihood of having "a lot" of support for this policy, while non-Millennials have a 75.8% likelihood of the same.[13] Millennials, in comparison to non-Millennials, are more likely to have "some" (8.8% versus 5.2% respectively) or "a little" support (4.5% versus 2.5% respectively). Moreover,

Millennials have nearly double the likelihood of having no support for this policy than older adults—4.5% versus 2.5% respectively.

While Millennials have a negative relationship with support for gun control, individuals with liberal political ideology, the unemployed, those with a positive government worldview, and females are all *more* likely to support background checks and waiting periods before the purchase of a gun. Liberal individuals have a 79.2% likelihood of having "a lot" of support for gun control, while moderates and conservatives have a 64.4% likelihood of the same. Similarly, individuals with the maximum positive government worldview factor score have an 86.6% likelihood of "a lot" of support for this policy while those with the minimum score have a 48.3% likelihood of the same. As expected, liberal individuals and those who favor government intervention to solve social and economic problems are supportive of increased government regulation of gun purchases. Unemployed individuals have a 76.6% likelihood of having "a lot" of support as well, compared to a 65.9% likelihood of the same among employed individuals. Females, too, are more likely to have "a lot" of support—76.5% likelihood, compared to 64.2% for men. This resonates with the findings of past studies (i.e., Pew Research Center 2014d; Spitzer 2015) that show women are more supportive of gun control.

Turning back to Millennials, it is important to examine support for gun control policy among subgroups of this age cohort. Figure 8.3 presents descriptive statistics across the measures of diversity, ideology/worldview, and economic hardship. Among race/ethnic groups, we find that white Millennials are least supportive (although a majority still has "a lot" of support) of gun control, while Latinos and African Americans have greater support. In fact, a higher percentage of Latinos and African Americans have "a lot" of support than Millennials on average (shown by the horizontal dotted line). Foreign-born Millennials have the most support for gun control, followed by liberals and those with a positive government worldview.[14] Even Millennials who are unemployed and have a negative economic outlook have a greater percentage of those who have "a lot" of support for gun control than Millennials on average. In all, we find that Millennial opinion is not monolithic on this issue; rather, there are multiple dynamics within this age cohort that influences, to varying degrees, support for gun control.

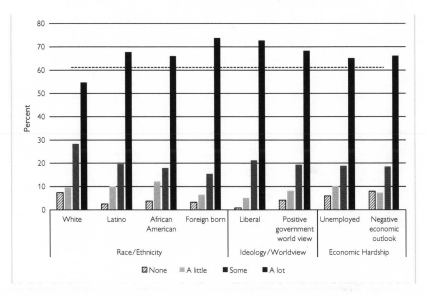

FIGURE 8.3. Support for Gun Control across Millennial Subgroups

Note: Average responses shown for each Millennial subgroup—White (n = 335), Latino (n = 158), African American (n = 106), foreign born (n = 61), liberal (n = 231), positive government worldview (n = 290), unemployed (n = 218), and negative economic outlook (n = 340). The dotted line represents the percentage of all Millennials who have "a lot" of support (61.2%). Positive government worldview for the purposes of this graph refers to individuals with a factor score that is in the top 50% (top two quartiles).

Legalization of Marijuana

The regression results on attitudes about marijuana indicate that Millennials are statistically more likely to support a federal policy legalizing marijuana for recreational use than older adults. Predicted probabilities report that Millennials, on average, have a 39.7% likelihood of having "a lot" of support for the legalization of marijuana compared to a 31% likelihood of the same among non-Millennials. Millennials, too, have a higher likelihood of saying they have "some" support for legalization of marijuana, 26.1% compared to 25.8% among older adults. Along the same trend line, Millennials, compared to non-Millennials, have a lower likelihood of only "a little" support (13.4% versus 15.4% respectively) or no support (20.8% versus 27.8% respectively) for legalization of marijuana.

In additional to Millennials, individuals with liberal political ideology and a positive government worldview are more likely to support marijuana legalization. Liberals have a 43% likelihood of having "a lot" support for this policy, compared to a 30.7% likelihood among moderates and conservatives. Those with the maximum positive government worldview factor score have a 46.7% likelihood of "a lot" of support, while individuals with the minimum score have a 25.4% of the same. In contrast, individuals who are unemployed and hold a negative economic outlook are less likely to have "a lot" of support for the legalization of marijuana—29.6% among the unemployed and 32.3% among those with a poor economic outlook, compared to 38.6% among the employed and 39.3% among those with a positive economic outlook. Education, too, influences support. Individuals with less than high school education have a 44.1% likelihood of "a lot" of support for the legalization of marijuana, while those with a bachelor's degree have a 32%, and those with a professional or PhD degree have a 27.7% likelihood of the same. This may reflect lower marijuana usage rates among those with postgraduate education (McCarthy 2016).

While Millennials are more likely to support the legalization of marijuana, there are differences among subgroups on this issue as well. Figure 8.4 displays the descriptive statistics for support across Millennial subgroups. We see that liberal, followed by African American, Millennials have the highest level of support for the legalization of marijuana, while foreign-born Millennials maintain the lowest level support. Latino Millennials exhibit levels of support that are below the aggregate and are the lowest among race/ethnic groups, compared to their white and African American counterparts. These findings mirror differences in attitudes across these groups generally, without age cohort differentiation. They also underscore that this particular social issue has ethnic and racial undertones even for Millennials.

Right to Abortion

Regression results indicate that Millennials are not statistically distinct from older adults in their beliefs about abortion rights. This comports with studies that have found abortion is the outlier in the trend of greater

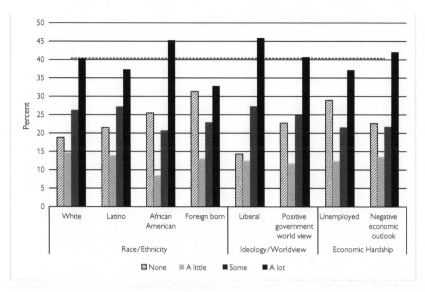

FIGURE 8.4.   Support for Legalization of Recreational Marijuana Use across Millennial Subgroups

Note: Average responses shown for each Millennial subgroup—White (n = 335), Latino (n = 158), African American (n = 106), foreign born (n = 61), liberal (n = 231), positive government worldview (n = 290), unemployed (n = 218), and negative economic outlook (n = 340). The dotted line represents the percentage of all Millennials who have "a lot" of support (40.4%). Positive government worldview for the purposes of this graph refers to individuals with a factor score that is in the top 50% (top two quartiles).

cultural liberalism, particularly evident among young people (Jelen and Wilcox 2003; Putnam and Campbell 2010). While young adults are permissive and tolerant on sexual issues (i.e., gay marriage, premarital sex), they are conservative on the issue of abortion. Instead of generation effects, we find pro-abortion beliefs are associated with being foreign born, having a liberal political ideology, and maintaining a positive government worldview. Income levels, gender, and marital status also positively influence opinions about abortion rights.

Predicted probabilities illustrate that the gap between liberals and moderates/conservatives on the issue is quite large. Liberals have a 63.3% likelihood of "a lot" of support for abortion rights, compared to a 32.6% likelihood of the same among moderates and conservatives. The latter group has a 23.8% likelihood of no support, while liberals have nearly no chance of no support—a slight 0.08% likelihood. Those with the

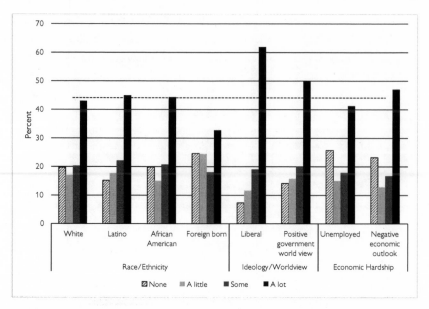

FIGURE 8.5.   Support for Women's Right to an Abortion across Millennial Subgroups

Note: Average responses shown for each Millennial subgroup—White (n = 335), Latino (n = 158), African American (n = 106), foreign born (n = 61), liberal (n = 231), positive government worldview (n = 290), unemployed (n = 218), and negative economic outlook (n = 340). The dotted line represents the percentage of all Millennials who have "a lot" of support (44.1%). Positive government worldview for the purposes of this graph refers to individuals with a factor score that is in the top 50% (top two quartiles).

maximum positive government worldview factor score have a 58.3% likelihood of "a lot" support for abortion rights, while those with the minimum score have a 30.6% of the same. The likelihood of no support drops to 9.8% among those with the maximum score and 25.5% among those with the minimum score. In contrast to liberals and those with a strong positive government worldview, being foreign born reduces the likelihood of support. The likelihood of having "a lot" of support for abortion rights is 27.3% among individuals who are foreign born, while those who were born in the United States have a 35.7% likelihood of the same. Foreign-born individuals have an even higher likelihood of no support for legal abortions—31.5% versus 23.8% among native-born individuals. These same trends are evident among Millennial subgroups.

Figure 8.5 displays the distribution of support for women's right to an abortion across Millennial subgroups. We see that, among Millennials, being liberal and having a positive government worldview are the characteristics that exhibit the most support for abortion rights. Millennials with these characteristics are more likely than Millennials on average to say they have "a lot" of support for the policy (average noted by the horizontal dotted line). While foreign-born young adults have noticeably lower than average support for abortion rights, levels of support do not considerably diverge among race/ethnic groups.

Returning to the regression results including Millennials and non-Millennial respondents, we find many of the control variables exerting a significant influence on abortion opinions. Individuals with higher incomes are more likely to support a woman's right to a legal abortion, as are females. Individuals that make less than $20,000 a year have a 32.1% likelihood of "a lot" of support for abortion rights, while individuals who make $50,000–$75,000 a year have a 46.7%, and those who make more than $100,000 a year have a 57% likelihood of the same. Females have a 49.8% likelihood of "a lot" of support for abortion rights in contrast to a 37.9% likelihood among males. Males, on the other hand, are more likely to have no support for abortion rights—a 19.9% likelihood compared to 13.5% among females. Married individuals are also less likely to support abortion rights—a 33.2% likelihood of a "a lot" of support versus a 36.8% likelihood of the same among their non-married counterparts and a 25.9% likelihood of no support versus a 22.9% likelihood among those not married.

The issue of abortion rights is heavily value laden, including specific religious values not captured by the variables included in our regression model. Past studies have established that Roman Catholics and evangelical Protestants are staunchly against abortion (Cox and Jones 2011; Masci 2016). We find evidence to support this in our survey data, particularly among "born again" (evangelical) Christians.[15] Slightly more non-Millennials (51.8%) identify as "born again" than Millennials (48.3%). As shown in Figure 8.6, among this Millennial subgroup, about one-third has "a lot" of support for abortion rights and one-third maintains no support—much weaker support than is evident in the aggregate adult population. Slightly fewer "born again" Millennials (13.3%) have no support for abortion rights than their older counterparts (16.8%).[16] This demonstrates that religious beliefs serve as cleavages in abortion attitudes that cut across generation identities.

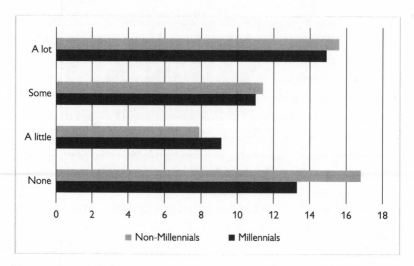

FIGURE 8.6.   Support for Right to Abortion among "Born Again" Christian Millennials & Non-Millennials

Note: Percentage of Millennials (n = 207) and non-Millennials (n = 222) supporting right to an abortion among self-identified "born again" Christians shown.

Millennials: Ideologically Positioned to Be Democrats, but Weakly Attached

While Millennials are known for their liberalness on social issues, the results of the analyses presented in this chapter demonstrate that this liberalness is distinct from that of older adults. It is innately tied to their race/ethnic diversity and concerns for social justice. On the issue of gun control and the legalization of marijuana, focus group participant statements and statistical analyses highlighted the influence of race/ethnicity on stances regarding these issues. Moreover, traditional liberal labels do not neatly fit Millennial stances on contemporary social issues. The majority of Millennials support gun control but lag in support compared to non-Millennials, and even liberal Millennials are behind in their support when compared to older liberals (72.7% versus 83.7%, respectively, say they have "a lot" of support). The same is true for abortion rights. While Millennials on average are similar to non-Millennials in their support for abortion rights, liberal Millennials lag behind older liberals (61.9% versus 69.6%, respectively, have "a lot" of support). On the other hand, Millennials outpace older adults in their support for the legalization of marijuana; even among liberals, younger adults favor the policy more than older adults (45.9% versus 41.3%, respectively, say they have "a lot" of support).

While this simply may be a matter of degree, it seems to point to a constellation of beliefs on social issues that are not fully captured by traditional liberal ideology and, perhaps, not fully addressed by the Democratic Party. This is lamentable for those who want to expand the party base because our survey results indicate that Millennials are positioned to be a strong constituency for the Democratic Party. Our data show that among Millennials, there are more individuals who self-identify as liberal than moderate and conservative (43.3%, 32.6%, and 24% respectively) *and* liberal Millennials significantly outnumber older adult liberals (43.3% versus 31.8% respectively). Conversely, though, we find that only slightly more Millennials than older adults identify with the Democratic Party (38.7% versus 38.1% respectively). The catch is Millennials do not feel strongly attached to political parties. When asked—*How strongly do you feel like you belong to a political party?*—the modal response among Millennials is "not at all" on a scale of where 0 indicates "not at all," a 50 means "neutral," and a 100 represents "extremely belong." Non-Millennials, on the other hand, are more evenly distributed in their responses across the political party attachment scale.[17]

Weak political party attachment is partly related to political engagement—an issue we turn to in the next chapter. It is also connected to the policy platform of the two main political parties in our country. Our analyses indicate that Millennial liberalness has gradations, and that there are specific social issues, like the legalization of marijuana as well as economic and political issues—ranging from jobs to student loan debt to immigration, all examined throughout this book—that have a large impact on Millennials. How well parties and politicians are able to tap into these nuances in order to court Millennials remains a very open question.

Conclusion: Millennials and Social Issues—Can They Find a Political Home?

Millennials are often touted as not only the most liberal generation in American history (Thompson 2016) but also the most progressive cohort, at least in the last fifty years (CIRCLE 2009). Our findings, with respect to social issues, indicate that these proclamations are perhaps a bit overstated.[18] In this chapter, we find that Millennials, in general, are much more liberal than non-Millennials on attitudes about the legalization of marijuana but are less likely to support gun control and trend closer to the attitudes of the rest of the population when it comes to abortion. Further, we show that even the most liberal Millennials lag behind in their support for gun control and abortion rights (liberal Millennials only outpace liberal non-Millennials in support for marijuana legalization). We also find that it is somewhat simplistic to discuss Millennial attitudes about these social issues in general terms, since this cohort is so diverse. Distinctions across Millennial subgroups exist on two of the three issues examined. On gun control, white Millennials are least supportive of restrictive policies, while African Americans and Latinos show greater support. Further, African American Millennials display the highest level of support for the legalization of marijuana, while Latino Millennials are least supportive of these policies.

The presidential campaign of Bernie Sanders resonated deeply with young adults during the 2016 election because he spoke directly to the Millennial Generation on many of the issues that matter to them. Further, his "gruffness, didacticism, and indifference to appearance...are central to his appeal" (Talbot 2015). This made him quite genuine to a generation desperately seeking authenticity in politics. On the other hand, the "authentic" label was hardly one people were willing to ascribe to Hillary Clinton. She also lost many Millennials with her diluted social and political agenda—including her stance on marijuana. Nevada state Senator Tick Segerblom, an outspoken legalization advocate and Sanders delegate at the Democratic convention, in a recent *Washington Times* article (Wolfgang 2016), sums up the root of the problem in this way:

> The big thing is millennials. They're sitting on their hands saying, "What difference does it make [who I vote for]?" If you have someone who can articulate an issue that they can see makes a difference in their lives, and shows the candidates are in tune with where the country is going, that helps with their turnout, their enthusiasm.

The question remains, however, if the Democratic Party can offer Millennials representation on the issues they care about. Clinton, as the

Democratic Party's presidential candidate, missed the mark in many regards. Our analyses show that Millennials have their own brand of social liberalness, one that has nuances with respect to the genesis of their attitudes, which should be carefully weighed and addressed if we are to fully engage this generation in mainstream political institutions.

CHAPTER 9

A Force in Waiting? Millennials and Political Engagement

To be honest I don't really feel that engaged in the process. I mean, everyone does have the freedom to vote, which I guess does give you some . . . What's the word? Like it gets you involved somewhat, being able to vote, but personally I feel that there's a lot more that I could do and other people my age could do. I think it's more, a lot of people just don't feel that motivated to take part in that whole process, other than voting, which even some people our age don't even feel like they do because it's not going to make much of a difference.

—Chris, Millennial focus group participant from Washington, DC.

Millennials have outpaced Baby Boomers to become the largest generation in the United States;[1] by the 2020 presidential election, they will be the largest generation in the US electorate (Fry 2016b). They are the most highly educated generation in US history (White House 2014), a factor that has been consistently linked to meaningful political participation (Brady, Verba, and Schlozman 1995; Mayer 2011). As "digital natives" growing up in the Information Age, never before has a generation had more and better tools at their disposal to make their voices heard in the political process. Further, as we have shown throughout this book, the Millennial Generation has a unique set of values, including the belief that government has a positive role to play in addressing crucial domestic and international problems that prompts them to look to government for solutions. They also share a deep sense of social justice, intertwined with being the most racially and ethnically diverse adult generation in

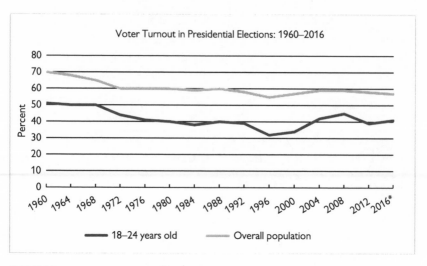

FIGURE 9.1.   Young People Vote at Lower Rates than the Rest of the Population

Note: Turnout rates for 2016 are estimates based on calculations from exit poll data. Data taken from US Census Bureau (various years) and the Center for Information and Research on Civic Learning and Engagement (2016).

American history, which leads them to be advocate for government policies to reduce inequalities (Roosevelt Institute 2013). All these factors set the stage for Millennials to make an indelible mark in politics. So far, however, this cohort's potential has not been met; rather, in many respects, Millennials behave similarly to young adults of generations before them. To illustrate this, Figure 9.1[2] displays voter turnout for 18–24 year olds, compared to the overall US population, for presidential elections over the past fifty years.

The figure clearly shows that young people (aged 18–24 years) consistently vote at lower rates than the rest of the US population (those 25 years and older). Millennials overall also follow this trend—voting at lower rates than older adults (Fry 2016c). While there was an uptick in voter turnout among this age cohort in the 2008 election, the numbers in the last two presidential elections have reflected declining rates of turnout. Thus, Millennials have been accused of treating electoral politics like Hollywood movies, only showing up for "the blockbusters" (Thompson 2016), and have been criticized for their political "slacktivism" (Gendron and Lienesch 2015). Many contend this generation is politically disenchanted and disengaged (Dalton 2016). Is this characterization fair?

The short, simple answer is "yes." Millennials, like young adults before them, turn out to vote at lower rates than older adults. Even Millennials recognize their own lack of engagement in this area, as evidenced by the quote at the start of this chapter. On the other hand, this characterization is missing nuances that are particular to this generation and critical for understanding the political future of our country. As we will discuss and explore in this chapter, Millennials may be less engaged than older adults by conventional measures, but they value representation and realize the importance of political outcomes. Moreover, some scholars posit that Millennials are no less engaged than past generations, but that this cohort displays different norms of citizenship and are more likely to follow what Dalton (2016) calls a model of "engaged citizenship." This model involves less traditional forms of political activities in favor of more direct and individual actions such as volunteering, boycotting, canvassing, and supporting referendums. In contrast, Dalton notes that older generations are more likely to follow a model of "duty-based citizenship," which stresses activities that maintain the existing political order such as voting, campaign contributions, and respect for and support of authority figures and existing institutional arrangements.

While we recognize that there are non-traditional forms of political participation important to democracy—and that Millennials have a propensity to be engaged in those at higher rates—here we mainly unpack Millennial disengagement with traditional institutions. We do this because we believe that by exploring the dynamics of traditional political (dis) engagement among young adults we can tap into what may improve their participation and, thus, the overall health of our democracy. Even scholars such as Dalton (2016), who tout the importance of alternative forms of engagement, also recognize that traditional form of participation should not be ignored. In fact, he argues that a healthy democracy needs a balance between "engaged citizenship" and "duty-based citizenship." Politics as we know it is not likely to significantly change in the near future. As evidenced by the 2016 presidential election, there is much that the American electorate, and by extension American society, is grappling with, and Millennials are embedded in the struggle.

The 2016 presidential election brought to the forefront two unconventional candidates in Donald Trump and Bernie Sanders, both who sought to take the country in a different direction. With a populist tone to both campaigns, Trump's "Make America Great Again" slogan—appealing to the strength of America's past—clashed with Sanders' "A Future We can Believe In" mantra—which saw greatness in what was ahead for America, rather than in what had been left behind. Because of their approaches and policy proposals (e.g., Trump: building of the wall along the southern border; Sanders: free college for all), both candidates, perhaps not surprisingly, drew interest from typically less engaged segments of the population. Millennials were overwhelmingly supportive of Sanders whose policies aligned with their liberal leanings (Blake 2016), specifically addressing the economic hardship they have experienced and the distrust in political institutions they maintain. Therefore, many young adults were disappointed with the choice of Clinton over Sanders as the Democratic Party presidential candidate, and the 2016 election, thus, became another facet of their disenchantment and cynicism with politics.

Our interest in this chapter is to explore Millennial political disengagement and disenchantment. Rather than treat it as an unwavering fact (and a fate), we unpack recent trends in political participation, comparing Millennials to non-Millennials, and explore what it might take for Millennials to be more engaged. We utilize our original 2015 survey for the majority of the analyses in the chapter and pivot to data from an original survey conducted a few weeks after the 2016 election to explore Millennial attitudes and beliefs specific to that event. We begin our exploration with a summary of factors that shape political engagement, paying particular attention to how the Millennial Generation fits into this narrative.

Factors that Influence Political Engagement

There are many reasons why individuals do not engage in politics. Some of these reasons involve personal choice, and others are based on external constraints. By far, the literature shows that the greatest external impediments to political participation and engagement have to do with socioeconomic status (SES) (Campbell et al. 1960; Lindquist 1964; Verba and Nie 1972; Wolfinger and Rosenstone 1980). Rosenstone and Hanson (2002) argue that those with higher SES (e.g., income, education, occupational status, and social networks) are more likely to engage with politics because they are able to underwrite the cost of engagement that facilitate participation; these individuals are more likely to "have the skills to master political subject matter and facilitate involvement in politics" (Tam Cho et al. 2006: 977). Further, those with a higher SES likely glean greater benefits from political engagement than those with lower SES (Campell, et al. 1960)—this is where resources meet efficacy to produce greater involvement. Research shows that SES also distinguishes "passive" from "active" participants in the democratic process. For example, Lindquist (1964) argues that while American democracy benefited from the expansion of voting rights to more groups, this is a "passive" form of participation; a more "active" type of participation, such as running for political office, is still greatly distinguished by SES status and continues today.

As the most educated cohort in history, Millennials, more so than previous generations, have overcome one of the major obstacles to engaging in politics. However, Millennials, unlike the immediate generations before them, experienced the Great Recession, an economic downturn that depressed their employment as they entered the job market and continues to affect their earnings (Carnevale et al. 2013; Glinski 2015). These experiences are represented in the figures reported in Table 9.1. We observe that Millennials, compared to the two previous generations when they were young, have higher levels of education but greater percentages of those unemployed and those not in the labor force altogether, as well as lower household income than Baby Boomers.

Beyond education and SES, scholars have noted that resources such as civic skills are important predictors of political activity (Verba, Scholzman, and Brady 1995). Verba, Scholzman and Brady (1995: 273) argue that while civic skills are acquired early in life, they "are honed in the non-political institutions of adult life—the workplace, voluntary associations, and churches." The ability to acquire civic skills depends largely on one's exposure to people and institutions that cultivate such skills, and not everyone has equal opportunities for this type of exposure. For example, churches play an important, but varying, role in the civic socialization of individuals, as different groups, such as racial and ethnic minorities, have benefited from this association more than others.

Minority populations, in particular African Americans and Latinos, have long struggled to be politically engaged at rates similar to those of whites (Verba, Scholzman, and Brady 1995). Though this gap is smaller or disappears altogether when we control for certain factors (Shingles 1981), this points to a number of reasons why participation disparities exist among minority groups. First and foremost, SES is lower for minorities, compared to whites. For example, wage gap disparities persist among African Americans and Latinos, compared to whites. Black men earned 73% of white men's hourly earnings in 2015 and Latino men earned 69% of white men's hourly earnings—a number that has actually decreased in the past thirty years (Salyer 2016). Further, as we discussed in Chapter 4 on education, African Americans and Latinos lag significantly behind in college graduation rates, with 47% of white students obtaining at least an Associate's degree in 2015, compared to 32% of blacks and 23% of Latinos (Ryan and Bauman 2016). We observe similar disparities in other measures such as living below the poverty line, earning a minimum wage, and high school drop-out rates (higher levels of each for African Americans and Latinos, compared to whites).

Beyond SES, minorities also often struggle to develop the civic skills that are important determinants of political activity. For African Americans, in particular, churches play a compensatory role for lack of SES and non-SES resources (Rosenstone and Hansen 2002). Protestant churches have (and

TABLE 9.1.   Comparison of SES across Generations When They Were Young

		Millennials in 2014	Gen Xers in 1998	Boomers in 1980
Household Income	Median, in 2013 dollars	$61,003	$63,365	$60,068
Male Education	Less than high school	15%	19%	19%
	High School diploma	31%	33%	40%
	Some college	34%	31%	24%
	Bachelor's degree or more	21%	18%	17%
Female Education	High School incomplete	10%	12%	13%
	High School diploma	24%	30%	46%
	Some college	37%	35%	22%
	Bachelor's degree or more	27%	20%	14%
Male Labor Force	Civilian employed	68%	78%	78%
	Unemployed	8%	6%	8%
	Not in labor force	22%	14%	12%
Female Labor Force	Civilian employed	63%	69%	60%
	Unemployed	6%	5%	5%
	Not in labor force	31%	26%	35%

Note: Millennials are those born in 1981–1996; Gen Xers are those born in 1965–1980; and Baby Boomers are those born in 1946–1964. Some figures do not add to 100% or slightly exceed 100% because of rounding. The percent of labor force in Armed Forces excluded because percentages were less than 1% for females. Source is Pew Research Center (2015e).

continue to have) an important role in fostering the civic skills needed for political engagement among the African American community (e.g., Kim and McKenry 1998). In contrast, Latinos, who are mostly Catholic, have derived less civic training from their church affiliations.[3] This is due to structural differences between Protestant and Catholic congregations as well as differences in the historical treatment of these groups that prompted church-led civic and political activity (i.e., the Civil Rights Movement). While African Americans have been better able to compensate for SES and non-SES deficiencies, Latinos, when compared to whites and African Americans, participate less because they, on average, have fewer resources and, thus, higher costs associated with political engagement. These trends in minority participation continue to be evident among Millennials. Polls reported that Latino Millennial voter turnout in the 2012 election lagged behind that of whites and African Americans—37.8% compared to 47.5% and 55%, respectively (Krogstad et al. 2016). This underscores that Latinos continue to lack the resources needed for participation, while African American young adults have effectively deployed resources for voting, pushing their participation to higher levels.

The Influence of the Millennial Generation Persona on Political Engagement

In addition to the traditional factors shaping political participation discussed above, we expect Millennial political engagement to be influenced by this cohort's persona or generational frame. The Millennial Generation persona is comprised of values and unique experiences shared by this age cohort. To a large degree, this persona is characterized by shared political ideology. Although Millennials are less likely than older adults to feel like they belong to a political party (Gilman and Stokes 2014), they are more likely to identify as liberal. Almost three in ten Millennials (29%) describe themselves as liberal, compared to just two in ten of Gen Xers (20%) and less than one-fifth of older adults (Pew Research Center 2010a). The majority of Millennials believe the government should be more involved in order to make college affordable, help the poor, create jobs, provide a basic standard of living, protect the environment, and address climate change (Reason-Rupe 2014). Millennials are more likely to address issues from a cosmopolitan or global perspective, and they seek to reinforce principles of social justice and tolerance (Zogby and Kuhl 2013; Dalton 2016). Related to their cosmopolitanism, Millennials espouse a collectivist worldview that sees government as a platform (Ben-Yehuda 2010) for solving problems and improving the lives of citizens, both in the United States and around the world (Molyneux and Teixeira 2010).[4] Although Millennials are less attached to political parties (and other institutions), this does not mean a detachment from a desire to improve the world or disengaging from government intervention. In fact, Millennials view government as "nothing less than the greatest tool at society's disposal to address the collective action problems of today" (Roosevelt Institute 2013: 8). They get lost, however, in the politics and political process of how to best utilize this tool. We unpack this engagement, or lack thereof, in the next section.

Trends in Millennial Political (Dis)Engagement

As we discussed above, the running narrative of Millennials paints a picture that young adults today are disenchanted and disengaged from politics. By some standards, this picture is no different than it was nearly 20 years ago when headlines read "A Politics for Generation X: Today's young adults may be the most politically disengaged in American history" (Halstead 1999). This particular article, featured in *The Atlantic*, pointed to falling wages and increased inequality, the unaddressed threat of global warming, and loss of social and political trust as reasons for apathy among young adults at that time. Many of these factors, as we have argued throughout this book, continue to frustrate young adults. However, despite these shared socioeconomic and political trends, we know that the politics of Millennials are different from Gen Xers. Census data shows that young adults in the past decade have voted at higher rates than those in the 1990s (File 2014),[5] and our own previous research has established that Millennials are more ideologically liberal than the generations before them at the same age (Ross and Rouse 2015). We also contend that there are characteristics of Millennial political engagement, connected to their shared persona that includes being digital natives and global citizens, that sets them apart from the generations before them and from older adults today. To establish this, we evaluate Millennial political engagement, in comparison to older adults,[6] in two ways—first, by assessing trends in Millennial attachment and involvement in traditional political institutions; and second, by exploring self-perceptions of political engagement. We rely on our original survey, conducted in 2015, to analyze these dynamics.[7]

Millennial (Dis)Engagement with Traditional Political Institutions

Political party affiliation and voting are hallmarks of democracy and democratic participation. If we are going to tap into levels of political engagement, it is first important to start with these benchmarks. To assess political party affiliation, we asked respondents to indicate on a scale, 0 to 100, how strongly "you feel like you belong to a political party." Higher numbers on the scale indicate "more strongly;" a 0 indicates "not at all," a 50 means "neutral," and a 100 represents "extremely belong."[8] The mean value for Millennials is 47.03, while the mean for non-Millennials was 54.40, indicating that Millennials are skewed toward less party attachment, while non-Millennials lean toward feeling more strongly affiliated with political parties.[9] A difference of means test indicates the difference between Millennials and non-Millennials on party attachment to be statistically significant.[10]

It is clear that Millennials are less attached to traditional political parties than older adults. Our focus group respondents shed light on why this is may be the case. Jeff, a Millennial focus group participant from Washington, DC, said, "I think that they're [traditional political parties] two, like they're both extreme, and I don't really want to affiliate with either extreme . . . there's no middle ground." Nia, also from DC, elaborated on this sentiment, stating:

> I don't think that I affiliate with either party . . . because my parents were Democrats I was just like, okay, I'm a Democrat. Now I feel like no one relates to me. I feel like, I don't want to say because they're older, but like some of their views are so old fashioned and they haven't taken into consideration how much times have changed with like technology and just how our generation tends to be more open-minded. I don't really relate to either one of them.

Carmen, like Nia—a Millennial Democrat from DC—said, "It's gotten to the point where I feel like I don't trust either party enough to put myself in their pocket." Carmen's concerns about trust were echoed by Chrishana from New Orleans. When asked if she felt like she belonged to the mainstream political parties, Chrishana said, "No, I feel they all lie. It doesn't matter, they all lie." Don, a Millennial from Los Angeles, California, expressed distrust about the interests political parties represent. He had this to say:

> I think that both parties represent their own interest, which is to continually get re-elected. They offer it and are informed by really savvy statisticians and business consultants, and their agenda obviously is a banner that is supposed to appeal to enough people to get them elected. I don't feel served by either party. I'm disenchanted with our politics in general. I voted for an independent in our last election.

Nicholas from New Orleans also feels disenchanted by special interests. He said, "It's [the political party system] like two faces of the same coin. And the coin's still made of money, and that's the interest." These findings underscore that Millennials feel detached from traditional political parties because they distrust them, they do not feel the parties are very different from one another, and they feel neither major party represents their interests.

Millennials are not only detached from traditional political parties but results of our survey indicate that they, in comparison to older adults, are also less likely to vote. We asked survey participants—"Are you registered to vote?" and "Have you voted in elections in the past four years?" Responses indicate that 80.1% of Millennials are registered to vote, compared to 86.5% of non-Millennials; 62.4% of Millennials reported voting in election during the past four years, while 81.3% of non-Millennials said the same. We also asked survey participants if they are likely to vote in the next (2016) presidential election. Among Millennials, 11.65% said "no," 14.98% said "maybe," and 73.38% said "yes;" among non-Millennials, 7.69% said "no," 9.17% said "maybe," and 83.14% said "yes." The differences between Millennials and non-Millennials on all three of these measures—voter registration, voter turnout, and vote intention—is

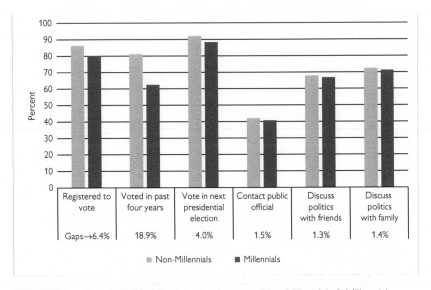

FIGURE 9.2.   Gaps in Political Participation between Non-Millennials & Millennials

Note: Bars represent percentage of non-Millennials and Millennials who say they: are registered to vote; voted in an election in the past four years; maybe or will vote in the next presidential election (2016); have contacted a public official via traditional and/or social media means; discuss politics with friends sometimes, often, or all the time; and discuss politics with family sometimes, often or all the time. The total number of observations are: register to vote—625 non-Millennials and 612 Millennials; voted in the past four years—620 non-Millennials and 602 Millennials; vote in next presidential election—611 non-Millennials and 601 Millennials; contact public official, discuss politics with friends, and discuss politics with family—630 non-Millennials and 621 Millennials.

statistically significant.[11] However, as shown in Figure 9.2, the gap between non-Millennial and Millennial voter registration and intentions for future voting is not as large as the gap in voter turnout (6.4%, 4%, and 18.9% respectively). Moreover, Millennials keep pace with older adults in other forms of conventional participation, including contacting public officials and discussing politics with friends and family. Therefore, it appears that Millennials are not completely apathetic when it comes to traditional politics.

Evidence of the importance of traditional political engagement among Millennials is further supported by responses to the survey question, "In your opinion, which brings about the most political change?" Possible responses included: "voting," "petitioning or protesting an issue," "contacting an elected official or politician through traditional means," "contacting an elected official or politician through email or social

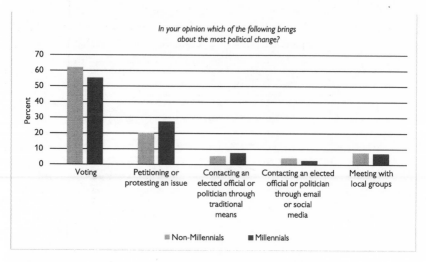

FIGURE 9.3. Perceptions of Forms of Political Participation in Bringing about Political Change

Note: Bars represent percentage of non-Millennials and Millennials in each category. Total number of observations for non-Millennials is 630 and for Millennials is 621.

media," and "meeting with local groups." Responses given by Millennials and non-Millennials are shown in Figure 9.3. We see that the majority of Millennials (55.4%) cite voting as bringing about the most political change, which clearly demonstrates that young adults consider this traditional form of participation the most valuable means of political expression and change. However, we also note a greater percentage of Millennials, in comparison to non-Millennials, cite protest and petition as bringing about the most political change (27.5% versus 20.2%, respectively)—and this difference is statistically significant.[12] Similar to Dalton's (2016) model of "engaged citizen," we find that Millennials, are more likely than older adults to value unconventional forms of political expression and change.

Taken together, the findings thus far have shown that Millennials are less attached to mainstream political parties and have lower rates of voter registration, voter turnout, and less intention to vote in future elections. While at first blush, this seems to confirm the accepted narrative that Millennials are disengaged, digging deeper, we find the gaps between Millennials and older adults in voter registration and intentions to vote (in the next presidential election) are not as large as the lag in voter turnout. Moreover, rates of participation among Millennials in contacting public officials and discussing politics with friends and family are nearly equal to that of older adults. This points to value in traditional politics, confirmed by the fact that Millennials cite voting as the form of participation that brings about most political change. Millennials are active in and ascribe some importance to traditional politics, but we also see that they value and desire alternatives to mainstream political institutions. This is sharply evident in their detachment from political parties and expressed need for better political party representation, as well as the importance they place on unconventional forms of political participation, namely protest and petition. These trends point to a young adult cohort that is interested in being political engaged but finding current politics and political opportunities as falling short of their expectations. To explore this further, we pivot to self-evaluations of political engagement as they are equally telling of Millennials' interactions with the political system.

Pathways to Millennial Political Participation: Exploring Self-Evaluations of Engagement

To assess perceptions of personal political engagement, we asked survey respondents—"Do you feel like you are engaged in the political system or politics?" Possible responses included "no," "somewhat," and "yes." As shown in Figure 9.4, we find slight differences between the Millennials and non-Millennials. In all, about one in four of Millennials and non-Millennials say they are not engaged in the system and one in three say they are engaged.[13] The majority of both groups—Millennials and non-Millennials—feel either not or only somewhat engaged. A difference of means test indicates there is not a statistically significant difference between Millennials and non-Millennials on this measure.[14] Confirming the trends discussed above, Millennials are not wildly disengaged from the traditional political system—or, rather, they are not more disengaged than older adults. *Are there differences among the two groups in the composition of this disengaged sub-sample?*

The disengaged sub-sample—those who say they do not feel or only somewhat feel engaged in the political system or politics—is large: 70.1% of

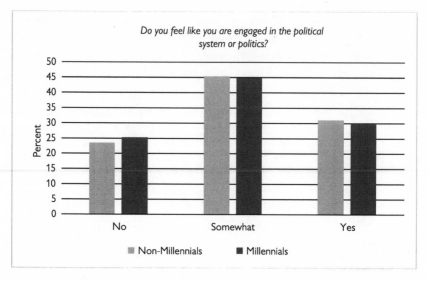

FIGURE 9.4.   Self-Evaluation of Political Engagement among Millennials & Non-Millennials

Note: Bars represent percentage of non-Millennials and Millennials in each category. Total number of observations for non-Millennials is 630 and for Millennials is 621.

Millennials and 68.9% of non-Millennials. To assess who these individuals are, we compare this group to the entire survey sample, across three sets of factors, all measured using questions from our 2015 survey: race/ethnicity, ideology/worldview, and economic hardship.[15] As discussed earlier in this chapter, race and ethnic minorities face disadvantages in the incentives, transaction costs, and rules surrounding political engagement. We hone in specifically on Latinos and African Americans as they comprise the majority of minority groups in our country. Political ideology (i.e., being liberal or conservative) and worldview on the role of government may also influence being or feeling engaged as some, for example those who see the government as having a positive role to play in solving social and economic problems (i.e., collectivist worldview), may have a greater proclivity for participation than others. We also assess economic hardship, specifically a negative economic outlook—saying the economy is worse today than it was twenty years ago—and being unemployed, as it may pose barriers to participation that are related to physical (e.g., transportation) and attitudinal (e.g., apathy) limitations.

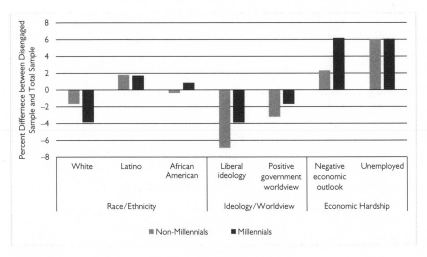

FIGURE 9.5. Composition of the Disengaged Sub-Sample

Note: Bars indicate if the subgroup is over (above the zero line) or under (below the zero line) represented in the disengaged sub-sample, as compared to the full sample of Millennials and non-Millennials.

Figure 9.5 illustrates the representation of each characteristic in the sub-sample of the disengaged for non-Millennials (light gray bars) and Millennials (dark gray bars). The estimates were calculated by subtracting the percent of the total survey sample from the percent of the disengaged sub-sample.[16] Bars above the zero line designate that there are more individuals sharing this characteristic (over-representation) in the disengaged sub-sample than in the entire group, whereas bars below the zero line denote that there are less individuals (under-representation) with that factor in common. The findings of this descriptive analysis indicate that there are more Latinos and economically hard pressed (i.e., negative economic outlook, unemployed) individuals in both the Millennial and non-Millennial disengaged sub-sample, although those with a negative economic outlook are more highly over-represented among Millennials. This is likely related to the economic hardships this generation has felt as a result of the Great Recession, including long-term effects on earnings, employment, and job satisfaction.[17] In contrast to this, whites, liberals, and those with a positive government worldview are under-represented in the disengaged sub-sample. Older adult liberals are particularly engaged, as are white Millennials. The one point of divergence between Millennials and non-Millennials is the engagement of African Americans in both groups. Older African Americans are slightly more engaged, while younger African Americans, like Latinos, are less engaged. This points to a real need to reach out to Millennial minorities, as well as those who feel economically hard pressed. *What would it take to get these groups as well as others in the disengaged sub-sample more involved in politics?*

To explore political disengagement in more depth, we asked a follow-up question in the survey of the disengaged sub-sample (those respondents that indicated they are not engaged or only somewhat engaged in politics)—"What would it take to make you more engaged in the political system or politics?" Responses were opened-ended, allowing for rich data collection. Using a grounded theory approach (Strauss and Corbin 1998), we identified emergent themes among Millennials and non-Millennials, then refined and integrated these among and between subgroups.[18] Ten themes emerged from the data—to be more engaged, both young and older adult respondents indicated they need the following: 1) address transaction costs of political participation; 2) better political representation, representatives, and outcomes; 3) different or improved political institutions or systems; 4) feel like I make a difference in the political system; 5) greater relevance of politics to me; 6) improved information and understanding of political system and politics; 7) improved interest in politics and political system; 8) more trust, honesty, and accountability of politicians, less politics; 9) nothing, not interested, or not applicable; and 10) not sure or don't know.[19] Table 9.2 presents the percentage of responses in each category for Millennials and non-Millennials, separately. Note that the themes are ranked in order of frequency of response.

Among Millennials, the most common response to what it would take to be more politically engaged include "not sure or don't know" and "nothing, not interested, or not applicable." Thirty percent of young adults feel this way, underscoring their disenchantment and detachment from traditional political institutions, but Millennials are not alone in this sentiment. An even higher percentage of older adults feel the same— 18.9% of non-Millennials also gave a response that falls into the category of "nothing, not interested, not applicable," and nearly the same percentage of older adults, in comparison to Millennials, (14%) said they are "not sure or don't know" what it would take for them to be more engaged.

Millennials and non-Millennials also share a focus on better political representation and increased honesty and accountability of politicians as drivers for improved engagement. Among Millennials, 14.5% cited better representation and 12.2% more honesty; a greater percentage of non-Millennials said the same—19.4% and 16.4%, respectively. For older adults, these issues emerged as very important; better representation ranked as the number one issue and honesty the third most important. Observations that fell into the category of "better political representation, representatives,

TABLE 9.2. Methods to Improve Political Engagement

What would it take to make you more engaged in the political system or politics?

		Percent Responses (N)	
Millennials			
1	not sure or don't know	15.0%	(60)
2	nothing, not interested, or not applicable	15.0%	(60)
3	better political representation, representatives, and outcomes	14.5%	(58)
4	more trust, honesty, and accountability of politicians, less politics	12.2%	(49)
5	greater relevance of politics to me	10.0%	(40)
6	improved information and understanding of politics/political system	9.7%	(39)
7	address transaction costs of political participation	7.0%	(28)
8	improved interest in politics and political system	7.0%	(28)
9	feel like I make a difference in the political system	5.2%	(21)
10	different or improved political institutions or systems	4.5%	(18)
		N	428
Non-Millennials			
1	better political representation, representatives, and outcomes	19.4%	(83)
2	nothing, not interested, or not applicable	18.9%	(81)
3	more trust, honesty, and accountability of politicians, less politics	16.4%	(70)
4	not sure or don't know	14.0%	(60)
5	address transaction costs of political participation	6.8%	(29)
6	greater relevance of politics to me	6.3%	(27)
7	improved information and understanding of politics/political system	6.1%	(26)
8	improved interest in politics and political system	5.1%	(22)
9	different or improved political institutions or systems	4.4%	(19)
10	feel like I make a difference in the political system	2.6%	(11)
		N	434

Note: Percent of responses shown with total number of observations in parentheses. Rank of theme noted next to theme label. See Appendix 9.B for more details on coding and number of observations.

and outcomes" included responses ranging from "better candidates with better solutions to make the country thrive" to "for politicians to actually start representing the majority of people in their constituency, instead of the vocal, often extreme, few" to "more results from the politician's we vote into our government." Examples of responses that were categorized as "more trust, honesty, and accountability of politicians, less politics" include: "more honesty and integrity among our leaders," "politicians working together," "if everyone would at least focus on something together instead of being so divided," and "a more direct way to contact politicians where one can know their response is seen/heard."

Intertwined with the issues of representation and honesty is relevance. Many Millennials and non-Millennials feel like politics is out of touch. The theme of "greater relevance of politics to me" registered with 10% of the responses given by Millennials. Slightly fewer—6.3%—non-Millennials gave responses that fell into this category. Young and older adults expressed sentiments along these lines: "a politician that I could really relate to and follow" or "something that affects me personally." Millennials, in particular, were sensitive to relevance among their age cohort, stating for example: "if they would try to relate to my generation," "relevance to age group discussions," "if my age demographic was reached out to more in a sincere way," and "problems more related to my generation." This underscores the central argument of this book—the Millennial Generation persona distinctly shapes the politics of this age cohort. As a generation who is distinctly more diverse, tolerant, ideologically liberal, and cosmopolitan, specific problems raised by Millennials included: student loans, drug legalization, the economy, gay marriage, healthcare, violence, gun control, security, and veteran assistance. As other scholars have emphasized, it is important that politicians court Millennials and that they show interest in issues that matter most to this generation (Gilman and Stokes 2014; Dalton 2016) in order to increase their political engagement.

Millennials also stood out as distinct from older adults in the manner in which they discussed information and knowledge as important to their political engagement. Nearly 10% of Millennial responses touched upon the theme of "improved information and understanding of politics and the political system," while only 6.1% of non-Millennials gave similar responses. This included, among both groups, general mentions of "understanding the issues better" as well as a few comments related to media bias, such as "being able to read non-bias[ed] news articles or watch on TV."[20] Millennials, unlike older adults, made specific reference to the accessibility of information; there were five comments along these lines, citing, for example, "make it [politics] less complicated" and "ease of ways to get information on local elections" as ways to improve engagement.[21] This indicates that Millennials' information needs are not being met in ways that enable and motivate them to be politically engaged. Being "digital natives," it is likely that Millennials have distinct expectations of information sources in comparison to older adults. While our survey does not provide the data needed to probe this further, there is evidence that information, as related to political engagement, entails differing dynamics for Millennials and non-Millennials.

Additional analyses of our survey data reveals a distinction between Millennials who are engaged, on one hand, and not/somewhat engaged, on the other hand, in their primary source of political information. As shown in Table 9.3, among Millennials, network and cable TV news programs as the primary source of political news is significantly correlated with feeling engaged.[22] In contrast, there is a significant correlation between social networks for political news—social media and discussions with friends and family as the primary source of information—and feeling only somewhat or not engaged. The same correlations are not evident for older adults, although among non-Millennials radio as a primary source of political information is correlated with those who feel engaged.

In all, we find that Millennials are slightly less engaged in traditional institutions than older adults. They report lower attachment to political parties as well as lower voter registration and turnout—all of which are statistically significant differences. However, we also find that Millennials do not feel any more or less engaged in politics than non-Millennials. And about one in three of both groups simply do not know or are not interested in what it would take to get them more engaged. Millennials, however, do indicate that improving representation, honesty, and relevance could make them feel more engaged. Moreover, Millennials expressed a need for more political information and knowledge—and in accessible forms. Analysis indicates that improving TV news, specifically, could boost Millennial political engagement, particularly if it touched upon issues salient to their

TABLE 9.3.   Political Information Sources among Millennials and Non-Millennials & Correlations with Feeling Politically Engaged

Source of political information and news	Millennials		Non-Millennials	
	Percent citing as primary source of info and news	Correlation with feel engaged in politics	Percent citing as primary source of info and news	Correlation with feel engaged in politics
Network and cable TV news programs	45.57%	0.093*	61.75%	−0.028
Newspapers—print or online	16.26%	0.064	17.62%	0.004
Social media (i.e., Twitter and Facebook)	27.86%	−0.101*	10.48%	−0.017
Discussions with friends and family	8.37%	−0.096*	5.71%	−0.033
Radio news programs	1.93%	0.010	4.44%	0.121*
	N = 621		N = 630	

Note: Percentages reported are those among the group that say the source is where they get "most" of their political information and news. The correlation coefficients reported are estimated from pairwise correlations with a variable constructed from the question "Do you feel like you are engaged in the political system or politics?" The variable is coded 1 for responses of "yes" and 0 for responses of "somewhat" and "no." Statistical significance denoted as * $p<0.05$.

generation. Millennials have shown that when they feel a connection with a candidate and the issues a candidate is supporting, they will engage. We saw this with the 2008 election and the overwhelming Millennial support for President Barack Obama. This was also evident in the 2016 presidential election. We explore this case study next.

The Presidential Election of 2016: A Case Study in Millennial Political Engagement

The presidential election of 2016 offered a chance for a political revolt, and perhaps for some, a chance for revolution. Despite being an unlikely pairing—a 74-year-old, Jewish man and young, "hipster" voters—the Democratic primary candidate, Bernie Sanders' message resonated deeply with Millennials. Sanders touted a reinvention of the American Dream, one that would address issues that Millennials care about, including student loan debt, income inequality, free college education, and kicking "big money" out of politics. Many viewed Sanders' popularity with young voters as "reminiscent of the Obama campaign, fueled in large part by the young people its 'change' message managed to engage" (Burns 2016). Donald Trump emerged as the change candidate on the right. Some of his stances, like Sanders's, offered young voters alternatives to the status quo and tapped into their economic concerns. This included the anthems of "America First" and "drain the swamp," in which he promised to bring jobs back to Americans and clean up Washington, DC. Despite these appeals, Millennials overwhelmingly supported Sanders late into the primary election season. A Gallup Poll from April 2016 showed that 55% of Millennials still favored Sanders over the presumptive and eventual Democratic Party nominee, Hillary Clinton (38%), or the front-running Republican counterpart, Donald Trump (22%) (Norman 2016). When Clinton was named the Democratic Party candidate in July, the dynamics of the election shifted for Millennials. We explore this, using an original survey conducted a few weeks after the 2016 election. Specifically, we examine Millennial voter turnout and vote choice, as well as perceptions of change and feeling the system is rigged. We find that the 2016 election serves as a case study to understand why young adults are disenchanted and disengaged with the political system.

Voter Turnout and Vote Choice

Millennials did not buck the general trend of low participation in the 2016 presidential election. While there were many distinct features of their engagement in this election, their turnout remained predictably lower, compared to the rest of the voting eligible population. Responses of self-reported turnout[23] in our survey indicate that 67.5% of Millennials voted, considerably less than the 81.1% of older adults' voter turnout. This difference is statistically significant.[24] An additional 16.2% of Millennials and 10.6% of non-Millennials said they "thought about voting this time, but didn't." The question remains, then, what kept them from the polls? Reasons for not voting among Millennials and non-Millennials are shown in Figure 9.6. The plurality of both non-Millennials' (40%) and Millennials' (33%) top choice for not voting is "I could not support any of the candidates." Undoubtedly, for many Millennials, this harkened to their loss of Sanders as a candidate. Slightly more Millennials (17% and 15%) than non-Millennials (11% and 14%) felt their vote would not matter to

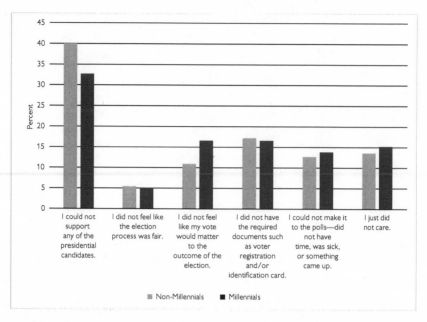

FIGURE 9.6.   Reasons for Not Voting in the 2016 Presidential Election

Note: Bars represent the percentage of non-Millennials and Millennials giving reasons for not voting. The total number of observations for non-Millennials is 110 and 217 for Millennials.

the outcome of election and did not care about voting. However, there are no statistically significant differences between non-Millennials and Millennials on these measures.[25] These results reinforce that Millennials and older adults had similar reasons for why they did not cast a ballot in the 2016 election. Even though there was a higher percentage of Millennials who did not turn out, there is no appreciable difference in the reasons for disengagement. This highlights, yet again, the similarities in what it would take for Millennials and non-Millennials to be more engaged, discussed in the previous section. Both groups shared a desire for better representation and representatives, greater honesty and accountability, and a general feeling of disinterest or not knowing what it would take to be more engaged.

Among those who did turn out to vote, our survey indicates more Millennials voted for Hillary Clinton than Donald Trump. Figure 9.7 displays vote choice among Millennials and non-Millennials. Almost six in ten Millennials (58%) voted for Hillary Clinton, compared to under

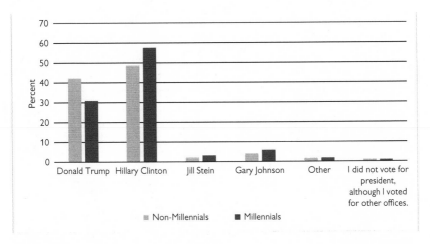

FIGURE 9.7. Presidential Candidate Vote Choice among Non-Millennials & Millennials

Note: Bars represent the percentage of non-Millennials and Millennials vote choice. The total number of observations for non-Millennials is 473 and 450 for Millennials.

half of non-Millennials (49%). Conversely, 42% of non-Millennials voted for Trump compared to 31% of Millennials. More Millennials (11% combined) than non-Millennials (8% combined) voted for a third-party candidate. The difference in Trump and Clinton votes between Millennials and non-Millennials is statistically significant;[26] however, there is no statistically significant difference between Millennials and non-Millennials on third-party voting.[27]

Responses to the survey question that asked participants reasons for their choice of presidential candidate further underscore that representation is important to the American voting public. The survey asked—"Rate the following reasons behind your choice for president. I chose my candidate for president because . . . I am loyal to my political party; I agree with my candidate's proposed policies; I strongly opposed the other candidate(s); I trust my candidate; my candidate cares about people like me; the next president will choose a justice for the Supreme Court; and while I usually don't vote, a vote for my candidate was particularly important this election." Ratings included: "not at all important," "slightly important," "moderately important," "very important," an "extremely important." Responses are shown in Figure 9.8. The largest percent of Millennials (24%) and non-Millennials (27%) say the most important reason for their vote is that

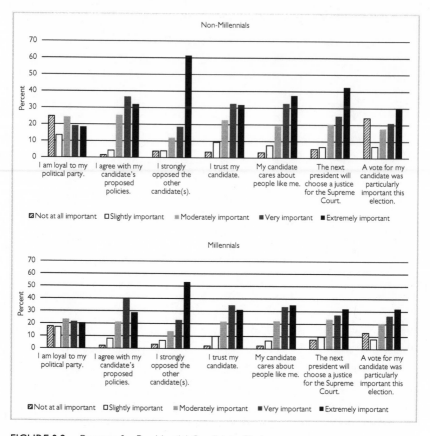

FIGURE 9.8.   Reasons for Presidential Candidate Choice

Note: Bars represent the percentage of responses in each category. The top graph corresponds to non-Millennial responses, and the bottom graph represents Millennial responses. The total number of observations for non-Millennials is 468 and 446 for Millennials.

they genuinely agreed with their preferred candidate's policy proposal. This was followed by voting against the other candidate—Millennials (23%) and non-Millennials (26%). A majority of both non-Millennial (six in ten) and Millennials (more than five in ten) said opposing other candidates is extremely important reason for their vote. While there is not a statistically significant difference between non-Millennials and Millennials in agreeing with the candidate's policies,[28] the difference almost reaches statistical significance for vote against another candidate (p<0.069).[29]

Further analysis indicates that Trump voters, in particular, were motivated by voting against the opposition candidate. In fact, 62.24% of

Trump voters said strongly opposing the other candidates was "extremely important," while only 56.24% of Clinton voters said the same. There is a statistically distinct difference in opposition voting among non-Millennials who voted for Donald Trump, compared to all other voters.[30] The same is not true for Millennial Trump voters or for non-Millennial or Millennial Clinton voters, although for Millennial Clinton voters the difference approaches statistical significance (p<0.0831).[31] This underscores that opposition voting was a strong motivating force for both Millennials and non-Millennials but particularly for older Trump supporters.

Change and Feeling the System Is Rigged

The 2016 presidential election was largely characterized by the idea of change—punctuated by Donald Trump's campaign of "Make American Great Again," a call to take the country back to a different, and for some, a better time, and Bernie Sanders's campaign that promoted change by looking forward to America's future. Thus, much of the politics of the 2016 election season were framed as a need for something different because the current way of doing things was not working.[32] To examine how this narrative may have resonated with Millennials, in comparison to older adults, we assess expressed desire for political and economic change as well as feelings that the current system is rigged.

Two questions captured political and economic change in the survey— "How much do you want significant change to American political system?" and "How much do you want significant change to American economic system?" Possible responses included: "not at all," "somewhat," and "very much." A majority of both Millennials (52%) and non-Millennials (50%) "very much" want change to the political system. Likewise, a majority of both Millennials (57%) and non-Millennials (55%) say they "very much" want economic change. While there are slightly more Millennials who express a desire for change, the differences between Millennials and non-Millennials on these measures are not statistically significant.[33]

When it comes to belief that the system is rigged, Millennials do stand out as distinct from older adults. Fifty-seven percent of Millennials agreed with the statement—"Our system is rigged against people like me."[34] Fewer older adults—50.8%—said the same, and this difference is statistically significant.[35] Let us look more closely at the composition of the sub-sample of Millennials that feel like the system is rigged against them. Similar to the analysis presented in the previous section, we examine three sets of factors: race/ethnicity, ideology/worldview, and economic hardship.[36] We break race and ethnicity into white, Latino, and African American categories. Liberal ideology is included, as is cosmopolitan identity or the feeling of being a "citizen of the world." We examine cosmopolitan identity in place of collectivist worldview because our 2016 survey did not directly ask questions related to this concept. Economic hardship is measured as negative economic outlook—perception that the economic today is worse off than twenty years ago—and unemployment status—not working part or full time.

The results, shown in Table 9.4, indicate that the majority (over 50%) of Millennials across all characteristics believe the system is rigged. This belief is most prevalent among African American Millennials—80.7% believe the system is rigged against them. Pairwise correlations confirm that there is a race/ethnic dynamic at play among young adults with the significant negative correlation of white, on one hand, and the significant positive correlation of African American, on the other hand, with the belief that the system is rigged.[37] We observed similar trends with attitudes about feeling disengaged from politics (discussed in the previous section), underscoring that minority Millennials perceive they are largely being left out of the political system. This is likely indicative of a latent component

TABLE 9.4.   Millennials that Believe the System Is Rigged against Them

		Percent of Millennials that believe the system is rigged.	Correlation with: "Our system is rigged against people like me."
Race/Ethnicity	White	52.0%	−0.117*
	Latino	56.8%	−0.001
	African American	80.7%	0.181*
Ideology/Worldview	Liberal ideology	61.3%	0.067
	Cosmopolitan identity	55.5%	0.020
Economic Hardship	Negative economic outlook	54.5%	−0.033
	Unemployed	55.7%	−0.016

Note: Sample is restricted to Millennials only (n = 667). Percentages reported are those among the group that agree the system is rigged against them. The percentage reported for cosmopolitan identity is the percent of those who are very strongly (self-placement of 10 on a 0 to 10 scale) with being a citizen of the world. Pairwise correlation coefficients are reported with statistical significance denoted as * p<0.05.

of disengagement among minority Millennials that is not only related to lower levels of SES or a lack of civic skills among this group, but also tied to a dearth of political efficacy and salience for young African American adults.

Conclusion: Millennials—Dormant Power or Growing Influence?

The Millennial Generation, simply by their sheer numbers (now the largest cohort and soon to be the largest voting cohort), have a lot of potential for exerting influence across the American political system (Howe and Strauss 2000; Zogby and Kuhl 2013; Gilman and Stokes 2014). It is still unclear, however, if and how their political power will materialize and how we measure its success. Based on our analyses in this chapter, Millennials are less attached to political parties and are less likely to vote or have the intent to vote than older adults. A simple conclusion to draw from these findings would be to say that given their cynicism about or apathy for traditional political institutions, this cohort is unlikely to join numerical strength with influence any time soon.

Some scholars and political pundits express concern that today's young adults are lacking in civic education, and by extension, civic skills and/ or attachment necessary to exert such influence. For example, Galston (2004) cites both a decrease in common measures of engagement (e.g., voting) or what Dalton (2016) terms "duty-based citizenship," as well as a decline in less-discussed trends such as keeping up with politics, discussing politics, and acquiring political knowledge from traditional news sources as leading to less politically engaged youth. The consequences, Galston (2004: 263) says, are that ". . . their disengagement increases the already powerful political tilt toward the concerns of the elderly." Our analyses in this chapter confirm some of the trends in low political engagement among Millennials. However, we also find that although Millennials vote at lower rates, a majority of this cohort see it as an important vehicle for bringing about political change. Thus, we also explored what it would take from the political system and actors to engage Millennials more fully. We found that Millennials want better representation and political outcomes. They want politics to be less political and for elected officials to be less politician and more representative. They would like to see more accountability and honesty in politics, and they want politicians to speak to the issues of their generation. Bernie Sanders was supported by a large number of Millennials because he addressed issues that resonated with young adults in a transparent and straightforward way. When the election shifted to Clinton versus Trump, enthusiasm among Millennials waned and they were less interested in turning out to vote. This, however, does not necessarily mean that we should conclude that Millennials are not interested or engaged in politics and that they cannot or will not exert their political influence in the future.

There is much agreement about how Millennials have discovered alternate ways to be involved. While we do not measure this directly in our survey, we see signs of these alternatives in our qualitative data and as an extension of their persona, specifically their cosmopolitan identity and in affirmation of their principals of social justice and tolerance. Many young adults have espoused what Dalton (2016) terms "engaged citizenship" and found more easily accessible ways to participate—through activities such as volunteering, consumer activism, and via the civic use of social media (e.g., promote political material and encourage others to get involved) (Center for Information & Research on Civic Learning and Engagement 2011; Gilman and Stokes 2014; Dalton 2016). However, the concern about Millennials embracing alternative forms of participation is whether these activities are as effective as traditional forms of engagement at influencing policy and holding those in power accountable, both of which are, according to our analyses, important to Millennial political engagement. Galston (2004: 263) says of this concern that young people may understand "why it matters to feed a hungry person at a soup kitchen," but they may not understand "why it matters where government sets eligibility levels for food stamps . . ." This could be an important distinction if a focus on individual activities does not translate into collective action that improves or addresses broad-based social policies. This concern circles back to why there is a value to traditional political institutions and why the lack of Millennial attachment to political parties should be disconcerting.

We must recognize that, as Gilman and Stokes point out, Millennials "as a generation raised in a period of instant information and unlimited options do not feel they have to be fixed in the economic marketplace or in politics" (Gilman and Stokes 2014: 58). Their detachment of political parties and independent tendencies evidence that they do not care whether a solution comes from Democrats or Republicans, or even that it has to be government led. They believe that the government has a positive role to play in solving socioeconomic problems, but their political attachments are more fluid. Further, unlike recent generations before them, Millennials have experienced significant economic hardship as a result of the Great Recession. While they are more educated than any previous generation, they also exhibit higher unemployment and labor force participation rates, as well as lower overall income. In particular, our results highlighted how these factors may have a disproportionate impact on the political engagement of Millennial minorities.

Perhaps, though, we should stop lamenting the lack of overall political engagement of Millennials within the traditional framework and instead focus on the development of pathways to engage them more fully. As our analyses indicate, this is especially critical for specific groups of young adults, including race/ethnic minorities and those that are economically hard pressed. These pathways should incorporate the issues that are salient to these groups (and to young adults in general) and address improved representation and accountability. Moreover, legitimate political space should be carved out for non-traditional political activities of young adults, and voices coming from these spaces should be heard by older adults and those in power. Far from being the death of democracy, a shift in what it means to be a good citizen is acceptable, perhaps even desirable. A balance of citizenship norms, Dalton points out, between duty-based and engaged citizenship creates a healthy democracy. When, and perhaps if, we are able to create pathways of engagement for young voters and come to terms with a balance in the two-model framework of citizenship, then we will see Millennials emerge as the expected force in our political system—sooner rather than later.

CHAPTER 10

Millennials—"Waiting on the World to Change" or Grasping Their Political Power?

In the mid-2000s, prominent singer and songwriter John Mayer wrote and sang about American youth being dissatisfied and disenchanted with the state of the world, but feeling fairly helpless in their ability to bring about change, and having little faith in the current system to make a difference. The words in the song, *Waiting on the World to Change*, reflect many of the sentiments we have observed among Millennials. However, as the findings of the analyses in this book point out, political dissatisfaction does not afflict Millennials with poor attitudes about important issues or a lack of overall interest in political engagement, despite this insinuation by some observers.[1] Instead, we find that Millennials, in their own way—exhibited through the traits of their particular persona—are deeply concerned about political, economic, and social challenges.

As we argue from the onset of this book, Millennials possess a unique persona, identity, or frame that defines this generation, distinguishes them from other age cohorts, and helps explain their political attitudes, policy preferences, and levels of engagement. This generational identity is rooted in cultural or value shifts that are a product of social, economic, and/or political events, which also include prospects about the future and shared experiences at the same point in life. Central to this persona is diversity. It is impossible to assess the politics of Millennials without first acknowledging the demographic shift that has occurred in the United States over the past thirty years. A discussion of Millennial political attitudes and policy preferences without considering diversity is like talking about democracy without understanding how people vote. Diversity penetrates general Millennial attitudes in terms of their tolerance, cosmopolitanism, and collectivist worldview, and it also differentiates attitudes across Millennial subgroups. Beyond diversity, it is also difficult to ignore that Millennials are the most educated generation in history, coupled with being the first digital natives. These factors extend their ability and knowledge. Furthermore, Millennials have come of age blanketed by technology, with information at their fingertips, and a level of connectedness not imagined several decades ago. Their knowledge, developed and honed in this digital revolution, dictates the way Millennials think about politics and how they engage in the political process. Also crucial to the Millennial identity are the events of September 11, 2001, when many belonging to this cohort were at a formative age in their development. The events of that day had long-term consequences and have helped frame for Millennials how they think about the United States and the rest of the world. These are but a few examples of the factors that comprise the Millennial identity, which are unique influences on this generation and have contributed to how they approach politics. We cover these factors in detail in Chapter 1, but here it is important to reemphasize the significance of the Millennial persona to our narrative about the distinct political perspectives of this generation.

Key Findings: Understanding Millennial Politics through the Millennial Generation Persona

Leveraging the Millennial persona and its explanatory power, we embarked on the journey of examining the attitudes of Millennials on important and specific issues, as well as their levels of engagement with the political process. The opinions of Millennials, however, are not examined in a vacuum; rather, we compare and contrast the preferences of this cohort against those of non-Millennials and we explore variations across Millennial subgroups. No other book to date has taken this approach—offering an in-depth examination of the political attitudes and policy preferences of the Millennial Generation and further dissecting these attitudes to account for variations across different segments of this cohort. We recognize, in particular, the paucity of research in accounting for the effects of race and ethnicity on generational political attitudes.

It is no coincidence that we started our substantive exploration of issue attitudes by examining how Millennials think about the economy (Chapter 3). As the "Children of the Great Recession," Millennials have experienced economic hardship unlike any other generation since those of the Great Depression. These burdens have impacted the attitudes of Millennials beyond just the economy. In other words, economic factors pervade opinions about other issues as well (e.g., educational reform). Analyzing opinions about the economy, we find that although Millennials have been disproportionately impacted by the recession, they are generally economically cautious (compared to non-Millennials). They prefer middle-of-the-road policies, especially when it comes to issues such as healthcare, Social Security, and overall government spending. However, as we have consistently emphasized, Millennials are not created equal. We observe differences in economic preferences among Millennials when we take race and ethnicity into account. Minority Millennials' economic attitudes look more like those of older adults of their similar race/ethnic group rather than like those of white Millennials. In other words, minority Millennials are more likely to favor greater government spending, increasing the minimum wage, and bringing incremental changes to Social Security.

We next explored the attitudes of Millennials concerning the issue of education (Chapter 4). We approached the narrative of this chapter with the backdrop of Millennials being the most educated generation in American history and the challenges that come along with educating a very diverse student body. Once again, as we saw with the economy (and certainly related), the Millennial Generation experienced inordinate levels of educational hardships in the form of devalued degrees and unprecedented amounts of student loan debt. The main takeaway with respect to Millennial attitudes about education is that it is one of the most important priorities for this cohort. This, of course, is not a surprise, given the impact education has had on the lives of Millennials (both good and bad). However, what may be somewhat surprising is how consistent their support is for government-led student loan debt forgiveness, even in the face of other factors that usually mitigate support for government spending. The preference for government action on student loan debt is even greater among African American and Latino Millennials—those who are more significantly impacted by current education policies.

Following our analysis of Millennials and education, we turn to this cohort's attitudes about foreign policy (Chapter 5). In this chapter, we emphasize the significant role that the events of September 11, 2001 have played in the formation of their worldviews. The effects of that day are certainly not limited to attitudes about foreign policy, but they do have a pronounced influence in how Millennials view their own security, their perspective about the world, and the United States' relationship with other countries. Add to this the fact that Millennials have grown up in an area of globalization and technological revolution which brings them in close and instant contact with the rest of the world. The impact of these and other factors lead to our general findings which show that, while Millennials have similar foreign policy priorities (e.g., ISIS, trade deficit, China, North Korea) as non-Millennials, their intensity for the importance of these issues is not as strong. The order and intensity of these priorities also vary across Millennials subgroups and other factors such as gender and cosmopolitan identity. Furthermore, Millennials are more likely than non-Millennials to prefer diplomatic solutions for solving international problems. These findings further emphasize the idea that Millennials have a more global than nationalistic approach to foreign policy (especially given their diversity), and in general, prefer cooperation with the rest of the world rather than conflict.

From issues related to foreign policy, we then transition to an evaluation of Millennial attitudes about immigration (Chapter 6). Here the diversity of the Millennial Generation is inexorably intertwined with their opinions about immigration policies, and as we say, this diversity is redefining what it means to live in a "melted pot" and soon, a majority–minority country. We find that Millennials are more supportive of policies that expand immigration rights—allowing undocumented childhood arrivals to stay in the country and supporting in-state tuition for undocumented immigrants—while non-Millennials are more likely to support tougher immigration enforcement policies, including E-Verify (requiring all companies to verify the legal status of workers before employing them) and border security. Support for policies that expand immigration rights is even higher among Millennial minorities, especially among Latino Millennials (as we would expect). Despite an overarching focus in our country on tougher immigration policies such as building a wall along the southern US border, immigration raids that may include targeting undocumented immigrants

without a criminal record, and banning immigrants from certain countries, the largest generation is largely not in favor of such policies. This is
something that politicians will have to reconcile now and in the future.

In Chapter 7, we turn our focus to another politically volatile issue: climate change. We show that while almost a quarter of the US population
do not believe in climate change, this is not the case among the Millennial
Generation. In fact, Millennials have the highest belief in climate change
(80% among those 18 to 29 year olds, according to 2015 National Surveys
on Energy and the Environment) among any age group. This strong
belief serves as a backdrop for analyzing Millennial climate change policy
preferences in comparison to older adults. We find that Millennials are
statistically more likely than older adults to attribute climate change to
anthropogenic (human-induced) causes. Given this, one would expect
Millennials to favor policies such as increased taxes and penalties for
corporations that pollute, pursuing the production of alternative energy
sources, and increased regulation of carbon emission for automobiles,
since many climate advocates argue that these policies mitigate the effects
of man-made climate change. However, our findings on support for these
policies among Millennials were a bit surprising. Millennials express less
support than non-Millennials for these climate change initiatives. Why is
this the case, given that many factors of the Millennial persona—climate
change belief, liberalness, positive worldview—should point to Millennial
support for such prescriptions? While there is not one specific and obvious
reason for these findings, we point to a few factors that may contribute
to these results. We argue that Millennials struggle to translate climate
change values into specific policy choices and instead pivot to a different
set of solutions when it comes to climate change. Since Millennials do not
have much trust in traditional political institutions (discussed in depth
in Chapter 9), their preference may not be for government-led answers.
The near political future is not promising for climate change solutions at
the federal government level; therefore, Millennials may be right to look
for non-government or local government-based solutions to the climate
change problem.

In Chapter 8, we conclude our analysis of Millennials' policy attitudes
by turning our attention to three "hot button" social issues: gun control,
legalization of marijuana, and right to abortion. Here we emphasize the
significance of the Millennial Generation's liberalness (an important part

of the Millennial persona) to understand variation in these policy prefer-ence, in relation to non-Millennials and across Millennial subgroups. Do Millennials follow their liberal tendencies when it comes to attitudes about these issues? The answer is, it depends. We find that the effect of liberalness for Millennials on these social issues is nuanced, varying in degrees and affecting Millennial subgroups differently. On the issue of gun control, we find that among Millennials, whites are the least supportive of gun control policies, while African Americans and Latino Millennials are much more supportive—both groups showing greater support for gun control policies than the average Millennial. Millennials are much more consistently liberal on the legalization of marijuana, compared to non-Millennials. However, attitudes on these issues diverge a bit across racial and ethnic lines as well. African Americans are by far the most supportive Millennial subgroup when it comes to the legalization of marijuana, while Latino Millennials are the least supportive (below the aggregate for Millennials). And on the issue of abortion rights, Millennials look a lot like the broader popula-tion, including African American and Latino Millennials who have similar opinions on the issue, compared to older members of their race/ethnic group. Among both Millennials and non-Millennials, ideology exerts a disproportionate and similar effect on attitudes about this issue—those who are more liberal are more likely to support abortion rights. These findings, coupled with results about other issues show that Millennials have their own brand of liberalness that is nuanced, is guided by a set of values heavily influenced by their generation persona, and does not follow a single or direct track. Again, for politicians and political parties to appeal to Millennials, they not only need to realize how ideological nuances play out with respect to specific policy preferences but also understand that these preferences can vary across Millennial subgroups, in a way that some-times tempers ideology in favor of other important factors.

Our final chapter goes a step further, beyond attitudes about a partic-ular set of issues, to examine whether and how Millennial may or may not be able to affect the policy preferences they exhibit. To do this, we exam-ined levels of political engagement of Millennials and their attitudes about traditional political institutions (Chapter 9). In this chapter, we preface our discussion with the importance of Millennials soon becoming the largest voting cohort in the country (by 2020). Whether this benchmark is symbolic or substantive still remains to be seen. Millennials participate, by traditional measures (e.g., voting), at lower levels than non-Millennials. In this sense, Millennials are no different than other generations when they were young. If we end the story here, then the obvious and easy conclusion would be that Millennials are less engaged and more apathetic about politics than non-Millennials and perhaps life cycle effects will change this in predictable ways (e.g., vote more as they age). However, our analyses do not support this overall conclusion. Our results do show that Millennials are less attached to traditional political parties and are less likely to vote, compared to non-Millennials. We also find, though, that Millennials still believe in the value of voting and see it at as a way to bring about political change. They also participate at similar levels to older adults in other traditional forms of participation such as contacting elected officials. Millennials do express a desire for better representation and improved political outcomes, especially on issues that matter to their generation (e.g., Bernie Sanders). Overall, these results are more a repudiation of electoral choices (recall that Millennials voted at higher rates for President Obama, especially in 2008) than of the general electoral process or traditional politics.

Overall, Millennials do not feel less engaged in the political process than non-Millennials. However, as in other scenarios, we do find differences across Millennial subgroups—Latinos and African Americans are less politically engaged than their white counterparts. The lack of political engagement is clearly not a generational issue; minorities have long lagged behind the engagement levels of non-Hispanic whites. With the Millennial Generation, we have seen some improvement in socioeconomic factors that have historically affected this trend, primarily greater educational achievement. The Great Recession, though, has hindered this progress. Millennials, in a sense, have taken one step forward and two steps back—a reality that has not spared their interest and ability to be politically engaged.

We concluded the chapter on political engagement through the lens of the 2016 election, treating it as the most recent case study of Millennial engagement. First and foremost, we found that Millennials continued their general trend of voting at lower rates, compared to the rest of the population. When we explored reasons for not voting, a plurality of Millennials (as well as non-Millennials) said they could not support any of the candidates. This further reinforces the fact that this cohort is disengaged primarily with electoral options and not necessarily the electoral process. Second, although not surprising, our survey shows that Millennials overwhelmingly supported Hillary Clinton (58%) over Donald Trump (31%) in the 2016 general election. While Hillary Clinton captured a majority of the Millennial vote, this rate was lower than what President Obama received in both 2008 and 2012 (Khalid 2016). Clearly the choices for president were less than ideal for Millennials, and many stayed home once Bernie Sanders was out of the running. Finally, since the rhetoric of "change" dominated the 2016 presidential campaign, we probed Millennials' attitudes about their belief that the system is rigged. We find that Millennials are indeed more likely than non-Millennials to feel like the system is set up against them. This sentiment is even more pronounced among minority Millennials, particularly African Americans.

The 2016 Election-Revisited: Policy Support and Issue Concerns

As we write this, President Donald Trump has assumed office and his policy agenda is taking shape in the first one hundred days of his administration. What are Millennials' opinions about his agenda priorities and what are their biggest concerns during his presidency? A few additional findings from our post-election survey,[2] administered in November 2016, help us answer these questions.

We asked respondents to indicate support, on a 0 to 100 scale—running from no support to complete support, for five policy areas that were prominent during the 2016 election.[3] These included: *trade*—"withdrawal from NAFTA, the Trans-Pacific Partnership (TPP), and other international trade deals;" *healthcare*—"repealing the Affordable Care Act (Obamacare);" *terrorism*—"concerned with the threat of ISIS;" *immigration*—"building a wall along the U.S. border with Mexico;" and *environment*—"federal government action to aggressively address climate change." Figure 10.1 illustrates support among Millennials and non-Millennials for these policy areas.

Generally, Millennials are unsupportive of Trump's prominent policy proposals, and their stances reinforce what we have learned about them in the analyses throughout this book—they value diversity, are ideologically liberal, feel connected to the global community, and support government action to promote the collective good. We see that Millennials are less supportive than older adults in withdrawal from international

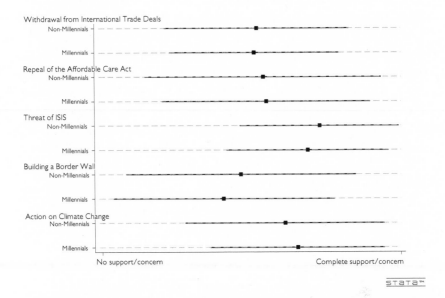

FIGURE 10.1. Support for Prominent Policy Proposals of the 2016 Presidential Campaign

Note: The dot represents the average response among the subgroup (Millennial or non-Millennial), and the bar indicates the range of responses, from minimum value to maximum value. Questions were asked as follows: "Indicate on the scale below how much you support [policy], with 0 meaning 'no support' and 100 meaning 'complete support.'"

trade deals and building a wall along the US–Mexico border. They are also less concerned with the threat of ISIS and, therefore, more likely to be reluctant to support military action. They are slightly more supportive of repealing the Affordable Care Act. Despite the fact that the policy has provided expanded healthcare coverage for their generation and that a majority of this age cohort remains committed to coverage for all adults, Millennials have been just as unhappy with the law as older adults (Pew Research Center 2014a). Millennial attitudes on this may change as the details of altering the healthcare law under Trump and a Republican-led Congress become clearer (this question was asked at a time when Trump had promised, during the campaign, "healthcare for all"). Millennials are also more supportive of aggressive action to mitigate climate change, including "placing a price on carbon, methane and other greenhouse gases

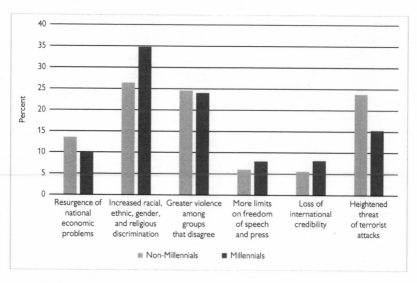

FIGURE 10.2.   Concerns about the Trump Presidency

Note: The bars indicate the percentage of respondents saying that issue concerns them the most, among each subgroup (Millennials, shown in light gray, and non-Millennials, shown in dark gray). Question was asked as follows: "Thinking of the next four years in our country under the leadership of President Donald Trump, which one of these concerns you the most?"

and massive investment in renewable energy sources like wind and solar." Given Millennials' expressed support for policies that President Donald Trump is at the very least unlikely to prioritize (or at worst, oppose), it will be a challenge to boost Millennial engagement (at least in a traditional sense). As we noted, Millennials want better representation on the issues they care about in order to be engaged, and the landscape on the national level looks a bit bleak for this prospect, at least in the near future.

In addition to these policy stances, we also asked survey respondents what concerns they have for a Trump administration. The survey asked— *Thinking of the next four years in our country under the leadership of President Donald Trump, which one of these concerns you the most? Resurgence of national economic problems; increased racial, ethnic, gender, and religious discrimination; greater violence among groups that disagree; more limits on freedom of speech and press; loss of international credibility; or heightened threat of terrorist attacks.* The issues prompted reflected the political discourse at the time of the 2016 election. Responses across Millennial and non-Millennial groups are shown in Figure 10.2.

Recall that Donald Trump ran as a presidential candidate, in part, on the heightened threat of terrorism and the need to "get tough on terror." Surprisingly, though, terrorism is not at the top of the list of concerns for either Millennials or non-Millennials during his presidency. Rather, both Millennials and non-Millennials say that "increased racial, ethnic, gender, and religious discrimination" is the issue they are most uneasy about during Trump's time in office. However, significantly more Millennials are worried about increased discrimination than non-Millennials; over a third of Millennials (34.8%) expressed this concern, compared to just over a quarter (26.4%) of non-Millennials. Concerns over increased discrimination are followed by uneasiness that there will be "greater violence among groups that disagree." A similar number of both Millennials (24.0%) and non-Millennials (24.5%) flagged this concern. Terrorism ranks third on the list of issues that make respondents uneasy about the Trump presidency—with Millennials (15.3%) expressing less uneasiness about "the heightened threat of terrorism" than non-Millennials (23.8%).

It is clear that the Trump presidency evokes anxiety about how marginalized groups in society will be treated during his time in office and how Americans will deal with escalating political, economic, and social tensions. Millennials, in particular, are uneasy about the next four (or eight) years. Given their size, diversity, and propensity for tolerance, we may need to rely on this generation to set the tone and discourse of the country, sooner rather than later.

Conclusion: Millennials—Waiting on the World to Change?

The answer to the question at the beginning of the chapter—Are Millennials waiting on the world to change or realizing their power and taking action?—is not a simple one. The response is somewhere in between, and the full impact of their numerical power and political potential still remains to be seen. What we can say, though, is that Millennials are not the political doormats that many make them out to be. Therefore, if we want this generation to lead the way and to save us from the current political quagmire (in terms of apathy, polarization, gridlock, and social tensions), we first need to give them credit for the qualities and potential they possess and then help guide them into the spotlight. This means that overemphasizing a traditional political path to participation and underemphasizing alternative options is *not* the likely path to greater Millennial engagement. Our system disincentivizes Millennials from stepping up in many ways, especially running for elected office. With the amounts of money that need to be raised, the commitment involved, and the level of undue scrutiny that is placed on candidates, the benefits for Millennials do not outweigh the costs (Shames 2017). Moreover, they are disgusted with money in politics, and this only contributes to their distrust of political institutions. This is lamentable as we need this generation to start putting their imprint on the institutions of government. Former President Barack Obama, in his first public appearance after leaving office, spoke to students at the University of Chicago and said:

> I'm spending a lot of time thinking: What is the most important thing I can do for my next job? And what I'm convinced of is that although there are all kinds of issues I care about and all kinds of issues I intend to work on, the single-most important thing I can do is to help, in any way I can, prepare the next generation of leadership to take up the baton and take their own crack at changing the world.[4]

It is not just the former leader of the free world that should take up this challenge, but rather, it is incumbent on the non-Millennial generations to help this cohort find its way and lead us into the latter part of the twenty-first century. This is accomplished by providing Millennials with guidance and encouragement, helping them avoid mistakes made by previous generations, and simply getting out of their way. We cannot and should not force them into traditional political spaces, labels, or policy prescriptions. Instead, Millennials need to be given the opportunity to see just how their values may be translated into meaningful changes in our politics, economy, and society. The John Mayer song referenced at the beginning of this chapter ends with a line not only about how a rising generation will be the one to rule over the population, but also how, in the meantime, the generation waits for the world to change. We have already seen Millennials overtake Baby Boomers in population size; they will be the biggest voting bloc in the 2020 election. It is now time to stop waiting for change; it is time for Millennials to grasp their political power.

Appendices

Appendices to Chapter 2: Studying the Politics of the Millennial Generation

Appendix 2.A: 2015 Survey Questionnaire

1. In your opinion, which of the following is the most important issue to your age group or generation?
   a. Drug legalization
   b. The economy
   c. Education
   d. The environment
   e. Gay marriage
   f. Gun control
   g. Healthcare
   h. Immigration
   i. Terrorism
   j. Other (type in response)

2. What year were you born?
   1901–1997

3. What is your gender?
   a. Male
   b. Female

4. Are you of Hispanic or Latino background, such as Cuban, Dominican, Mexican, Puerto Rican, Salvadoran, Central American, South American or other Spanish background?
   a. No
   b. Yes

5. What is your race?
   a. White or Caucasian
   b. White Hispanic
   c. African American
   d. Asian American
   e. Pacific-Islander American
   f. American Indian
   g. Other (type in answer)

6. Were you born in the United States or in a US territory (i.e., Puerto Rico, Guam or Virgin Islands) or in another country?
   a. I was born in another country.
   b. I was born in the United States or a US territory.

7. What is your marital status?
   a. Married or in a domestic partnership/civil union
   b. Widowed
   c. Divorced
   d. Separated
   e. Never married

8. What is the highest degree or level of school that you have completed?
   a. Less than high school
   b. Some high school
   c. High school
   d. Some college
   e. Associate's degree
   f. Bachelor's degree
   g. Master's degree
   h. Professional or doctoral degree

9. Are you currently employed?
    a. No
    b. Part time (work less than 40 hours per week)
    c. Full time (work 40 hours or more per week)

10. Last year, that is from January 1, 2014 to December 31, 2014, what was your total family income from all sources, before taxes?
    a. Less than $20,000
    b. $20,000 to under $30,000
    c. $30,000 to under $50,000
    d. $50,000 to under $75,000
    e. $75,000 to under $100,000
    f. $100,000+
    g. I don't know.

11. We hear a lot of talk these days about liberals and conservatives. Here is a 7-point scale on which the political views that people might hold are arranged from extremely liberal to extremely conservative. Where would you place yourself on this scale or haven't you thought much about this?
    a. Extremely liberal
    b. Liberal
    c. Slightly liberal
    d. Moderate; middle of the road
    e. Slightly conservative
    f. Conservative
    g. Extremely conservative
    h. I haven't thought much about it.
    i. I don't know.

12. Do you consider yourself a Republican, Democrat, or Independent?
    a. Republican
    b. Democrat
    c. Independent
    d. Other (type in response)
    e. I do not consider myself part of any party.

13. Move the following scale to indicate how strongly you feel like you belong to a political party. Higher numbers indicate more strongly. A 0 indicates "not at all", a 50 means "neutral", and a 100 represents "extremely belong".

14. What religion do you most closely associate with (if any)?
    a. Protestant
    b. Roman Catholic
    c. Judaism
    d. Muslim
    e. Mormon
    f. Orthodox
    g. Buddhist
    h. Hindu
    i. None
    j. Other (type in response)

15. Do you consider yourself a "born again" Christian?
    a. No
    b. Yes

16. Are you registered to vote?
    a. No
    b. Yes
    c. I don't know.

17. Have you voted in elections in the past 4 years?
    a. No
    b. Yes
    c. I don't know.

18. Do you feel like you are engaged in the political system or politics?
    a. No
    b. Somewhat
    c. Yes

    *If "yes," skip to question 20.

19. What would it take to make you more engaged in the political system or politics? (Please type your response.)

20. Where do you get most of your political information and news?
    a. Network and cable TV news programs.
    b. Newspapers—print or online.
    c. Social media—for example, Twitter and Facebook.
    d. Discussions with friends and family.
    e. Radio news programs.

21. Have you ever contacted an elected official or politician through traditional means like a letter or phone call or through email or social media?
    a. No
    b. Yes—traditional means (i.e., letter or phone call)
    c. Yes—email or social media (i.e., Twitter or Facebook)
    d. Yes—traditional means and email/social media

22. In your opinion, which of the following brings about the most political change?
    a. Voting.
    b. Petitioning or protesting an issue.
    c. Contacting an elected official or politician through traditional means.
    d. Contacting an elected official or politician through email or social media.
    e. Meeting with local groups.

23. How often do you discuss politics and policy with your friends?
    a. Never
    b. Rarely
    c. Sometimes
    d. Often
    e. All of the time

24. How often do you discuss politics and policy with your family?
    a. Never
    b. Rarely
    c. Sometimes
    d. Often
    e. All of the time

25. Are you likely to vote in the next presidential election in 2016?
    a. No
    b. Maybe
    c. Yes
    d. I don't know.

26. If you vote in the next presidential election, how important might the following issues be to your vote? For each issue, indicate if it would be important, somewhat important, or not important.
    a. Education
    b. The economy
    c. Immigration
    d. The environment
    e. Healthcare
    f. Gay marriage
    g. Gun control
    h. National security
    i. Privacy rights
    j. Income inequality
    k. The minimum wage
    l. Government waste/corruption
    m. International conflict

27. Considering our country's economy, which of the following is the most important issue to your generation or age group?
    a. Unemployment and job scarcity.
    b. Federal government debt.
    c. Cost of entitlement programs (Social Security and Medicare).
    d. Rising cost of education.
    e. Increasing gap between the wealthy, the middle class, and the poor.
    f. Lack of long-term job and retirement security.

28. Thinking about the national economy, do you believe our country is better or worse off than it was twenty years ago for people of your age?
    a. Worse
    b. About the same
    c. Better
    d. Don't know

29. For the following pair of statements, select the one that most closely aligns (agrees) with your personal opinion.
    a. Cutting government spending is the only way to change our economic outlook. OR More government spending is needed to alleviate the economic hardships Americans are suffering.
    b. Making some changes to Social Security will ensure retirement for everyone. OR Overhaul of our Social Security program is needed.
    c. The free market will resolve unemployment with enough time. OR The government should do more to stimulate job growth.

30. Are you currently paying or have paid student loan debt?
    a. No
    b. Yes

    *If answer "no," skip to question 32.

31. What is the total amount of student loan debt you owe or owed?
    a. Below $10,000
    b. Between $11,000–$20,000
    c. Between $21,000–$30,000
    d. Between $31,000–$40,000
    e. Between $41,000–$50,000
    f. Between $50,000–$100,000
    g. Above $100,000
    h. Don't know

32. Considering our country's healthcare system, which of the following is the most important issue to your generation or age group?
    a. Cost of health insurance and prescription drugs
    b. Regulations tied to the Affordable Care Act (Obama Care)
    c. Quality of food and nutrition
    d. Rates of obesity and other preventable diseases
    e. Availability of health services
    f. Cost of health services
    g. Quality of health services

33. For the following pair of statements, select the one that most closely aligns (agrees) with your personal opinion.
    a. Insurance and pharmaceutical companies drive up the cost of our healthcare. OR Insurance and pharmaceutical companies improve the safety and quality of our healthcare.
    b. The government should require that all individuals have healthcare. OR Healthcare coverage is best left up to individuals to decide.
    c. The government should do more to reduce the costs of healthcare to individuals. OR The government should leave it up to the free market to determine healthcare costs.

34. Considering our country's education system, which of the following is the most important issue to your generation or age group?
    a. Standardized testing
    b. Overall quality of education
    c. Gap between the wealthy and those who have less in the quality of education obtained
    d. Cost of higher education/college
    e. College and workplace preparedness

35. For the following pair of statements, select the one that most closely aligns (agrees) with your personal opinion.
    a. The government should forgive all student loans. OR Individuals should have to pay back all the student loan debt they incurred.
    b. Standardized testing ensures uniform educational outcomes. OR Standardized testing impairs teaching and learning.
    c. Higher education should be reformed to decrease costs and increase quality. OR Higher education is functioning well to keep up with economic and student demands.

36. Considering international matters, which of the following is the most important issue to your generation or age group?
    a. Establishment of an Islamic state by extremists
    b. Global terrorism
    c. Israel–Palestine conflict
    d. Russia–Ukraine conflict

  e. Syrian civil war

  f. Dealing with Iran

  g. Continued conflict in Iraq and Afghanistan

  h. Ebola or other disease outbreak

  i. Refugee crises (Sudan, Syria, Iraq, etc.)

37. What are you more likely to support as a solution to international conflicts?

  a. Diplomatic methods of negotiations or sanctions.

  b. Armed/militarized action or force.

38. Considering the environment, which of the following is the most important issue to your generation or age group?

  a. Pollution of the air, waters, and land.

  b. Global climate change.

  c. Dependence on fossil fuels like coal, natural gas, and oil.

  d. Global exploitation of forests and lands to extract natural resources.

  e. Loss of biodiversity and rising extinction.

39. How much do you support or are likely to support the following federal government policy? (None, A little, Some, A lot)

  a. Increased taxes and penalties for polluting by corporations.

  b. Aggressively pursue the production and use of alternative energy sources.

  c. Increased regulation of carbon emissions for automobiles.

40. From what you've read and heard, is there solid evidence of global warming and climate change, or not?

  a. No, there is not solid evidence.

  b. There is some/mixed evidence.

  c. Yes, there is solid evidence.

  * If answer "no," skip to question 42.

41. What do you think? The earth is getting warmer mostly because of . . .

  a. Natural patterns in the earth's environment.

  b. Human activity such as burning fuels.

  c. I don't know.

42. For the following pair of statements, select the one that most closely aligns (agrees) with your personal opinion.

    a. The growing number of immigrants from other countries threatens traditional American customs and values. OR Immigrants strengthen the diversity of our country.

    b. Immigrants take jobs away from Americans. OR Immigrants only take jobs Americans do not want to do.

    c. Illegal immigrants threaten our nation's security. OR Illegal immigrants do not threaten our safety.

    d. The federal government should reform immigration policy to reduce the number of newcomers coming into our country. OR The federal government should keep immigration policy the way it is now.

43. How much do you support or are likely to support the following federal government policy? (None, A little, Some, A lot)

    a. Require that all companies verify the legal status of workers before employing them.

    b. Strengthen border security and extend wall or fence along the US–Mexico border.

    c. Allow undocumented children and childhood arrivals under the age of 30 years to stay in the United States permanently.

    d. Allow in-state tuition and fees at state universities for undocumented immigrants who arrived in the United States as children.

44. How much do you support or are likely to support the following federal government policy? (None, A little, Some, A lot)

    a. Mandate for increased minimum wage.

    b. Requirement for background checks and waiting periods before purchase of a gun.

    c. Marijuana for recreational use by adults.

    d. Women's right to an abortion.

Appendix 2.B: 2016 Post-Election Survey Questionnaire

1. What year were you born?
   1902–1998

2. What is your gender?
   a. Male
   b. Female

3. Are you of Hispanic or Latino background, such as Cuban, Dominican, Mexican, Puerto Rican, Salvadoran, Central American, South American or other Spanish background?
   a. No
   b. Yes

4. What is your race?
   a. White or Caucasian
   b. White Hispanic
   c. African American
   d. Asian American
   e. Pacific-Islander American
   f. American-Indian
   g. Other (type in answer)

5. Were you born in the United States or in a US territory (i.e., Puerto Rico, Guam, or Virgin Islands) or in another country?
   a. I was born in the United States or a US territory.
   b. I was born in another country.

6. What is your marital status?
   a. Married or in a domestic partnership/civil union
   b. Widowed
   c. Divorced
   d. Separated
   e. Never married

7. What is the highest degree or level of school that you have completed?
   a. Less than high school
   b. Some high school
   c. High school

    d. Some college

    e. Associate's degree

    f. Bachelor's degree

    g. Master's degree

    h. Professional or doctoral degree

8. Are you currently employed?

    a. No

    b. Part time (work less than 40 hours per week)

    c. Full time (work 40 hours or more per week)

9. Last year, that is from January 1, 2015 to December 31, 2015, what was your total family income from all sources, before taxes?

    a. Less than $20,000

    b. $20,000 to under $30,000

    c. $30,000 to under $50,000

    d. $50,000 to under $75,000

    e. $75,000 to under $100,000

    f. $100,000+

    i. I don't know.

10. We hear a lot of talk these days about liberals and conservatives. Here is a 7-point scale on which the political views that people might hold are arranged from extremely liberal to extremely conservative. Where would you place yourself on this scale or haven't you thought much about this?

    a. Extremely liberal

    b. Liberal

    c. Slightly liberal

    d. Moderate; middle of the road

    e. Slightly conservative

    f. Conservative

    g. Extremely conservative

    h. I haven't thought much about it.

    i. I don't know.

11. Do you consider yourself a Republican, Democrat, or Independent?

    a. Republican

    b. Democrat

    c. Independent

    d. Other (type in response)

    e. I do not consider myself part of any party.

12. How strongly do you feel like you belong to a political party? Slide the scale running from 0 ("not at all belong") to 10 ("extremely belong") to match your belief.

13. What religion do you most closely associate with (if any)?

    a. Protestant

    b. Roman Catholic

    c. Judaism

    d. Muslim

    e. Mormon

    f. Orthodox

    g. Buddhist

    h. Hindu

    i. None

    j. Other (type in response)

14. Do you consider yourself a "born again" Christian?

    a. No

    b. Yes

15. In terms of what's important about you, how much do you identify with each of the following? Slide the scales running from 0 ("not at all") to 10 ("very strongly") to match your beliefs.

    a. A citizen of the United States

    b. A citizen of the world

    c. A follower of your religious faith

    d. A member of your race

    e. Part of your ethnic group

    f. Your gender

16. Which of these identities is most important to you?

    a. A citizen of the United States

    b. A citizen of the world

    c. A follower of your religious faith

    d. A member of your ethnic group

    e. Your gender

17. Are you registered to vote?
    a. No
    b. Yes
    c. I don't know.

18. In talking to people about elections, we often find that a lot of people weren't able to vote because they weren't registered, they were sick, or they just didn't have the time. Which of the following statements best describes you?
    a. I did not vote (in the election this November).
    b. I thought about voting this time, but didn't.
    c. I usually vote, but didn't this time.
    d. I voted in this year's election.

    *If "I voted in this year's election" is selected, skip to question 20.

19. What was the biggest reason you did not vote?
    a. I could not support any of the presidential candidates.
    b. I did not feel like the election process was fair.
    c. I did not feel like my vote would matter to the outcome of the election.
    d. I did not have the required documents such as voter registration and/or identification card.
    e. I could not make it to the polls—did not have time, was sick, or something came up.
    i. I just did not care.

20. Which presidential candidate did you vote for?
    a. Donald Trump
    b. Hillary Clinton
    c. Jill Stein
    d. Gary Johnson
    e. Other candidate (type in response)
    f. I did not vote for a presidential candidate, although I voted for other offices.

    *For all responses except for Trump, skip to question 22.

21. How important was each of the following in your vote for Trump? (Not at all important, Slightly important, Moderately important, Very important, Extremely important)
    a. Trump was the candidate most likely to take on the establishment, both Democrat and Republican.
    b. Trump was the Republican candidate.
    c. Trump was the best choice among bad candidates.

22. Rate the following reasons behind your choice for president. I chose my candidate for president because . . . (Not at all important, Slightly important, Moderately important, Very important, Extremely important)
    a. I am loyal to my political party.
    b. I agree with my candidate's proposed policies.
    c. I strongly opposed the other candidate(s).
    d. I trust my candidate.
    e. My candidate cares about people like me.
    f. The next president will choose a justice for the Supreme Court.
    g. While I usually don't vote, a vote for my candidate was particularly important this election.

23. Now, which of these is the most important reason for your vote? Please choose one.
    a. Party loyalty.
    b. Impact on the makeup of the Supreme Court.
    c. I genuinely agree with my preferred candidate's proposed policies.
    d. A vote against another candidate(s).
    e. I have trust in my candidate.
    f. My candidate cares about people like me.
    g. While I usually don't vote, I felt a vote for my candidate was particularly important this election.

24. How satisfied are you with the outcome of the presidential election? Slide the scale running from 0 ("extremely dissatisfied") to 10 ("extremely satisfied") to match your belief.

25. Thinking of the next four years in our country under the leadership of President Donald Trump, how concerned are you with the following? Slide the scales running from 0 ("not at all concerned") to 10 ("extremely concerned") to match your beliefs.
    a. Resurgence of national economic problems.
    b. Increased racial, ethnic, gender, and religious discrimination.
    c. Greater violence among groups that disagree.
    d. More limits on freedom of speech and press.
    e. Loss of international credibility.
    f. Heightened threat of terrorist attacks.

26. Now, which one of these concerns you the most? Please choose one.
    a. Resurgence of national economic problems.
    b. Increased racial, ethnic, gender, and religious discrimination.
    c. Greater violence among groups that disagree.
    d. More limits on freedom of speech and press.
    e. Loss of international credibility.
    f. Heightened threat of terrorist attacks.

27. How much do you agree with this statement? Our system is rigged against people like me.
    a. Strongly disagree
    b. Somewhat disagree
    c. Somewhat agree
    d. Strongly agree

28. Which of the following is closest to your view?
    a. I am generally comfortable with our political system.
    b. I think our political system needs change, but it should be gradual.
    c. I think our political system needs revolutionary change.

29. How much do you want significant change to American political system?
    a. Very much
    b. Somewhat
    c. Not at all

30. How much do you want significant change to American economic system?
    a. Very much
    b. Somewhat
    c. Not at all

31. In your opinion, which of the following is the most important issue to your age group or generation?
    a. Drug legalization
    b. The economy
    c. Education
    d. The environment
    e. Gay marriage
    f. Gun control
    g. Healthcare
    h. Immigration
    i. Terrorism
    j. Other (type in response)

32. Thinking about the national economy, do you believe our country is better or worse off than it was twenty years ago for people of your age?
    a. Better
    b. About the same
    c. Worse
    d. I don't know.

33. Indicate on the scale below how much you support withdrawal from NAFTA, the Trans-Pacific Partnership (TPP), and other international trade deals, with 0 meaning "no support" and 100 meaning "complete support".

34. Indicate on the scale below how much you support repealing the Affordable Care Act (Obamacare), with 0 meaning "no support" and 100 meaning "complete support".

35. Indicate on the scale below how much you support a federal government loan forgiveness program for student loans, with 0 meaning "no support" and 100 meaning "complete support".

36. Indicate on the scale below how much you are concerned with the threat of ISIS, with 0 meaning "not at all concerned" and 100 meaning "extremely concerned".

37. Indicate on the scale below how much you support building a wall along the US border with Mexico with 0 meaning "no support" and 100 meaning "complete support".

38. Indicate on the scale below how much you support federal government action to aggressively address climate change—including placing a price on carbon, methane and other greenhouse gases and massive investment in renewable energy sources like wind and solar—with 0 meaning "no support" and 100 meaning "complete support".

39. From what you've read and heard, is there solid evidence of global warming and climate change, or not?
    a. Yes, there is solid evidence.
    b. There is some/mixed evidence.
    c. No, there is not solid evidence.

    *If "no" is selected, skip to question 41.

40. What do you think? The earth is getting warmer mostly because of...
    a. Human activity such as burning fuels.
    b. Natural patterns in the earth's environment.
    c. I don't know.

41. For the following four pairs of statements, select the one that most closely aligns (agrees) with your personal opinion.
    a. The growing number of immigrants from other countries threatens traditional American customs and values. OR Immigrants strengthen the diversity of our country.
    b. Immigrants take jobs away from Americans. OR Immigrants only take jobs Americans do not want to do.
    c. Illegal immigrants threaten our nation's security. OR Illegal immigrants do not threaten our safety.
    d. The federal government should reform immigration policy to reduce the number of newcomers coming into our country. OR The federal government should keep immigration policy the way it is now.

42. What do you think should be done with most illegal immigrants working in the United States?
    a. Offer a chance to become legal workers.
    b. Offer a chance to become legal citizens.
    c. Deport them to their home countries.
    d. Nothing—things are fine as is.

43. How much do you support or are likely to support the following federal government policies? (None, A little, Some, A lot)
    a. Mandate for increased minimum wage.
    b. Requirement for background checks and waiting periods before purchase of a gun.
    c. Marijuana for recreational use by adults.
    d. Women's right to an abortion.

Appendix 2.C: 2016 Nielsen Survey

1. Generally speaking, do you think of yourself as a:
   a. Republican
   b. Independent
   c. Democrat
   d. Other
   e. No preference

   *If Republican or Democrat, skip to question 3.

2. Do you think of yourself as closer to the:
   a. Republican Party
   b. Democratic Party
   c. Neither

3. Which of the following describes your ethnic background best?
   a. Black or African American
   b. Hispanic American
   c. Asian American
   d. Anglo American
   e. Jewish American
   f. Arab American
   g. Israeli American
   h. American with ancestry from a Muslim-majority country
   i. Two or more races
   j. Other

4. Do you have relatives, including distant relatives, who reside outside of the United States?
   a. Yes
   b. No

5. In terms of what's important about you, how much do you identify with each of the following on the scale presented? (Not at all, 1, 2, 3, 4, 5, 6, 7, 8, 9, Very strongly)
   a. A citizen of the United States
   b. A citizen of the world
   c. A follower of your religious faith

    d. A member of your race

    e. Part of your ethnic group

    f. Your gender

6. Which one of these identities is **most** important to you today? Please select one.

    a. A citizen of the United States

    b. A citizen of the world

    c. A follower of your religious faith

    d. A member of your race

    e. Part of your ethnic group

    f. Your gender

7. For each pair of statements below, please use the scale to indicate where your opinion falls with regard to the two statements. (1—statement 1, 2, 3, 4, 5—statement 2)

    a. The government should provide national health insurance that everyone pays into and has access to when going to their doctor. | The government should stay out of all healthcare insurance decisions, and let those who want to buy it themselves or get it through their employer.

    b. The government should do more to make healthcare affordable. | The government should leave it up to the free market to determine healthcare costs.

8. On a scale of 1–10, where 10 is very important and 1 is not important, how important are the following issues in American global priorities?

    a. The rise of China

    b. The assertiveness of Russia

    c. North Korea

    d. Iran

    e. Trade deficit

    f. The Israeli-Palestinian conflict

    g. The war on ISIS

    h. The war on al-Qaeda

    i. The civil war in Libya

    j. The civil war in Yemen

    k. US immigration policy
    l. The tense relations with Egypt and Saudi Arabia
    m. Other issue (please specify)

9. Which of the following issues should be America's top global priorities? Please select two.
    a. The rise of China
    b. The assertiveness of Russia
    c. North Korea
    d. Iran
    e. Trade deficit
    f. The Israeli–Palestinian conflict
    g. The war on ISIS
    h. The war on al-Qaeda
    i. The civil war in Libya
    j. The civil war in Yemen
    k. US immigration policy
    l. The tense relations with Egypt and Saudi Arabia
    m. Other issue (please specify)

Appendix 2.D: Focus Group Questions

1. Imagine President Obama is joining our session today. What do you want to tell him about your concerns?
2. Do you feel you belong to one of the two major parties— Democrat or Republican?
3. Do you feel that you are engaged with the political process?
4. What does "engaged in politics and the political process" mean to you?
5. In what ways do you engage in politics? Is social media a way to engage?
6. If you do feel that you are not engaged—what would it take for you to be more engaged?
7. Regarding the 2016 presidential race—do the presidential candidates appeal to you? How do you feel about those candidates who are "out of the box" or non-traditional, for example Donald Trump and Bernie Sanders?
8. What do you think is our nation's biggest economic issue? Why?
9. Thinking of the national economy, do you believe our country is better or worse off than it was twenty years ago for people of your age?
10. Considering our country's healthcare system, what is most important? Why?
11. Considering our country's education system, what is the most pressing issue facing our county? Why?
12. Considering international issues, what is the most important issue facing our country?
13. Do you think climate change is caused by human consumption or by nature?
14. What personal choices or trade-offs are you willing to make to mitigate climate change?
15. How do you feel about immigration into our country?
16. Do you feel that your generation is competing for jobs with immigrants?
17. Should employers take responsibility for unauthorized immigrant workers through programs like e-verify?
18. How do you feel about the legalization of marijuana?
19. How do you feel about the national legal recognition of same-sex marriage?
20. Is there anything else you would like to say about policy issues that are important to you?

Appendix 2.E: Descriptive Statistics

APPENDIX 2.E.1.   Descriptive Statistics: Original Survey 2015

Variable	N	Mean	Std. Dev.	Min	Max
Millennial	1,251	0.496	0.500	0	1
Latino	1,251	0.205	0.404	0	1
African American	1,251	0.153	0.360	0	1
Foreign born	1,251	0.086	0.282	0	1
Liberal ideology	1,112	0.373	0.484	0	1
Unemployed	1,251	0.412	0.492	0	1
Negative economic outlook	1,189	0.623	0.485	0	1
Positive government worldview	1,238	$-2.99E-09$	1	-1.693	1.768
Education	1,251	4.648	1.498	1	8
Income	1,196	3.269	1.568	1	6
Female	1,251	0.511	0.500	0	1
Married	1,251	0.484	0.450	0	1

APPENDIX 2.E.2.   Descriptive Statistics: Nielsen Survey 2016

Variable	N	Mean	Std. Dev.	Min	Max
Millennial	1,580	0.546	0.498	0	1
Latino	1,580	0.109	0.312	0	1
African American	1,580	0.101	0.302	0	1
Foreign relatives	1,578	0.378	0.485	0	1
Republican	1,580	0.385	0.487	0	1
Cosmopolitan identity	1,566	6.498	3.147	0	10
Education	1,580	4.767	1.450	1	7
Income	1,580	8.111	3.100	1	13
Female	1,580	0.530	0.499	0	1

Appendix 2.F: Principle Component Factor Analysis for "Positive Government Worldview"

1 Factor Retained
Factor:

Eigenvalue:	1.469
Proportioned Explained:	0.367

APPENDIX 2.F. Factor Loadings for Components of Positive Government Worldview

Variable	Factor Loading	Uniqueness
Support for more government spending as a way to alleviate economic hardships	0.611	0.627
Support for government requiring that all individuals have healthcare	0.681	0.537
Support for government doing more to reduce the cost of healthcare	0.662	0.562
Support for government forgiving all student loans	0.441	0.805

Variable Descriptions

Government Spending

Cutting government spending is the way to change our economic outlook = 0

More government spending is needed to alleviate the economic hardships Americans are suffering = 1

Healthcare Coverage

Healthcare coverage is best left up to individuals to decide = 0

The government should require that all individuals have healthcare = 1

Healthcare Cost

The government should leave it up to the free market to determine healthcare costs = 0

The government should do more to reduce the costs of healthcare to individuals = 1

Loan Forgiveness

Individuals should have to pay back all student loan debt they incurred = 0

The government should forgive all student loans = 1

Appendices to Chapter 3: Children of the Great Recession

APPENDIX 3.A. Ordered Logistic Regression Results for Government Spending

Dependent variable: *Indicate your preference: Cutting government spending is the only way to improve our economic outlook (coded 1); a policy in-between (coded 2); more government spending is needed to alleviate economic hardships Americans are suffering (coded 3).*

Millennial	−0.114
	(0.107)
Latino	−0.175
	(0.169)
African American	0.107
	(0.167)
Foreign relatives	0.062
	(0.108)
Republican	−1.780**
	(0.124)
Cosmopolitan identity	0.025
	(0.018)
Education	0.183**
	(0.039)
Income	−0.025
	(0.018)
Female	0.033
	(0.106)
Constant cut1	0.201
	(0.259)
Constant cut2	1.696**
	(0.264)
N	1,528
Pseudo R^2	0.10

Notes: Ordered logistic regression estimated. Coefficients reported with standard errors in parentheses. Statistical significance denoted as ** $p<0.01$ and * $p<0.05$.

APPENDIX 3.B.   Ordered Logistic Regression Results for
Minimum Wage

Dependent variable: *How much do you support or are likely to support the following federal government policy? Mandate for increased minimum wage. Responses coded: 1 = none, 2 = a little or some, and 3 = a lot.*

Millennial	−0.108
	(0.140)
Latino	0.094
	(0.177)
African American	0.910**
	(0.229)
Foreign born	0.404
	(0.221)
Liberal ideology	0.608**
	(0.155)
Unemployed	−0.291
	(0.153)
Negative economic outlook	−0.519**
	(0.145)
Positive government worldview	0.800**
	(0.079)
Education	−0.105*
	(0.050)
Income	−0.216**
	(0.052)
Female	0.287*
	(0.143)
Married	0.089
	(0.146)
Constant cut1	−3.562**
	(0.355)
Constant cut2	−0.976**
	(0.329)
N	1,035
F-value	18.19
Prob > F	0.0000

Notes: Ordered logistic regression estimated. Coefficients reported with standard errors in parentheses. Statistical significance denoted as ** $p<0.01$ and * $p<0.05$

APPENDIX 3.C.   Logistic Regression Results for Social Security Reform

Dependent variable: *For the following pair statements, select the one that most closely aligns (agrees) with your personal opinion. Making some changes to Social Security will ensure retirement for everyone (coded 0). Overhaul of our Social Security program is needed (coded 1).*

Millennial	0.257
	(0.138)
Latino	−0.130
	(0.190)
African American	0.309
	(0.216)
Foreign born	0.138
	(0.256)
Liberal ideology	−0.047
	(0.160)
Unemployed	−0.245
	(0.158)
Negative economic outlook	0.232
	(0.148)
Positive government worldview	−0.353**
	(0.078)
Education	0.016
	(0.054)
Income	0.105
	(0.055)
Female	−0.102
	(0.148)
Married	−0.261
	(0.151)
Constant cut1	0.958**
	(0.326)
N	1,032
F-value	3.56
Prob > F	0.0000

Notes: Logit regression estimated. Coefficients reported with standard errors in parentheses. Statistical significance denoted as ** $p<0.01$ and * $p<0.05$.

APPENDIX 3.D.   Ordered Logistic Regression Results for Healthcare Cost

Dependent variable: *Indicate your preference: The government should do more to make healthcare affordable (coded 1); a policy in-between (coded 2); the government should leave it up to the free market to determine healthcare costs (coded 3).*

Millennial	−0.024
	(0.105)
Latino	−0.232
	(0.171)
African American	−0.199
	(0.176)
Foreign relatives	0.104
	(0.106)
Republican	1.908**
	(0.121)
Cosmopolitan identity	−0.077**
	(0.017)
Education	−0.092*
	(0.037)
Income	0.052**
	(0.018)
Female	−0.169
	(0.104)
Constant cut1	−0.537*
	(0.255)
Constant cut2	1.966**
	(0.263)
N	1,530
Pseudo R^2	0.13

Notes: Ordered logistic regression estimated. Coefficients reported with standard errors in parentheses. Statistical significance denoted as ** $p<0.01$ and * $p<0.05$

Appendices to Chapter 4: Moving on Up?

APPENDIX 4.A. Logistic Regression of Attitudes about Standardized Testing

Dependent variable: *Negative attitudes about standardized testing*
(0 = standardized testing ensures uniform education outcomes;
1 = standardized testing impairs teaching and learning)

Millennial	0.325*
	(0.140)
Latino	−0.210
	(0.186)
African American	−0.613**
	(0.214)
Foreign born	−0.806**
	(0.271)
Liberal ideology	0.480**
	(0.159)
Unemployed	−0.080
	(0.156)
Negative economic outlook	0.402**
	(0.146)
Positive government worldview	−0.022*
	(0.074)
Education	0.183**
	(0.053)
Income	0.080
	(0.054)
Female	0.517**
	(0.149)
Married	−0.132
	(0.152)
Constant	1.271
	(0.336)
N	1,034
F-value	5.45
Prob > F	0.000

Note: Logit regression estimated with robust standard errors. Coefficients reported with standard errors in parentheses. Statistical significance denoted as ** $p<0.01$ and * $p<0.05$.

APPENDIX 4.B.   Logistic Regression of Interactions between Millennial
Generation and Factors Influencing Attitudes about Student Loan Forgiveness

Dependent Variable: *Support for student loan forgiveness (0 = individuals should have to pay back all student loan debt; 1 = the government should forgive all student loans)*

	Coefficient	Standard Error
Millennial	1.243**	(0.357)
Latino	0.473	(0.266)
Latino*Millennial	0.266	(0.353)
African American	0.747**	(0.268)
African American*Millennial	−0.093	(0.393)
Foreign relatives	0.079	(0.354)
Foreign relatives*Millennial	−0.225	(0.476)
Liberal ideology	0.363	(0.217)
Liberal ideology*Millennial	0.092	(0.300)
Unemployed	−0.281	(0.195)
Unemployed*Millennial	0.534	(0.290)
Negative economic outlook	0.251	(0.204)
Negative economic outlook*Millennial	−0.453	(0.292)
Government spending	0.159	(0.212)
Government spending*Millennial	−0.164	(0.300)
Healthcare coverage	0.275	(0.215)
Healthcare coverage*Millennial	−0.171	(0.296)
Healthcare cost	0.732**	(0.228)
Healthcare cost*Millennial	−0.579	(0.320)
Education	−0.020	(0.054)
Income	−0.135*	(0.053)
Female	−0.000	(0.150)
Married	0.039	(0.151)
Constant	−0.786*	(0.385)
N	1,035	
F	4.410	
Prob > F	0.000	

Note: Logit regression estimated with robust standard errors. Coefficients reported with standard errors in parentheses. Statistical significance denoted as **p<0.01 and *p<0.05.

Appendix to Chapter 5:
The 9/11 Generation

APPENDIX 5.A Ordered Logistic Regression for Foreign Policy Preferences

Dependent Variable: *Preferred method for solving international conflict*
(1 = dove, 2 = mixed, 3 = hawk)

	Coefficient	Standard Error
Millennial	0.236	(0.392)
Latino	0.428	(0.341)
Latino*Millennial	−0.730	(0.405)
African American	0.478	(0.319)
African American*Millennial	−0.242	(0.393)
Foreign relatives	−0.021	(0.167)
Foreign relatives*Millennial	−0.278	(0.226)
Republican	1.542**	(0.170)
Republican*Millennial	−0.329	(0.227)
Cosmopolitan identity (1)	0.034	(0.415)
Cosmopolitan identity (2)	−0.956*	(0.425)
Cosmopolitan identity (3)	0.027	(0.470)
Cosmopolitan identity (4)	−0.347	(0.376)
Cosmopolitan identity (5)	−0.574*	(0.284)
Cosmopolitan identity (6)	−0.380	(0.342)
Cosmopolitan identity (7)	−0.850**	(0.321)
Cosmopolitan identity (8)	−0.489	(0.316)
Cosmopolitan identity (9)	−1.416**	(0.408)
Cosmopolitan identity (10)	−0.736**	(0.273)
Cosmopolitan identity (1)*Millennial	0.174	(0.857)
Cosmopolitan identity (2)*Millennial	0.859	(0.671)
Cosmopolitan identity (3)*Millennial	−0.771	(0.688)
Cosmopolitan identity (4)*Millennial	0.885	(0.618)
Cosmopolitan identity (5)*Millennial	0.335	(0.450)
Cosmopolitan identity (6)*Millennial	−0.487	(0.517)
Cosmopolitan identity (7)*Millennial	−0.138	(0.483)
Cosmopolitan identity (8)*Millennial	−0.527	(0.480)
Cosmopolitan identity (9)*Millennial	0.622	(0.574)
Cosmopolitan identity (10)*Millennial	−0.258	(0.431)
Education	−0.229**	(0.040)
Income	−0.000	(0.019)
Female	0.159	(0.110)
Constant cut1	−0.804**	(0.316)
Constant cut2	1.192**	(0.317)
N	1,524	
Pseudo R^2	0.099	

Notes: Ordered logistic regression estimated. Coefficients reported with standard errors in parentheses. Statistical significance denoted as ** $p<0.01$ and * $p<0.05$.

Appendices to Chapter 6: The Melted Pot

APPENDIX 6.A. Linear Regression of Millennial Generation Immigration Intolerance

Dependent variable: *Immigration intolerance factor score*	
Latino	−0.360**
	(0.102)
African American	−0.066
	(0.133)
Foreign born	−0.308*
	(0.139)
Liberal ideology	−0.406**
	(0.092)
Unemployed	0.113
	(0.101)
Negative economic outlook	−0.112
	(0.087)
Positive government worldview	−0.076
	(0.048)
Education	−0.087*
	(0.036)
Income	0.072*
	(0.032)
Female	−0.033
	(0.092)
Married	−0.004
	(0.087)
Constant	0.439*
	(0.191)
N	481
R^2	0.127

Note: Linear regression estimated with robust standard errors. Coefficients reported with standard errors in parentheses. Statistical significance denoted as ** $p<0.01$ and * $p<0.05$. Sample restricted to Millennial Generation observations.

APPENDIX 6.B. Logistic Regression of Millennial Generation Support for Immigration Reform

Dependent variable: *Support for immigration reform to reduce the number of newcomers into the United States (1 = yes; 0 = no)*

Latino	−0.445
	(0.232)
African American	0.114
	(0.295)
Foreign born	−0.108
	(0.318)
Liberal ideology	−0.891**
	(0.206)
Unemployed	0.162
	(0.226)
Negative economic outlook	0.322
	(0.199)
Positive government worldview	−0.074
	(0.108)
Education	−0.073
	(0.083)
Income	0.179*
	(0.076)
Female	−0.269
	(0.207)
Married	0.025
	(0.202)
Constant	0.398
	(0.448)
N	482
Pseudo R^2	0.068

Note: Logistic regression estimated. Coefficients reported with standard errors in parentheses. Statistical significance denoted as ** $p<0.01$ and * $p<0.05$. Sample restricted to Millennial Generation observations.

Appendices to Chapter 7: Millennials to the Rescue?

APPENDIX 7.A.   Ordered Logit Regression Results for Evidence of Global Warming

Dependent variable: *From what you've read and heard, is there solid evidence of global warming and climate change, or not? 1 = no solid evidence; 2 = some/mixed evidence; 3 = yes solid evidence*

Millennial	0.079
	(0.136)
Latino	−0.045
	(0.174)
African American	−0.208
	(0.212)
Foreign born	−0.192
	(0.233)
Liberal ideology	0.903**
	(0.158)
Born again Christian	−0.609**
	(0.142)
Unemployed	−0.172
	(0.152)
Negative economic outlook	−0.518**
	(0.147)
Positive government worldview	0.657**
	(0.078)
Education	0.004
	(0.054)
Income	0.030
	(0.051)
Female	0.058
	(0.140)
Married	0.129
	(0.147)
Constant cut1	−2.465**
	(0.355)
Constant cut2	0.062
	(0.338)
N	1,035
F-value	13.52
Prob > F	0.000

Notes: Ordered logistic analysis estimated with survey weights to correct for Millennial oversample. Coefficients reported with standard errors in parentheses. Statistical significance denoted as: ** $p<0.01$ and * $p<0.05$.

APPENDIX 7.B.   Logistic Regression Results for Global Warming Cause

Dependent variable: *What do you think? The earth is getting warmer mostly because of . . . natural patterns in the Earth's environment (coded 0) or human activities such as burning (coded 1).*

Millennial	0.321*
	(0.148)
Latino	0.113
	(0.195)
African American	0.075
	(0.222)
Foreign born	0.579*
	(0.283)
Liberal ideology	0.533**
	(0.165)
Born again Christian	−0.112
	(0.162)
Unemployed	0.009
	(0.164)
Negative economic outlook	−0.070
	(0.155)
Positive government worldview	0.396**
	(0.083)
Education	0.078
	(0.058)
Income	−0.015
	(0.057)
Female	−0.326*
	(0.157)
Married	0.106
	(0.160)
Constant	−0.268
	(0.357)
N	917
F-value	5.01
Prob > F	0.000

Notes: Logistic analysis estimated with survey weights to correct for Millennial oversample. Coefficients reported with standard errors in parentheses. Statistical significance denoted as ** $p<0.01$ and * $p<0.05$

Appendices to Chapter 8: Their Own Brand of Liberal

APPENDIX 8.A.   Ordered Logit Regression Results for Gun Control

Dependent variable: *How much do you support or are likely to support the following federal government policy? Requirement for background checks and waiting periods before purchase of a gun. Possible responses: none (coded 1), a little (coded 2), some (coded 3), and a lot (coded 4).*

Millennial	−0.595**
	(0.149)
Latino	0.123
	(0.191)
African American	0.259
	(0.254)
Foreign born	0.304
	(0.271)
Liberal ideology	0.742**
	(0.172)
Unemployed	0.530**
	(0.176)
Negative economic outlook	0.188
	(0.148)
Positive government worldview	0.557**
	(0.087)
Education	−0.067
	(0.059)
Income	0.031
	(0.057)
Female	0.596**
	(0.153)
Married	0.275
	(0.157)
Constant cut1	−2.782**
	(0.411)
Constant cut2	−1.601**
	(0.390)
Constant cut3	−0.269
	(0.375)
N	1,035
F-value	12.71
Prob > F	0.0000

Notes: Ordered logit regression estimated. Coefficients reported with standard errors in parentheses. Statistical significance denoted as ** $p<0.01$ and * $p<0.05$.

APPENDIX 8.B.   Ordered Logit Regression Results for Legalization
of Marijuana

Dependent variable: *How much do you support or are likely to support the following federal government policy? Marijuana for recreational use by adults. Possible responses: none (coded 1), a little (coded 2), some (coded 3), and a lot (coded 4).*

Millennial	0.382**
	(0.121)
Latino	0.024
	(0.170)
African American	0.001
	(0.199)
Foreign born	−0.389
	(0.217)
Liberal ideology	0.535**
	(0.133)
Unemployed	−0.403**
	(0.138)
Negative economic outlook	−0.304*
	(0.123)
Positive government worldview	0.274**
	(0.068)
Education	−0.103*
	(0.047)
Income	−0.005
	(0.048)
Female	−0.125
	(0.129)
Married	−0.160
	(0.135)
Constant cut1	−1.779**
	(0.289)
Constant cut2	−1.098**
	(0.287)
Constant cut3	−0.025
	(0.286)
N	1,035
F-value	7.11
Prob > F	0.0000

Notes: Ordered logit regression estimated. Coefficients reported with standard errors in parentheses. Statistical significance denoted as ** $p < 0.01$ and * $p < 0.05$.

APPENDIX 8.C.   Ordered Logit Regression Results for Right to Abortion

Dependent variable: *How much do you support or are likely to support the following federal government policy? Women's right to an abortion. Possible responses: none (coded 1), a little (coded 2), some (coded 3), and a lot (coded 4).*

Millennial	−0.166
	(0.129)
Latino	−0.123
	(0.170)
African American	0.215
	(0.199)
Foreign born	−0.607**
	(0.208)
Liberal ideology	1.271**
	(0.141)
Unemployed	−0.014
	(0.140)
Negative economic outlook	−0.066
	(0.129)
Positive government worldview	0.332**
	(0.069)
Education	−0.065
	(0.048)
Income	0.206**
	(0.050)
Female	0.486**
	(0.137)
Married	−0.290*
	(0.136)
Constant cut1	−0.868**
	(0.292)
Constant cut2	0.005
	(0.288)
Constant cut3	1.021**
	(0.287)
N	1,035
F-value	13.89
Prob > F	0.0000

Notes: Ordered logit regression estimated. Coefficients reported with standard errors in parentheses. Statistical significance denoted as ** $p < 0.01$ and * $p < 0.05$

Appendices to Chapter 9: A Force in Waiting?

APPENDIX 9.A. Variable Coding for Political Engagement Analysis

Variable	Survey Question	Coding	Survey Source
Millennial	What year were you born?	1 = born 1980–1997 0 = born before 1980	Original survey, 2015
Millennial	What year were you born?	1 = born 1980–1998 0 = born before 1980	Original survey, 2016
White	What is your race?	1 = white 0 = other	Original survey, 2015 Original survey, 2016
Latino	Are you of Hispanic or Latino background?	1 = yes 0 = no	Original survey, 2015 Original survey, 2016
African American	What is your race?	1 = African American 0 = other	Original survey, 2015 Original survey, 2016
Liberal ideology	Here is a 7-point scale on which the political views that people might hold are arranged from extremely liberal to extremely conservative. Where would you place yourself on this scale or haven't you thought much about this?	1 = liberal (1–3: extremely liberal, liberal, and slightly liberal) 0 = non-liberal (4–7: moderate, slightly conservative, conservative, and extremely conservative)	Original survey, 2015 Original survey, 2016
Positive government worldview	For the following pair of statements, select the one that most closely aligns (agrees) with your personal opinion. 1) Cutting government spending is the only way to change our economic outlook OR more government spending is needed to alleviate the economic hardships Americans are suffering; 2) Healthcare coverage is best left up to individuals to decide OR the government should require that all individuals have healthcare; 3) The government should leave it up to the free market to determine healthcare costs OR the government should do more to reduce the costs of healthcare to individuals; 4) Individuals should have to pay back all the student loan debt they incurred OR the government should forgive all student loans.	factor score where higher values indicate greater belief in the positive role of government	Original survey, 2015
Cosmopolitan identity	In terms of what's important about you, how much do you identify with being a citizen of the world?	0 "not at all" to 10 "very strongly"	Original survey, 2016
Unemployed	Are you currently employed?	1 = no 0 = work part or full-time	Original survey, 2015 Original survey, 2016

Variable	Question	Response coding	Source
Negative economic outlook	Thinking about the national economy, do you believe our country is better or worse off than it was twenty years ago for people of your age?	1 = worse 2 = about the same or better	Original survey, 2015 Original survey, 2016
Political party affiliation	Do you consider yourself a Republican, Democrat or Independent?	1 = Republican 2 = Democrat 3 = Independent 4 = Other (type in response) 5 = I do not consider myself part of any party.	Original survey, 2015
Party affiliation strength	Move the following scale to indicate how strongly do you feel like you belong to a political party. Higher numbers indicate more strongly. A 0 indicates "not at all", a 50 means "neutral", and a 100 represents "extremely belong".	0 = not at all 50 = neutral 100 = extremely belong	Original survey, 2015
Registered to vote	Are you registered to vote?	0 = no 1 = yes . = I don't know.	Original survey, 2015
Vote in past four years	Have you voted in elections in the past four years?	0 = no 1 = yes . = I don't know.	Original survey, 2015
Political change	In your opinion which of the following brings about the most political change?	1 = voting 2 = petitioning or protesting an issue 3 = contacting an elected official or politician through traditional means 4 = contacting an elected official or politician through email or social media 5 = meeting with local groups	Original survey, 2015
Feel engaged	Do you feel like you are engaged in the political system or politics?	1 = no 2 = somewhat 3 = yes	Original survey, 2015
Politically engaged	Do you feel like you are engaged in the political system or politics?	0 = no or somewhat 1 = yes	Original survey, 2015
Be more engaged	What would it take to make you more engaged in the political system or politics?	open-ended response	Original survey, 2015

(Continued)

APPENDIX 9.A. (Continued)

Variable	Survey Question	Coding	Survey Source
Source political information	Where do you get most of your political information and news?	1 = network and cable TV news programs 2 = newspapers - print or online 3 = social media - for example Twitter and Facebook 4 = Discussions with friends and family 5 = radio news programs	Original survey, 2015
Voter turnout	In talking to people about elections, we often find that a lot of people weren't able to vote because they weren't registered, they were sick, or they just didn't have the time. Which of the following statements best describes you?	0 = I did not vote (in the election this November); OR I thought about voting this time, but didn't; OR I usually vote, but didn't this time; or 1 = I voted in this year's election.	Original survey, 2016
Reason for not voting	What was the biggest reason you did not vote?	1 = I could not support any of the presidential candidates. 2 = I did not feel like the election process was fair. 3 = I did not feel like my vote would matter to the outcome of the election. 4 = I did not have the required documents such as voter registration and/or identification card. 5 = I could not make it to the polls—did not have time, was sick, or something came up. 6 = I just did not care.	Original survey, 2016
Presidential vote choice	Which presidential candidate did you vote for?	1 = Donald Trump 2 = Hillary Clinton 3 = Jill Stein 4 = Gary Johnson 5 = Other candidate (write in response) 6 = I did not vote for a presidential candidate, although I voted for other offices.	Original survey, 2016
Reasons for candidate choice: political party	Rate the following reasons behind your choice for president. I chose my candidate for president because . . . I am loyal to my political party.	1 = not at all important 2 = slightly important 3 = moderately important 4 = very important 5 = extremely important	Original survey, 2016

Reasons for candidate choice: policies	Rate the following reasons behind your choice for president. I chose my candidate for president because . . . I agree with my candidate's proposed policies.	1 = not at all important 2 = slightly important 3 = moderately important 4 = very important 5 = extremely important	Original survey, 2016
Reasons for candidate choice: opposition	Rate the following reasons behind your choice for president. I chose my candidate for president because . . . I strongly opposed the other candidate(s).	1 = not at all important 2 = slightly important 3 = moderately important 4 = very important 5 = extremely important	Original survey, 2016
Reasons for candidate choice: trust	Rate the following reasons behind your choice for president. I chose my candidate for president because . . . I trust my candidate.	1 = not at all important 2 = slightly important 3 = moderately important 4 = very important 5 = extremely important	Original survey, 2016
Reasons for candidate choice: care	Rate the following reasons behind your choice for president. I chose my candidate for president because . . . My candidate cares about people like me.	1 = not at all important 2 = slightly important 3 = moderately important 4 = very important 5 = extremely important	Original survey, 2016
Political change	How much do you want significant change to American political system?	1 = not at all 2 = somewhat 3 = very much	Original survey, 2016
Economic change	How much do you want significant change to American economic system?	1 = not at all 2 = somewhat 3 = very much	Original survey, 2016
System rigged	How much do you agree with this statement? Our system is rigged against people like me.	1 = strongly disagree 2 = somewhat disagree 3 = somewhat agree 4 = strongly agree	Original survey, 2016

Appendix 9.B: Qualitative Analysis of Political Engagement

Survey participants were asked—"Do you feel like you are engaged in the political system or politics?" Those who responded "no" or "somewhat" were asked the follow-up question—"What would it take to make you more engaged in the political system or politics?" The responses were open ended and coded by the authors into common themes. The responses coalesced around ten themes: 1) address transaction costs of political participation; 2) better political representation, representatives, and outcomes; 3) different or improved political institutions or systems; 4) feel like I make a difference in the political system; 5) greater relevance of politics to me; 6) improved information and understanding of political system and politics; 7) improved interest in politics and political system; 8) more trust, honesty, and accountability of politicians, less politics; 9) nothing, not interested, or not applicable; and 10) not sure or don't know. Some of the themes included sub-categories, shown in the table. Some observations (i.e., individual open-ended response) included more than one theme; in these cases, the observation was counted toward all themes mentioned. For example, the response "better candidates, more discussion on issues that I care about (like healthcare)" is coded as "better representatives" *and* "greater relevance of politics to me."

APPENDIX 9.B. Political Engagement Analysis: Emergent Themes

Themes with Sub-Categories	Millennial	Non-Mill.
1) Address transaction costs of political participation	28	29
actually participate	6	4
more incentives or motivation to participate	5	8
more opportunity, less barriers	8	8
more time—I'm too busy.	9	9
2) Better political representation, representatives, & outcomes	58	83
better outcomes or changes	9	10
better political candidates, representatives, leaders	38	54
better representation	11	19
3) Different or improved political institutions or systems	18	19
improved political institutions or systems	12	14
less money involved	6	5
4) Feel like I make a difference in the political system	21	11
5) Greater relevance of politics to me	40	27
more attention to specific issues	19	12
domestic issues	0	2
drug legalization	2	1
economy	11	3
environment	0	1
gay marriage	1	0
healthcare	2	1
housing	0	1
less violence	1	0
security/terrorism	1	2
veterans	1	1
greater relevance of issues or politicians	21	15
6) Improved information & understanding of political system	39	26
less media bias	4	3
make easier to get information and understand system	5	0
more information and or understanding	30	23
7) Improved interest in politics and political system	28	22
I'm just not interested and or don't care about politics.	12	17
make politics more interesting	14	1
motivation by drastic event or timing of election	2	4
8) More trust, honesty, and accountability of politicians, less politics	49	70
less political divisions	13	23
more accessibility	2	5
more trust, honesty and accountability (less corruption)	34	42
9) Not sure or don't know	60	60
10) Nothing, not interested, or not applicable	60	81
not applicable	10	5
Observations	401	428

Notes

Chapter 1

1. From "The Real Reason Millennials Love Bernie Sanders" in *Time* magazine, April 19, 2016.

2. Also known as Generation Y, Generation Me, and the iGeneration.

3. It is important to note that there is some disagreement about when a generation begins and ends. However, most generational scholars, social scientists, and popular authors agree that this time period largely encompasses the Millennial Generation (Straus and Howe 2000; P. Taylor 2014; Dalton 2016). As such, in our study, we designate Millennials as those born in 1981–1997. This aligns with the conventions adopted by the Pew Research Center (Fry 2016a).

4. We use the terms "Latino" and "Hispanic" interchangeably in this book.

5. From: Santhanam, Laura. 2015. "Here's why it's so hard to figure out how Millennials feel about racism." March 19. PBS Newshour. http://www.pbs.org/newshour/updates/data-reveal-complex-millennial-attitudes-race/

6. This reference is used to emphasize the importance of social media in the formative experiences of Millennials; it is not meant to suggest that all Millennials experienced this particular event.

7. Based on preliminary data from national exit polls about Millennial voter turnout in the 2016 election, the pattern for this cohort voting at higher rates at similar age than the previous generation seems to hold (even though Millennial turnout slightly decreased for this cycle) (The Center for Information and Research on Civic Learning and Engagement [CIRCLE] 2016).

8. This is also known as "period effect"—events (e.g. war) that simultaneously influence everyone, regardless of age (Dinas and Stoker 2014).

Chapter 2

1. Given the scope of this study, which includes in-depth analyses of multiple political issues, it is simply out of the purview of this book to analyze specific, older generations. We do, however, occasionally refer to data, typically provided by the Pew Research Center,

highlighting trends in attitudes across Millennials and older generations (e.g., Generation X, Baby Boomers, and Silent Generation). When presenting this information, we make clear the source and the birth years assigned to the generations (per the source).

2. This is an electronic book without page numbers (and not available in print format); therefore, we reference location of the quote.

3. According to a Qualtrics representative that we worked with to develop the survey, Qualtrics partners with numerous panel providers that have proprietary panels across the nation. Qualtrics endeavors to improve the quality and representative nature of its online sample by incorporating participants from online communities, social networks, and websites of all types. This is accomplished by going beyond the simple "river" approach to recruiting; participants are invited via banners, invitations, and messaging of all types but also go through rigorous quality controls before being included in any sample. Regarding participant incentives—Qualtrics offers a variety of incentives to increase the diversity of sample frames. Some people are motivated by cash, points, prizes, or sweepstakes or by being able to donate to charity; others are motivated by the chance to make a difference, learn or receive information, make their voice heard, have fun taking a survey, or help out. Qualtrics aims to respond to all of these individual motivations in order to provide a sample that is diverse and as representative as possible. Rewards offered may vary by survey length and the characteristics of the population targeted. Qualtrics uses a reasonable level of reward based on the amount of effort required.

4. In particular, we acknowledge that the sample we have drawn may be comprised of those who are more civically engaged (Kennedy et al. 2016). This will make findings of disengagement and disconnection from politics even more compelling.

5. We also used Indeed.com in Washington, D.C and placed an online advertisement in the New Orleans newspaper, the Times-Picayune. We assume there was some word-of-mouth advertising among interested participants.

6. This analysis predominantly focuses on conceptual analysis. Given the scope of the book, it is not possible to fully flesh out the relationships between themes identified. We hope that this analysis, however, may provide ample support for theory development in future studies.

7. See Hutchinson, et al. (2010) for a discussion of the utility of QSR-NVivo for qualitative analysis from a grounded theory perspective.

Chapter 3

1. The Millennial Generation refers to adults (aged 18 years and older) born in the early 1980s to the early 2000s. Specifically, this chapter's analyses include the birth year range of 1980–1998.

2. This dynamic is discussed further in Chapter 4, which focuses on education.

3. According to Business Cycle Dating Committee of the National Bureau of Economic Research, these are the official years on record of the most recent economic recession (Rampbell 2010). The aftershocks were felt for years to come, with unemployment peaking in 2010 (DeSilver 2015).

4. In 2010, Millennials, born 1980 and after, were 18–30 years old. Because of the way the Bureau of Labor Statistics aggregates data in age ranges, we cut off Millennials at age 29 years for reporting this specific statistic.

5. Unemployment rates were calculated using quarterly data, unadjusted seasonally, on total civilian labor force and number unemployed for each age category (18–29 years for Millennials and thirty years and older for Non-Millennials).

6. We recognize that Millennials, born 1980 and later, were not as old as 34 years across many of the years shown in the graph. However, we aggregate across these age groups based on the available data, clustered by age ranges. This also ensures we err on the side of caution as the figures are more conservative (show lower unemployment rates) with the inclusion of adults into their early thirties in the Millennial category. Moreover, this makes the statistics on recent years relevant to our discussion of Millennials as we have defined this age cohort as those aged 18–35 years in our study.

7. The survey was nationally representative and oversampled Millennials. See Chapter 2 for more details on the survey sample and methodology.

8. Our original survey is used to explore minimum wage and Social Security reform opinions; we use the Nielsen survey for data on government spending and healthcare costs attitudes. Our original survey asks a question about healthcare costs but presents the respondent with a dichotomous option. The Nielsen survey provides an ordinal response, and, therefore, provides greater variation to examine. Given this, we rely on the Nielsen survey for healthcare cost opinions.

9. We rely on data from two surveys in this chapter: 1) our original survey, conducted in 2015 and 2) the Nielsen survey, conducted in 2016. Our original survey codes Millennial as an individual born from 1980–1997. The Nielsen survey codes Millennials from age ranges and considers those 18–34 years to be Millennials (birth years 1982–1998).

10. See Chapter 2 for details on variable coding.

11. Given that our original survey and the Nielsen survey did not ask identical questions, the models for each are somewhat different. The model for the Nielsen survey analyses of government spending and healthcare cost includes the following independent variables: Millennial Generation, Latino, African American, foreign relatives, Republican, cosmopolitan identity, education, income, and gender. The model using data from our original survey for the analyses of minimum wage increases and Social Security reform include the following independent variables: Millennial Generation, Latino, African American, foreign born, liberal political ideology, unemployed, negative economic outlook, positive government worldview, education, income, gender, and marital status. See Chapter 2 the coding rationale of these variables.

12. See Online Appendices, available at https://doi.org/10.3998/mpub.9526877.fulcrum (Chapter 3, Appendix A) for the difference of means test results of government spending.

13. Foreign relatives are identified as those that live outside of the United States.

14. See Appendix 3.A for the results of this regression estimation.

15. See Online Appendices, available at https://doi.org/10.3998/mpub.9526877.fulcrum (Chapter 3, Appendix B) for a regression table reporting the results of analysis of government spending.

16. See Online Appendices, available at https://doi.org/10.3998/mpub.9526877.fulcrum (Chapter 3, Appendix C) for a figure depicting attitudes about government spending across race/ethnic groups.

17. See Online Appendices, available at https://doi.org/10.3998/mpub.9526877.fulcrum (Chapter 3, Appendix D) for the results of the difference of means test of minimum wage preferences.

18. See Appendix 3.B for a table of the regression results.

19. All predicted probabilities discussed in this chapter were estimated while holding all other variables in the model at their mean value.

20. See Online Appendices, available at https://doi.org/10.3998/mpub.9526877. fulcrum (Chapter 3, Appendix E) for a regression table reporting the results of analysis of minimum wage beliefs.

21. See Online Appendices, available at https://doi.org/10.3998/mpub.9526877. fulcrum (Chapter 3, Appendix F) for the results of the difference of means test for social security reform preferences.

22. See Appendix 3.C for a table of the regression results.

23. A logit model was estimated including the following variables: Millennial, Latino, African American, foreign born, liberal, unemployed, negative economic outlook, positive government worldview, education, income, female, and being married.

24. See Online Appendices, available at https://doi.org/10.3998/mpub.9526877. fulcrum (Chapter 3, Appendix G) for the regression results of the interaction model of social security reform.

25. For a table of these regression results with the sample restricted to Millennials, see Online Appendices, available at https://doi.org/10.3998/mpub.9526877.fulcrum (Chapter 3, Appendix H).

26. See Online Appendices, available at https://doi.org/10.3998/mpub.9526877. fulcrum (Chapter 3, Appendix I) for the results of the difference of means test of healthcare cost preferences.

27. For a table of the regression results, see Appendix 3.D.

28. The variables interacted with Millennial in the model were: Latino, African American, having foreign relatives, Republican Party affiliation, and cosmopolitan identity. Control variables included: education, income, and female.

29. See Online Appendices available at https://doi.org/10.3998/mpub.9526877.fulcrum, (Chapter 3, Appendix J) for a table of regression results including interactions for healthcare cost preferences.

30. Millennials, in comparison to non-Millennials, are more likely to favor a mixed policy when it comes to healthcare costs. The significant ($p<0.05$) marginal effect contrasts for this finding include: 5.04% among non-Latinos; 5.20% among non-African Americans; 5.07% among those without foreign relatives; 4.82% among non-Republicans; 4.95% among Republicans; and 5.05% among those with no cosmopolitan identity.

31. This area of study is ripe for future work that employs data specifically designed to capture the interconnections of economic stances and trust in traditional institutions. Unfortunately, this is beyond the scope of our analysis as our survey did not ask respondents their opinion of traditional institutions, including financial organizations such as Wall Street.

Chapter 4

1. Transcript of Bernie Sanders speech formally announcing his candidacy for the Democratic presidential nomination on May 26, 2015 (https://berniesanders.com/bernies-announcement/).

2. The Millennial Generation refers to adults (aged 18 years and older) born in the early 1980s to the early 2000s. Specifically, in the analyses of this chapter, the range of birth years is 1980–1997.

3. The Bureau of Labor Statistics (2012) marked the beginning of the recession as December 2007 and the end of the recession in June 2009.

4. According to the "Kids Count" data center from the Annie E. Casey Foundation, in 2015, 36% of African American children and 31% of Latino children lived in poverty, compared to 12% of non-Hispanic white children. Information can be found at: http://datacenter.kidscount.org/data/tables/44-children-in-poverty-by-race-and-ethnicity#detailed/1/any/false/573,869,36,868,867/10,11,9,12,1,185,13/324,323

5. According to National Center for Education Statistics (NCES), the characteristics for defining non-traditional students are not finite and continue to evolve.

6. See Chapter 2 for more information on Millennial and non-Millennial issue ranks.

7. See Online Appendices, available at https://doi.org/10.3998/mpub.9526877. fulcrum for distribution of responses on the importance of education to presidential vote (Chapter 4, Appendix A).

8. The results for the difference of mean test can be found in the Online Appendices, available at https://doi.org/10.3998/mpub.9526877.fulcrum (Chapter 4, Appendix B1).

9. A similar percentage of white (71%), African American (69%), and Latino (77%) Millennials believe that higher education needs to be reformed.

10. See Chapter 2 for more details on the coding of variables in the model.

11. The correlation between attitudes about standardized testing and student loan forgiveness (a component of the worldview factor score) is statistically significant at the $p<0.05$ level. However, the correlation is low (0.059), and the correlation between standardized testing and worldview is even lower (0.016).

12. See Appendix 4.A for a table of the ordered logistic regression results.

13. In calculating predicted probabilities for all analyses in the chapter, all other variables (except the variable of interest) are held at their mean value.

14. The predicted probability of an individual with a less than high school education having a negative attitude about standardized testing is 43.7%, while someone with a professional or doctorate degree has a 72.8% likelihood. An individual with a less than $20,000 annual income has a 55% likelihood of viewing standardized testing negatively, while an individual with a more than $100,000 income has a 64.6% of the same. Females have a 65.9% likelihood of saying standardized testing impairs learning, while males have a 53.6% of the same.

15. See Online Appendices, available at https://doi.org/10.3998/mpub.9526877.fulcrum for the results of the difference of means test between Millennials and non-Millennials on student loan forgiveness attitudes (Chapter 4, Appendix B2).

16. Details on the measurement of independent variables can be found in Chapter 2.

17. We do not utilize the worldview factor score in the model because the score contains a variable for education. Instead, we include the remaining variables that comprised the factor score as independent measures of attitudes about government. These include measures of attitudes about: more government spending to reduce economic hardships, government requirement for all to have healthcare coverage, and government action to reduce the cost of healthcare.

18. See Appendix 4.B for the logistic regression results.

Chapter 5

1. The Millennial Generation refers to adults (aged 18 years and older) born in the early 1980s to the early 2000s. Specifically, for the analyses of this chapter, the birth year range is 1982–1998.

2. Wagaman, Andrew. 2016. "For millennials, 9/11 and its aftermath shaped their view of the world." *The Morning Call*, September 11. Available at: http://www.mcall.com/news/local/mc-911-millenials-worldview-15-years-anniversary-20160911-story.html

3. This period also coincided with the development of scientific public opinion polling that was better able to gauge American attitudes about an array of issues including foreign policy (Holsti 1992).

4. The liberal-realist distinction is not the same thing as a liberal-conservative differentiation. The former refers to a strategy for dealing with foreign policy issues and the latter refers to a political ideology. While political ideology influences how one views issues of foreign policy, there are other factors that also contribute to foreign policy views.

5. This categorization results in four options: engagement through military force, engagement through cooperation, supporting both, or supporting neither option.

6. In political science, the "critical period" has sometimes been referred to as "impressionable years" which identifies a time of openness to political leanings and attitudes.

7. In the two figures, the dots represent the mean of each variable, the solid lines extend left from the mean minus one standard deviation and right from the mean plus one standard deviation, and the dashed lines extend from the minimum to maximum values (all variables from 1 to 10).

8. See Online Appendices, available at https://doi.org/10.3998/mpub.9526877.fulcrum for the results of the difference of means test for each of the five issues (Chapter 5, Appendix A). Mann-Whitney U (Wilcoxon rank sum) tests were also conducted and confirm the results of the difference of means tests.

9. These variables were measured using survey questions that asked respondents to self-identify across these factors. See Chapter 2 for coding of the variables.

10. We utilize difference of means tests to determine statistically significant differences between female and males, as well as Republicans and non-Republicans. See Online Appendices, available at https://doi.org/10.3998/mpub.9526877.fulcrum for the summary of results on global priorities for these Millennial subgroups (Chapter 5, Appendices B and C). Mann-Whitney U (Wilcoxon rank sum) tests were also conducted and confirm the results of the difference of means tests.

11. For the race and ethnic subgroups, we utilize one-way ANOVA and Tukey post-hoc test to determine statistically significant differences between groups. See Online Appendices, available at https://doi.org/10.3998/mpub.9526877.fulcrum for the summary of ANOVA results on global priorities for Millennial subgroups (Chapter 5. Appendices D and E).

12. We utilize a difference of means Wald test to determine if a statistically significant difference exists between Millennials and non-Millennials. See Online Appendices, available at https://doi.org/10.3998/mpub.9526877.fulcrum for the summary of the results (Chapter 5, Appendix F).

13. See Appendix 5.A for a table of the ordered logistic regression results.

Chapter 6

1. The Millennial Generation refers to adults (aged 18 years and older) born in the early 1980s to the early 2000s. Specifically, in this chapter's analysis, we consider Millennials to be those adults born from 1980 to 1997.

2. See Online Appendices, available at https://doi.org/10.3998/mpub.9526877. fulcrum for mean test results (Chapter 6, Appendix A) and for the distribution of immigration tolerance factor scores (Chapter 6, Appendix B).

3. Response options included: "none," "a little," "some," and "a lot."

4. Since ANOVA analysis is not supported with the use of sample weights, we run linear regressions to obtain race/ethnic Millennial subgroup means and two sample T-tests to determine statistically significant differences between specific subgroups. See Online Appendices, available at https://doi.org/10.3998/mpub.9526877.fulcrum (Chapter 6, Appendix C) for a summary of two sample T-test results.

5. See Chapter 2 for details about the 2016 survey methodology.

6. See transcript of Trump's immigration speech delivered on August 31, 2016 in Phoenix, Arizona http://www.nytimes.com/2016/09/02/us/politics/transcript-trump-immigration-speech.html

7. For details on the measurement of all independent variables, see Chapter 2.

8. We recognize that cosmopolitan identity, too, should influence immigration attitudes and that the feeling of being a "global citizen" is likely to vary among Millennials. Unfortunately, we do not have a measure of cosmopolitan identity in this survey and instead see it has a predominant explanatory factor of the differences between Millennials and non-Millennials. Millennials are more likely to be and feel more connected to the rest of the world, and this is coupled with the decreased levels of immigration intolerance found in the analyses conducted. Certainly exploring how cosmopolitan identity varies among Millennials and how it is related to individual attitudes is a fruitful endeavor for future studies to undertake.

9. See Appendix 6.A for a table of the linear regression results.

10. All predicted probabilities discussed were calculated while holding all other variables in the model at their mean values.

11. See Appendix 6.B for a table of the logistic regression results.

12. It is beyond the scope of this book to explore the durability of Millennial Generation attitudes as this requires longitudinal data not yet available.

Chapter 7

1. The Millennial Generation refers to adults (aged 18 years and older) born in the early 1980s to the early 2000s. Specifically, in this chapter's analysis, we consider Millennials to be those adults born from 1980 to 1997.

2. See Online Appendices, available at https://doi.org/10.3998/mpub.9526877. fulcrum (Chapter 7, Appendix A) for more on how the Republican Party's stance has changed.

3. A progressive sect of the evangelical community has emerged in the past decade, focused on the disproportionate effects of environmental degradation and extreme

weather events on the poor (Wilkinson 2012). However, this group is controversial among the broader evangelical leadership community.

4. See Chapter 2 for details on survey methodology.

5. This question was asked only of those who indicated there is some/mixed or solid evidence of global warming and climate change.

6. The difference of mean tests included survey weights to account for the over-sample of Millennials. See Online Appendices, available at https://doi.org/10.3998/mpub.9526877.fulcrum (Chapter 7, Appendix B) for the results of the difference of means tests.

7. See Chapter 2 for details on the coding of variables taken from our original survey. Born again Christian is a dichotomous variable, coded "1" for those who self-identified as having these beliefs and "0" for those who did not identify as "born again."

8. Specifically, this study examined egalitarian–communitarian values versus individualistic–hierarchical values. We see the former as akin to the collectivist worldview.

9. See Chapter 2 for a discussion of the survey methodology, including sample weights.

10. See Appendix 7.A for the ordered logistic regression results of global warming evidence.

11. See Online Appendices, available at https://doi.org/10.3998/mpub.9526877.fulcrum (Chapter 7, Appendix C) for the ordered logistic analysis results of global warming evidence with interactions.

12. The p-value for this marginal effect contrast is 0.057.

13. The p-value for this marginal effect contrast is 0.078.

14. The native-born population was estimated to be 87.1% in 2010 by the US Census Bureau.

15. The p-value for this marginal effect contrast is 0.059.

16. See Appendix 7.B for the logistic analysis results of global warming cause.

17. See Online Appendices, available at https://doi.org/10.3998/mpub.9526877.fulcrum (Chapter 7, Appendix D) for the logistic analysis results of global warming cause with interactions.

18. According to our survey, 59.7% of Latinos (compared to 57.1% of non-Latinos) believe in the anthropogenic causes of global warming, and 71% of foreign-born individuals (compared to 56.3% of native-born respondents) believe the same.

19. Analyses of the interaction of Millennial with liberal ideology, race/ethnicity, and worldview confirmed this.

20. For examples, see: Pew Research Center (2015b), "Beyond Distrust: How Americans View Their Government" http://www.people-press.org/2015/11/23/beyond-distrust-how-americans-view-their-government/

21. The Paris Agreement is an agreement by 195 countries and negotiated under the direction of the United Nations Framework Convention on Climate Change that deals with the reduction of greenhouse gases emissions to certain levels, starting in the year 2020. More information about the agreement can be found at: http://unfccc.int/paris_agreement/items/9485.php

Chapter 8

1. The Millennial Generation refers to adults (aged 18 years and older) born in the early 1980s to the early 2000s. Specifically, we consider Millennials to be adults born 1980 through 1997 (with our 2015 survey) or 1998 (with our 2016 survey).

2. See Chapter 2 for more details on this original survey, including methodology and variable coding.

3. Millennials are those born in 1980–1997 (aged 18–35 years at the time of the 2015 survey); non-Millennials are those born before 1980 (age 36 years and older at the time of the survey).

4. See Chapter 1 for a full discussion of the social liberalness and tolerance of Millennials as part of their generation persona, frame, or identity. We use the term "identity" loosely—not in the same sense as ethnic or racial identity—to refer to broadly shared values and beliefs among young adults.

5. See Chapter 2 for a discussion of the methodology of this survey.

6. This includes police violence against minority individuals. See Page & Shedrofsky (2016) for recent poll data on Millennial support of the Black Lives Matters Movement, activism spurred by multiple shootings by police of unarmed African Americans.

7. In 2011, the Texas state legislature eliminated funding for any clinic associated with an abortion provider (even if the clinic itself did not perform abortions). As a result, the state's family planning budget was cut by two-thirds, and eighty-two family planning clinics have closed across the state in the past five years (Goodwyn 2016).

8. See Chapter 2 for details on the justification of this model as well as variable coding.

9. As detailed in the previous section, the survey question asked: "How much do you support or are likely to support the following federal government policy?" Multiple policies were proposed, in turn, including: "requirement for background checks and waiting periods before purchase of a gun;" "marijuana for recreational use by adults;" and "women's right to an abortion."

10. See Chapter 2 for details on the methodology of this survey.

11. Because Millennials are oversampled in this survey, the regressions estimated are weighted to correct for this.

12. See Appendices 8.A, 8.B, and 8.C for tables reporting the regression results for gun control, legalization of marijuana, and right to abortion, respectively.

13. For all predicted probabilities reported in this chapter, all other variables were held at their means.

14. Positive government worldview here refers to individuals with a factor score that is in the top 50% (top two quartiles).

15. The survey asked respondents—"Do you consider yourself a born again Christian?" Possible responses included "yes" (coded 1) or "no" (coded 0).

16. Support for abortion rights was higher among Roman Catholic respondents but slightly lower than average support among all survey respondents. Among this subgroup, 38.7% say they have "a lot" of support for women's right to abortion, while 17.8% say they have no support. Notably, fewer Millennials offered no support in comparison to their non-Millennial, Roman Catholic counterparts (7% versus 10.8% respectively).

17. See Online Appendices, available at https://doi.org/10.3998/mpub.9526877.fulcrum (Chapter 8, Appendix A) for a figure of the distribution of responses to this party strength question among Millennials and non-Millennials.

18. While our examination of social issues is far from exhaustive, results across three diverse topics indicate enough variance in Millennial attitudes to question these assertions.

Chapter 9

1. The Millennial Generation refers to adults (aged 18 years and older) born in the early 1980s to the early 2000s (specifically, in our 2015 study, the range is 1980–1997 and in our 2016 study, the range is 1980–1998), and Baby Boomers are considered to be those adults born in 1946–1964.

2. Figure 1 provides estimates for 18–24 year-old voter turnout. Actual Current Population Survey calculations show that voter turnout in 2016 among nearly the same age range, 18–29 year olds, was 43.4% (McDonald 2017).

3. Scholars have shown that the Catholic Church has served to increase political participation among Latinos, particularly since for many Latinos, it may be the only form of "associational membership" (Jones-Correa and Leal 2001), but its effects still lag behind those of black churches.

4. For a more detailed discussion of cosmopolitan identity and collectivist world-view, see Chapter 1.

5. U.S. Census Bureau data reports that voter turnout for 18–29 year olds in 1996 (Generation Xers) was 39.6% while 18–29 year olds (Millennials) in 2012 had a 45.0% turnout rate (File 2014).

6. Unfortunately, data is not available to compare Millennials to older generations at the same age; this would require similar measures of engagement, ideally on the individual level. Such data does not, to our knowledge, exist. Therefore, we evaluate Millennial engagement in relation to older adults today.

7. See Chapter 2 for a discussion of the methodology of this survey.

8. Appendix 9.A summarizes the coding of all variables analyzed in this chapter.

9. See Online Appendices, available at https://doi.org/10.3998/mpub.9526877.fulcrum (Chapter 9, Appendix A) for histogram displaying the strength of political party attachment among Millennials and non-Millennials.

10. See Online Appendices, available at https://doi.org/10.3998/mpub.9526877.fulcrum (Chapter 9, Appendix B) for the results of the difference of means test for strength of political party attachment.

11. For difference of means test results, see Online Appendices, available at https://doi.org/10.3998/mpub.9526877.fulcrum Chapter 9: Appendix C for voter registration, Appendix D for voter turnout, and Appendix E for vote intention in the next presidential election.

12. See Online Appendices, available at https://doi.org/10.3998/mpub.9526877.fulcrum (Chapter 9, Appendix F) for the difference of means test between Millennial and non-Millennial protest and petition.

13. Only slightly fewer Millennials say they are engaged than non-Millennials (29.95% versus 31.11%, respectively) and slightly more Millennials than non-Millennials say they are not engaged (25.28% versus 23.49%, respectively).

14. See Online Appendices, available at https://doi.org/10.3998/mpub.9526877.fulcrum (Chapter 9, Appendix G) for the results of a difference of means test between Millennials and non-Millennials on political engagement.

15. See Chapter 2 for more details on the coding of these measures.

16. For example: among Millennials, whites comprise 53.95% of the total group but 50.11% of the disengaged sub-sample. The difference between the two

(50.11–53.95) is -3.84%. Among Millennials, those with a negative economic outlook total 58.32% of the sample but 64.5% of the disengaged sub-sample. The difference between the two (64.5–58.32) is 6.18%. Therefore, whites are under-represented, and those with a negative economic outlook are over-represented in the disengaged sub-sample.

17. See Chapter 3 for a more detailed discussion of the effects of the Great Recession on Millennials.

18. This qualitative analysis is predominantly a conceptual analysis. Given the scope of this chapter (and the book), it is not possible to fully flesh out the relationships between the themes identified. We hope that this analysis, however, may provide ample support for theory development in future studies.

19. See Appendix 9.B for more details on the coding of these responses. Sub-categories are listed as well as notes on methodology.

20. A total of four Millennials and three non-Millennials specifically mentioned media bias and information in their responses to what it would take to make them more politically engaged.

21. While this is only a handful of responses, it is notable because no comments were made related to the ease/accessibility of information by non-Millennials.

22. These pairwise correlations are restricted to the Millennial and non-Millennial sub-samples and, therefore, no weighting is needed.

23. See Appendix 9.A for details on coding of all variables reported.

24. See Online Appendices, available at https://doi.org/10.3998/mpub.9526877. fulcrum (Chapter 9, Appendix H) for the results of the difference of means tests between Millennials and non-Millennials on voter turnout in the 2016 election.

25. For the results of difference of means tests between Millennials and non-Millennials on reasons for not voting, see Online Appendices, available at https://doi. org/10.3998/mpub.9526877.fulcrum Chapter 9: Appendix I for "could not support candidate"; Appendix J for "vote does not matter"; and Appendix K for "do not care".

26. For the results of difference of means tests between Millennials and non-Millennials on Clinton and Trump voting, see Online Appendices, available at https:// doi.org/10.3998/mpub.9526877.fulcrum (Chapter 9, Appendix L and Appendix M).

27. See Online Appendices, available at https://doi.org/10.3998/mpub.9526877. fulcrum (Chapter 9, Appendix N) for the difference of means test between Millennials and non-Millennials on third-party voting.

28. See Online Appendices, available at https://doi.org/10.3998/mpub.9526877. fulcrum (Chapter 9, Appendix O) for the results of the difference of means test between Millennials and non-Millennials in voting because they agreed with their candidate's policies.

29. See Online Appendices, available at https://doi.org/10.3998/mpub.9526877. fulcrum (Chapter 9, Appendix P) for the difference of means test results between Millennials and non-Millennials on voting against the other candidate.

30. The mean importance of opposition voting (on a 0 "not at all important" to 5 "extremely important" scale) among non-Millennials who voted for Trump is 4.44; the mean among those who did not vote for Trump is 4.18. The results of the difference of means test is reported in Online Appendices, available at https://doi.org/10.3998/ mpub.9526877.fulcrum (Chapter 9, Appendix Q).

31. See Online Appendices, available at https://doi.org/10.3998/mpub.9526877. fulcrum for the difference of means test between Trump and non-Trump Millennial supporters on opposition voting (Chapter 9, Appendix R) and for Clinton and non-Clinton supporters on opposition voting among non-Millennials and Millennials (Chapter 9, Appendices S and T).

32. Hillary Clinton ran a campaign that emphasized building on the Obama administration's accomplishments, rather than on significant change. Some would argue that this was the wrong message in a climate where many voters were looking for something different.

33. See Online Appendices, available at https://doi.org/10.3998/mpub.9526877. fulcrum (Chapter 9, Appendix U and Appendix V) for the difference of means tests between Millennials and non-Millennials on political change and economic change.

34. This question was purposefully left vague to allow respondents to interpret "system" in their own personal way. This followed a series of questions about the presidential election, so we believe respondents were primed to think about "system" with some political perspective in mind. See Appendix 2.B for the survey questionnaire and Appendix 9.A for variable coding.

35. See Online Appendices, available at https://doi.org/10.3998/mpub.9526877. fulcrum (Chapter 9, Appendix W) for the results of the difference of means test between Millennials and non-Millennials in feeling the system is rigged.

36. Details on variable coding are provided in Appendix 9.A.

37. The correlations presented in Table 9.4 are restricted to the Millennial subsample and, therefore, do not require weighting. These same correlations are not significant for non-Millennials, further demonstrating that there is a distinct race and ethnic dimension to Millennial political disengagement.

Chapter 10

1. The Millennial Generation refers to adults (aged 18 years and older) born in the early 1980s to the early 2000s. Specifically, we consider Millennials to be adults born in 1980 through 1997 (with our 2015 survey) or 1998 (with our 2016 survey).

2. See Chapter 2 for a discussion of the methodology of this survey as well as the survey questionnaire.

3. These issues are all ones Donald Trump vowed to address during the 2016 presidential campaign. Some had specific solutions such as building a wall or withdrawing from NAFTA, while others were discussed more generally like doing something about terrorism or reversing Obama-era policies that addressed climate change.

4. Speech given on April 24, 2016. Information about the speech can be found at: https://news.uchicago.edu/article/2017/04/24/obama-focuses-inspiring-next-generation-leaders-return-uchicago

References

ABC News/Washington Post. 2015. "Trump Plan Is Supported in His Party but Widely Opposed outside the GOP." *ABC News/Washington Post Poll: Trump and Muslims*. December 14. http://www.langerresearch.com/wp-content/uploads/1174a1TrumpandMuslims.pdf

Abramowitz, Alan I., and Kyle L. Saunders. 2006. "Exploring the Bases of Partisanship in the American Electorate: Social Identity vs. Ideology." *Political Research Quarterly* 59 (2): 175–87.

Adams, Bob. 2004. "Gun Control Debate: Do Gun Bans Violate Americans' Second Amendment Rights?" *CQ Researcher*. November 12. http://library.cqpress.com/cqresearcher/document.php?id=cqresrre2004111200

Alden, Edward, and Rebecca Strauss. 2016. "Remedial Education: Federal Education Policy." *Council on Foreign Relations*. February. http://www.cfr.org/united-states/remedial-education-federal-education-policy/p30141?cid=otr-marketing_use-remedialeducation

Allen, Samantha. 2015. "Millennials Are the Gayest Generation." *The Daily Beast*. March 31. http://www.thedailybeast.com/articles/2015/03/31/millennials-are-the-gayest-generation.html

Allison, Tom. 2017. "Financial Health of Young America: Measuring Generational Declines between Baby Boomers & Millennials." *Young Invincibles*. January. http://younginvincibles.org/financial-health/

Alper, Becka A. 2015. "Millennials Are Less Religious than Older Americans, but Just as Spiritual." *Pew Research Center*. November 23. http://www.pewresearch.org/fact-tank/2015/11/23/millennials-are-less-religious-than-older-americans-but-just-as-spiritual/

Alvarez, Priscilla. 2016. "Clinton Takes a Page from Sanders's College Plan." *The Atlantic*. July 6. https://www.theatlantic.com/politics/archive/2016/07/bernie-sanders-hillary-clinton-college-tuition/490142/

Alvarez, Ramon M., and Tara Butterfield. 2000. "The Resurgence of Nativism in California? The Case of Proposition 187 and Illegal Immigration." *Social Science Quarterly* 81 (1): 167–79.

Ambrose, Stephen E., and Douglas Brinkley. 2010. *Rise to Globalism: American Foreign Policy Since 1938*, 9th edition. New York: Penguin Books.

American National Election Studies. 2008. *The ANES Guide to Public Opinion and Electoral Behavior*. Ann Arbor, MI: University of Michigan, Center for Political Studies.

American Student Assistance. 2013. "Life Delayed: The Impact of Student Debt on the Daily Lives of Young Americans." http://www.asa.org/site/assets/files/3793/life_delayed.pdf

Anand, Sowmya, and Jon A. Krosnick. 2003. "The Impact of Attitudes toward Foreign Policy Goals on Public Preferences among Presidential Candidates: A Study of Issue Publics and the Attentive Public in the 2000 Presidential Election." *Presidential Studies Quarterly* 33 (1): 31–71.

Anderegg, William R. L., James W. Prall, Jacob Harold, and Stephen H. Schneider. 2010. "Expert Credibility in Climate Change." *Proceedings of the National Academy of Sciences of the United States of America* 107 (27): 12107–09.

Anderson, Christopher J., and Pablo Beramendi. 2008. "Income, Inequality, and Electoral Participation." In *Democracy, Inequality, and Representation in Comparative Perspective*, edited by Pablo Beramendi, and Christopher J. Anderson, 278–311. New York: Russell Sage Foundation.

Apple, Michael W. 2002. *Power, Meaning and Identity: Essays in Critical Educational Studies*. New York: Peter Lang, Inc.

Armstrong, Thomas. 2013. "15 Reasons Why Standardized Tests Are Worthless." *American Institute for Learning and Human Development.* February 28. http://www.institute4learning.com/2013/02/28/15-reasons-why-standardized-tests-are-worthless-2/

Arnett, Jeffrey J. 2000. "Emerging Adulthood: A Theory of Development from the Late Teens through the Twenties." *American Psychologist* 55: 469–80.

Ayers, Sarah. 2013. "The High Cost of Youth Unemployment." Washington, DC: Center for American Progress. April 5. https://cdn.americanprogress.org/wp-content/uploads/2013/04/AyresYouthUnemployment1.pdf

Baer, Don, and Mark Penn. 2015. "The American Dream: Personal Optimists, National Pessimists." *The Atlantic.* July 1. http://www.theatlantic.com/national/archive/2015/07/aspen-ideas-american-dream-survey/397274/

Bahrampour, Tara. 2016. "Young People Now More Likely to Live with Parents than Partners." *The Washington Post.* May 24. https://www.washingtonpost.com/local/social-issues/young-people-more-likely-to-live-with-parents-now-than-any-time-in-modern-history/2016/05/24/9ad6f564-2117-11e6-9e7f-57890b612299_story.html?tid=a_inl&utm_term=.96edbbc59800

Baker, Reg, Michael J. Brick, Nancy A. Bates, Mike Battaglia, Mick P. Couper, Jill A. Dever, Krista J. Gile, and Roger Tourangeau. 2013. "Summary Report of the AAPOR Task Force on Non-probability Sampling." *Journal of Survey Statistics and Methodology* 1 (2): 90–143.

Basu, Rupa, and Bart Ostro. 2008. "A Multi-County Analysis Identifying the Vulnerable Populations for Morality Associated with High Ambient Temperature in California." *California Climate Change Center.* August. http://www.energy.ca.gov/2009publications/CEC-500-2009-035/CEC-500-2009-035-F.PDF

Battaglia, Michael P. 2008. "Nonprobability Sampling." *Encyclopedia of Survey Research Methods*. Thousand Oaks: SAGE Publications.

Beier, Margaret E., and Ruth Kanfer. 2015. "Generations at Work: Don't Throw the Baby Out with the Bathwater." *Industrial and Organizational Psychology* 8 (3): 387–90.

Ben-Yehuda, Gadi. 2010. "Millennials Want Better, Not Smaller Government; Implementation Is Key." *IBM Center for the Business of Government*. July 28. http://www.businessofgovernment.org/blog/millennials-want-better-not-smaller-government-implementation-key

Berman, Jillian. 2016. "America's Growing Student-Loan-Debt Crisis." *Marketwatch*. January 19. http://www.marketwatch.com/story/americas-growing-student-loan-debt-crisis-2016-01-15

Bernstein, Carl. 2007. *A Women in Charge: The Life of Hillary Rodham Clinton*. New York: Vintage Books.

Blake, Aaron. 2016. "More Young People Voted for Bernie Sanders than Trump and Clinton Combined—By a Lot." *The Washington Post*. June 20. https://www.washingtonpost.com/news/the-fix/wp/2016/06/20/more-young-people-voted-for-bernie-sanders-than-trump-and-clinton-combined-by-a-lot/?utm_term=.34a0e4367ecf

Bloome, Deirde. 2014. "Racial Inequality Trends and the Intergenerational Persistence of Income and Family Structure." *American Sociological Review* 79 (6): 1196–225.

Bobo, Lawrence, and Frederick Licari. 1989. "Education and Political Tolerance: Testing the Effects of Cognitive Sophistication and Target Group Affect." *Public Opinion Quarterly* 53: 285–308.

Borick, Christopher, Barry G. Rabe, and Sarah B. Mills. 2015. "Acceptance of Global Warming among Americans Reaches Highest Level since 2008." *Issues in Energy and Environment Policy*. October. http://closup.umich.edu/files/ieep-nsee-2015-fall-climate-belief.pdf

Borick, Christopher P., and Barry G. Rabe. 2014. "Weather or Not? Examining the Impact of Meteorological Conditions on Public Opinion Regarding Global Warming." *Weather, Climate, and Society* 6 (3): 413–24.

Bostrom, Ann, M. Granger Morgan, Baruch Fischhoff, and Daniel Read. 1994. "What Do People Know About Climate Change? 1. Mental Models." *Risk Analysis* 14 (6): 959–70.

Boykoff, Maxwell T. 2007. "From Convergence to Contention: United States Mass Media Representation of Anthropogenic Climate Change Science." *Transaction of the Institute of British Geographers* 32 (4): 477–89.

Brady, Henry E., Sidney Verba, and Kay Lehman Schlozman. 1995. "Beyond SES: A Resource Model of Political Participation." *American Political Science Review* 89 (2): 271–94.

Brainard, William C., and George L. Perry. 2004. "Brookings Paper on Economic Activity: 1." August 17. Washington, DC: Brookings Institution Press.

Braungart, Richard, and Margaret M. Braungart. 1986. "Life Course and Generational Politics." *Annual Review of Sociology* 12: 205–31.

Brooks, Clem, and Catherine Bolzendahl. 2004. "The Transformation of US Gender Role Attitudes: Cohort Replacement, Social Structure Change, and Ideological Learning." *Social Science Research* 33:106–33.

Brown, Meta, Andrew Haughwout, Donghoon Lee, Joelle Scally, and Wilbert van der Klaauw. 2015. "The Student Loan Landscape." *Liberty Street Economics*. February 18. http://libertystreeteconomics.newyorkfed.org/2015/02/the_ student_loan-landscape.html

Brownstein, Ronald. 2014. "How *Brown v. Board of Education* Changed—and Didn't Change—American Education." *The Atlantic*. April 25. https://www.theatlantic. com/education/archive/2014/04/two-milestones-in-education/361222/

Brownstein, Ronald. 2016. "Trump's Rhetoric of White Nostalgia." *The Atlantic*. June 2. http://www.theatlantic.com/politics/archive/2016/06/trumps-rhetoric-of-white-nostalgia/485192/?utm_source=atltw

Brulle, Robert J., Jason Carmichael, and J. Craig Jenkins. 2011. "Shifting Public Opinion on Climate Change: An Empirical Assessment of Factors Influencing Concern over Climate Change in the U.S., 2002-2010." *Climatic Change* 114: 169–88.

Buckley, Patricia, Peter Viechnicki, and Akrur Barua. 2015. "Issues by the Numbers: A New Understanding of Millennials: Generational Differences Reexamined." *Deloitte University Press*, October 16. https://dupress.deloitte. com/dup-us-en/economy/issues-by-the-numbers/understanding-millennials-generational-differences.html

Burns, Dasha. 2016. "For Millennials, Sanders Is a Grandpa Who Gets Them." *CNN*. January 18. http://www.cnn.com/2016/01/17/opinions/burns-millennials-bernie-sanders/

Burns, Peter, and James G. Gimpel. 2000. Economic Insecurity, Prejudicial Stereotypes, and Public Opinion on Immigration Policy. *Political Science Quarterly* 115 (2): 201–25.

Campbell, Angus, Philip E. Converse, Warren E. Miller, and Donald Stokes. 1960. *The American Voter*. New York: Wiley.

Campbell, John C., and John Strate. 1981. "Are Old People Conservative?" *The Gerontologist* 21 (6): 580–91.

Campbell, William K., Stacy M. Campbell, Lane W. Siedor, and Jean M. Twenge. 2015. "Generational Differences Are Real and Useful." *Industrial and Organizational Psychology*, 8 (3): 324–31.

Card, David. 1999. "The Causal Effect of Education on Earnings." In *Handbook of Labor Economics*, edited by Orley C. Ashenfeleter, and David Card, Vol. 3, Part A. Amsterdam The Netherlands: Elsevier Science, B.V.

Carmines, Edward G. and James Woods. 2002. "The Role of Party Activists in the Evolution of the Abortion Issue." *Political Behavior* 24 (4): 361–77.

Carnevale, Anthony P., Andrew R. Hanson, and Artem Gulish. 2013. "Failure to Launch: Structural Shift and the New Lost Generation." *Center on Education and the Workforce*. September. https://cew.georgetown.edu/cew-reports/failure-to-launch/

Center for Information & Research on Civic Learning and Engagement. 2011. "Youth Volunteering Rate Much Higher than in the 1970s and 1980s." March 3. http:// civicyouth.org/youth-volunteering-rate-much-higher-than-in-the-1970s-and-80s/

Center for Information & Research on Civic Learning and Engagement. 2016. "An Estimated 24 Million Young People Voted in 2016 Election." November 9. http://civicyouth.org/an-estimated-24-million-young-people-vote-in-2016-election/

Churchill, Aaron. 2015. "Bless the Tests: Three Reasons for Standardized Testing. *Thomas B. Fordham Institute*, March 18. https://edexcellence.net/articles/bless-the-tests-three-reasons-for-standardized-testing

CIRCLE (The Center for Information & Research on Civic Learning and Engagement). 2009. "Millennials Most Progressive Generation in 50 Years." *Around the Circle: Research and Practice*. September. http://civicyouth.org/wp-content/uploads/2009/08/v6.i2.3.pdf

Clement, Scott. 2015. "Millennials Are Just as Racist as Their Parents." *The Washington Post*. June 23. https://www.washingtonpost.com/news/wonk/wp/2015/06/23/millennials-are-just-as-racist-as-their-parents/

Colby, Sandra L., and Jennifer M. Ortman. 2015. "Projections of the Size and Composition of the U.S. Population: 2014-2060." Current Population Reports, P25-1143, U.S. Census Bureau, Washington, DC. http://www.census.gov/content/dam/Census/library/publications/2015/demo/p25-1143.pdf

Converse, Philip E. 1964. "The Nature of Belief Systems in Mass Publics." In *Ideology and Its Discontents*, edited by David Apter. New York: The Free Press of Glencoe.

Converse, Philip E., and Gregory B. Markus. 1979. "Plus ca Change . . . : The New CPS Election Study Panel." *American Political Science Review* 73: 32–49.

Corak, Miles. 2013. "Income Inequality, Equality of Opportunity, and Intergenerational Mobility." *Institute for the Study of Labor*, July. http://ftp.iza.org/dp7520.pdf

Couch, Kenneth A., and Thomas A. Dunn. 1997. "Intergenerational Correlations in Labor Market Status: A Comparison of the United States and Germany." *The Journal of Human Resources* 32 (1): 210–32.

Cox, Daniel, Eugene J. Dionne Jr., Robert P. Jones, and William A. Galston. 2011. "What It Means to be American: Attitudes towards Increasing Diversity in America Ten Years after 9/11." *Public Religion Research Institute*. September 6. http://www.prri.org/wpcontent/uploads/2011/09/Pluralism-2011-Brookings-Report.pdf

Cox, Daniel, and Robert P. Jones. 2011. "Committed to Availability, Conflicted about Morality: What the Millennial Generation Tells Us about the Future of the Abortion Debate and the Culture Wars." *PRRI*. https://www.prri.org/wp-content/uploads/2011/06/Millenials-Abortion-and-Religion-Survey-Report-1.pdf

CSPAN. 2016. "Hillary Clinton Campaign Rally in Miami, Florida." October 11. https://www.c-span.org/video/?416751-1/al-gore-campaigns-hillary-clinton-miami-florida

Dalton, Russell J. 2016. *The Good Citizen*. Los Angeles: CQ Press (2nd Edition).

Davenport, Coral, and Eric Lipton. 2016. "Trump Picks Scott Pruitt, Climate Change Denialist, to Lead E.P.A." *The New York Times*. December 7. http://www.nytimes.com/2016/12/07/us/politics/scott-pruitt-epa-trump.html

Dawson, Michael C. 1994. *Behind the Mule: Race and Class in African American Politics*. Princeton: Princeton University Press.

Democratic National Committee. 2017. "Education." https://www.democrats.org/issues/education

DeNavas-Walt, Carmen, and Bernadette D. Proctor. 2015. "Income and Poverty in the United States: 2014." Current Population Reports, P60-252, U.S. Census

Bureau, Washington, DC. https://www.census.gov/content/dam/Census/library/publications/2015/demo/p60-252.pdf

DeSilver, Drew. 2015. "For Young Americans, Unemployment Returns to Prerecession Levels." *Pew Research Center.* May 8. http://www.pewresearch.org/fact-tank/2014/07/07/1-in-10-americans-dont-give-a-hoot-about-politics/2/

Dinas, Elias, and Laura Stoker. 2014. "Age-Period-Cohort analysis: A Design-based Approach." *Electoral Studies* 33: 28–40.

Dispensa, Jaclyn M., and Robert J. Brulle. 2003. "Media's Social Construction of Environmental Issues: Focus on Global Warming—A Comparative Study." *International Journal of Sociology and Social Policy* 23 (10): 74–105.

Djube, Paul A., and Patrick Kieran Hunt. 2009. "Beyond the Lynn White Thesis: Congregational Effects on Environmental Concern." *Journal for the Scientific Study of Religion* 48 (4): 670–86.

Dokoupil, Tony. 2015. "Pope Francis Issue Radical Call for Climate Change Action." MSNBC, September 25. http://www.msnbc.com/msnbc/pope-francis-issues-radical-call-climate-change-action

Drake, Bruce. 2014. "6 New Findings about Millennials." *Pew Research Center.* March 7. http://www.pewresearch.org/fact-tank/2014/03/07/6-new-findings-about-millennials/

Dunlap, Riley E. 1998. "Lay Perceptions of Global Risk: Public Views of Global Warming in Cross-National Context." *International Sociology* 13 (4): 473–98.

Dunlap, Riley E., and Aaron M. McCright. 2008. "A Widening Gap: Republican and Democratic Views on Climate Change." *Environment: Science and Policy for Sustainable Development* 50 (5): 26–35.

The Economist. 2013. "Catching on at Last." *The Economist.* July 29. http://www.economist.com/news/briefing/21580136-new-technology-poised-disrupt-americas-schools-and-then-worlds-catching-last

Education Opportunity Network. 2016. "How Education Fares in the Democratic Party Platform." July 8. http://educationopportunitynetwork.org/how-education-fares-in-the-democratic-party-platform/

Education Reform Now. 2016. "The Democratic Party Education Platform Positions with Amendments Approved July 9, 2016." Edreformnow.org. July 12. https://edreformnow.org/wp-content/uploads/2016/07/Democratic-Ed-Platform-with-July-9-Amendments.pdf

Eilperin, Juliet. 2016. "Al Gore to Campaign for Clinton, Hoping to Galvanize Young Voters on Climate Change." *The Washington Post.* October 4. https://www.washingtonpost.com/news/energy-environment/wp/2016/10/04/al-gore-to-campaign-for-clinton-hoping-to-galvanize-young-voters-on-climate-change/?utm_term=.fe177277a73e

Equal Justice Works. 2013. "How Student Debt Affects Women, Minorities." *U.S. News.* May 1. https://www.usnews.com/education/blogs/student-loan-ranger/2013/05/01/how-student-debt-affects-women-minorities

Erkulwater, Jennifer L. 2012. "Political Participation over the Life Cycle." In *The Unheavenly Chorus: Unequal Political Voice and the Broken Promise of American Democracy*, edited by Kay L. Schlozman, Sidney Verba, and Henry E. Brady, 199–231. Princeton: Princeton University Press.

Erskine, Hazel G. 1963. "The Polls: Exposure to International Information." *Public Opinion Quarterly* 27: 658–62.

Espenshade, Thomas J. and Katherine Hempstead. 1996. "Contemporary American Attitudes towards U.S. Immigration." *International Migration Review* 30 (2): 535–70.

Experian. 2014. "Millennials Come of Age." June. http://www.experian.com/assets/marketing-services/reports/ems-ci-millennials-come-of-age-wp.pdf

Fang, Lee, and Alex Emmons. 2016. "Hacked Audio Reveals Hillary Clinton Sees Herself Occupying 'Center-Left to Center-Right'." *The Intercept*. September 30. https://theintercept.com/2016/09/30/hillary-clinton-center-right/

Federal Reserve Bank of New York. "Student Loan Debt by Age Group." Accessed July 20, 2016. https://www.newyorkfed.org/studentloandebt/index.html

File, Thom. 2014. "Young-Adult Voting: An Analysis of Presidential Elections, 1964–2012." *U.S. Census Bureau*, April. https://www.census.gov/prod/2014pubs/p20-573.pdf

Fingerhut, Hannah. 2016. "Millennials' Views of News Media, Religious Organizations Grow More Negative." *Pew Research Center*. January 4. http://www.pewresearch.org/fact-tank/2016/01/04/millennials-views-of-news-media-religious-organizations-grow-more-negative/

Finnie, Hannah and Simran Jagtiani. 2016. "Millennial Crave Economic Stability and Opportunity." Generation Progress. October 26. http://genprogress.org/ideas/2016/10/25/44656/millennials-crave-economic-stability-opportunity/

Fischer, Douglas. 2009. "Climate Change Hits Poor Hardest in the U.S." *Scientific American*. May. http://www.scientificamerican.com/article/climate-change-hits-poor-hardest/

Fleming, John. 2016. "Gallup Analysis: Millennials, Marriage and Family." *Gallup*. May 10. http://www.gallup.com/poll/191462/gallup%ADanalysis%ADmillennials%ADmarriage%ADfamily.aspx

Fletcher, Dan. 2009. "Brief History: Standardized Testing." *Time*. December 11. http://content.time.com/time/nation/article/0,8599,1947019,00.html

Foran, Clare. 2015. "A Year of Black Lives Matter." *The Atlantic*. December 31. http://www.theatlantic.com/politics/archive/2015/12/black-lives-matter/421839/

Fottrell, Quentin. 2014a. "40% of Unemployed Workers Are Millennials." *Market Watch*. July 7. http://www.marketwatch.com/story/40-of-unemployed-workers-are-millennials-2014-07-03

Fottrell, Quentin. 2014b. "Millennials Are the Most Underemployed Generation." *MarketWatch*. November 19. http://www.marketwatch.com/story/millennials-are-the-most-underemployed-generation-2014-11-19

Fox, Emily J. 2014. "Millennials Turn Up Heat against Low Wages." *CNN Money*. January 6. http://money.cnn.com/2014/01/06/news/economy/millennial-low-wages-protests/

Frand, Jason. 2000. "The Information Age Mindset: Changes in Students and Implications for Higher Education." *EDUCAUSE Review* 35 (5): 15–24.

Frey, William H. 2016. "Diversity Defines the Millennial Generation." *The Avenue*. Brookings Metropolitan Program. June 28. http://www.brookings.edu/blogs/the-avenue/posts/2016/06/28-diversity-millennial-frey#.V3fFdWi4TE.twitter

Fry, Richard. 2014. "The Changing Profile of Student Borrowers." *Pew Research Center.* October 7. http://www.pewsocialtrends.org/2014/10/07/the-changing-profile-of-student-borrowers/

Fry, Richard. 2016a. "For First Time in Modern Era, Living with Parents Edges Out Other Living Arrangements for 18 to 34 Year Olds." *Pew Research Center.* May 24. http://www.pewsocialtrends.org/2016/05/24/for-first-time-in-modern-era-living-with-parents-edges-out-other-living-arrangements-for-18-to-34-year-olds/

Fry, Richard. 2016b. "Millennials Overtake Baby Boomers as America's Largest Generation." *Pew Research Center.* April 25. http://www.pewresearch.org/fact-tank/2016/04/25/millennials-overtake-baby-boomers/

Fry, Richard. 2016c. "Millennials Match Baby Boomers as Largest Generation in U.S. Electorate, but Will They Vote?" *Pew Research Center.* May 16. http://www.pewresearch.org/fact-tank/2016/05/16/millennials-match-baby-boomers-as-largest-generation-in-u-s-electorate-but-will-they-vote/

Fry, Richard. 2017. "Millennials and Gen Xers Outvoted Boomers and Older Generations in 2016 Election." July 31. http://www.pewresearch.org/fact-tank/2017/07/31/millennials-and-gen-xers-outvoted-boomers-and-older-generations-in-2016-election/

Fullerton, Andrew S., and Jeffrey C. Dixon. 2010. "Generational Conflict or Methodological Artifact? Reconsidering the Relationship between Age and Policy Attitudes in the U.S. 1984-2008." *Public Opinion Quarterly* 74 (4): 643–73.

Funk, Cary, and Becka A. Alper. 2015. "Religion and Views on Climate Change and Energy Issues." *Pew Research Center.* October 22. http://www.pewinternet.org/2015/10/22/religion-and-views-on-climate-and-energy-issues/

Furman, Jason, and Matt Fielder. 2015. "4.5 Million Young Adults Have Gained Coverage since 2010, Improving Access to Care and Benefiting Our Economy." *The White House.* January 29. https://obamawhitehouse.archives.gov/blog/2015/01/29/45-million-young-adults-have-gained-coverage-2010-improving-access-care-and-benefitt

Galston, William A. 2004. "Civic Education and Political Participation." *PS: Political Science and Politics* 37 (2): 263–66.

Gamboa, Suzanne. 2015. "Donald Trump Announces Presidential Bid by Trashing Mexico, Mexicans. *NBC News.* June 16. http://www.nbcnews.com/news/latino/donald-trump-announces-presidential-bid-trashing-mexico-mexicans-n376521

Gandel, Stephen. 2016. "OMG, Young Millennials Are the Job Market's Biggest Losers." *Fortune.* March 4. http://fortune.com/2016/03/04/young-millennials-job-market-losers/

Gao, George. 2015. "63% of Republican Millennials Favor Marijuana Legalization." *Pew Research Center.* February 27. http://www.pewresearch.org/fact-tank/2015/02/27/63-of-republican-millennials-favor-marijuana-legalization/

Gates, Gary. 2011. "*How Many People Are Lesbian, Gay, Bisexual, and Transgender?*" The Williams Institute, UCLA School of Law. April. http://williamsinstitute.law.ucla.edu/research/census-lgbt-demographics-studies/how-many-people-are-lesbian-gay-bisexual-and-transgender/

Geiger, Abigail. 2016. "Support for Marijuana Legalization Continues to Rise." *Pew Research Center.* October 12. http://www.pewresearch.org/fact-tank/2016/10/12/support-for-marijuana-legalization-continues-to-rise/

Gendron, Charlotte and Rachel Lienesch. 2015. "Millennials and Political 'Slacktivism.'" *PRRI*. June 8. https://www.prri.org/spotlight/millennials-political-slacktivism/

Ghitza, Yair, and Andrew Gelman. 2014. "The Great Society, Reagan's Revolution, and Generations of Presidential Voting." working paper. http://www.stat.columbia.edu/~gelman/research/unpublished/cohort_voting_20140605.pdf

Gilman, Hollie R., and Elizabeth Stokes. 2014. "The Civic and Political Participation of Millennials." *Millennials Rising, New America Foundation.* https://s3.amazonaws.com/www.newamerica.org/downloads/The_Civic_and_Political_Participation_of_Millennials.pdf

Glinski, Nina. 2015. "Four Ways Millennials Are Still Scarred from the Recession." *Bloomberg.* February 23. https://www.bloomberg.com/news/articles/2015-02-23/four-ways-millennials-are-still-scarred-from-the-recession

Goodwyn, Wade. 2016. "Texas Try to Repair Damage Wrought upon Family Planning Clinics." *NPR.* January 28. http://www.npr.org/2016/01/28/464728393/texas-tries-to-repair-damage-wrought-upon-family-planning-clinics

Goren, Paul. 2005. "Party Identification and Core Political Values." *American Journal of Political Science* 49 (4): 882–97.

Goyal, Nikhil. 2016. "The Real Reason Millennials Love Bernie Sanders." *Time.* April 26. http://time.com/4299321/millennials-bernie-sanders/

Gramlich, John. 2016. "Trump Voters Want to Build the Wall, But Are More Divided on Other Immigration Questions." *Pew Research Center.* November 29. http://www.pewresearch.org/fact-tank/2016/11/29/trump-voters-want-to-build-the-wall-but-are-more-divided-on-other-immigration-questions/

Greenberg, Eric, and Karl Weber. 2008. *Generation We: How Millennial Youth Are Taking Over America and Changing Our World Forever.* Emeryville: Pachatusan.

Grose, Jessica. 2014. "For Many Millennials, Children Are Out of Reach." *The New York Times.* December 14. http://www.nytimes.com/roomfordebate/2014/12/25/is-it-smart-to-delay-adulthood/for-many-millenials-children-are-out-of-reach

Guth, James L., John C. Green, Lyman A. Kellstedt, and Corwin E. Smidt. 1995. "Faith and the Environment: Religious Beliefs and Attitudes on Environmental Policy." *American Journal of Political Science* 39 (2): 364–82.

Gwynn, Roberta C., and George D. Thurston. 2001. "The Burden of Air Pollution: Impacts among Racial Minorities." *Environmental Health Perspectives* 109 (4): 501–06.

Hainmueller, Jens, and Michael J. Hiscox. 2010. "Attitudes toward Highly Skilled and Low-skilled Immigration: Evidence from a Survey Experiment." *American Political Science Review* 104 (1): 61–84.

Halpin, John, and Karl Agne. 2009. "The Political Ideology of the Millennial Generation: A National Study of Political Values and Beliefs among 18-to-29-Year-Old Adults." *Center for American Progress.* https://cdn.americanprogress.org/wp-content/uploads/issues/2009/05/pdf/political_ideology_youth.pdf

Halstead, Ted. 1999. "A Politics for Generation X." *The Atlantic.* August. https://www.theatlantic.com/magazine/archive/1999/08/a-politics-for-generation-x/306666/

Harrell, Allison, Stuart Soroka, Shanto Iyengar, and Nicholas Valentino. 2012. "The Impact of Economic and Cultural Cues on Support for Immigration in Canada and the United States." *Canadian Journal of Political Science* 45 (3): 499–530.

Harvard Institute of Politics. 2015. "Harvard Youth Poll." http://iop.harvard.edu/youth-poll/past

Harvard Public Opinion Project. 2014. "Executive Summary: Survey of Young Americans' Attitudes toward Politics and Public Service: 25th Edition." *Harvard University Institute of Politics*. April 29. http://www.iop.harvard.edu/sites/default/files_new/Harvard_ExecSummarySpring2014.pdf

Harvey, John T. 2014. "Raising Minimum Wage Is Not The Answer." *Forbes*. July 6. https://www.forbes.com/sites/johntharvey/2014/07/06/raising-minimum-wage-not-the-answer/#460f39965b5c

Hasenfeld, Yeheskel, and Jane A. Rafferty. 1989. "The Determinants of Public Attitudes toward the Welfare State." *Social Forces* 67 (4): 1027–48.

Hays, Ron D., Honghu Liu, and Arie Kapteyn. 2015. "Use of Internet Panels to Conduct Surveys." *Behavior Research Methods* 47 (3): 685–90.

Hendley, Alexa A., and Natasha F. Bilmoria. 1999. "Minorities and Social Security: An Analysis of Racial and Ethnic Differences in the Current Program." *Social Security Bulletin* 62 (2): 59–64.

Hodges, Julianne. 2016. "Poll Finds Millennials More Concerned about Energy and the Environment." *They Daily Texan*. April 20. http://www.dailytexanonline.com/2016/04/20/poll-finds-millennials-more-concerned-about-energy-and-the-environment

Holland, Kelley. 2015. "The High Economic and Social Costs of Student Loan Debt." *CNBC*, June 15. https://www.cnbc.com/2015/06/15/the-high-economic-and-social-costs-of-student-loan-debt.html

Holsti, Ole R. 1992. "Public Opinion and Foreign Policy: Challenges to the Almond-Lippmann Consensus; Mershon Series: Research Programs and Debates." *International Studies Quarterly* 36: 439–66.

Holsti, Ole R., and James N. Rosenau. 1980. "Does Where You Stand Depend on When You Were Born? The Impact of Generation on Post-Vietnam Foreign Policy Beliefs." *Public Opinion Quarterly* 44 (1): 1–22.

Hopkins, Daniel J. 2010. "Politicized Places: Explaining Where and When Immigrants Provoke Local Opposition." *The American Political Science Review* 104 (1): 40–60.

Hopper, Paul. 2007. *Understanding Cultural Globalization*. Cambridge: Polity.

Howe, Neil. 2016. "What Do Millennials Think Can Fix Government? More Government." *Forbes*. January 15. http://www.forbes.com/sites/neilhowe/2016/01/15/what-do-millennials-think-can-fix-government-more-government/#4f6cb0ed6c96

Howe, Neil, and William Strauss. 2000. *Millennials Rising: The Next Great Generation*. New York: Vintage Books.

The Huffington Post. 2012. "The Republican Education Platform 2012 Emphasizes School Choice, Teacher Accountability." *The Huffington Post*. August 29. http://www.huffingtonpost.com/2012/08/28/2012-gop-education-platfo_n_1837670.html

Hulme, Mike. 2009. *Why We Disagree about Climate Change*. Cambridge: Cambridge University Press.

Hurwitz, Jon, and Mark Peffley. 1987. "How Are Foreign Policy Attitudes Structured? A Hierarchical Model." *American Political Science Review* 81 (4): 1099–20.

Hutchison, Andrew J., Lynee H. Johnston, and Jeff D. Breckon. 2010. "Using QSR-NVivo to Facilitate the Development of a Grounded Theory Project: An Account of a Worked Example." *International Journal of Social Research Methodology* 13 (4): 283–302.

Ingraham, Christopher. 2016. "Aging Baby Boomers Increasingly Embrace Marijuana, Heavy Alcohol Use." *The Washington Post*. December 18. https://www.washingtonpost.com/news/wonk/wp/2016/12/18/aging-boomers-increasingly-embrace-marijuana-heavy-alcohol-use/?utm_term=.4dccef8a0bd0

The Institute for College Access and Success. 2014a. "10th Annual Report: Student Debt and the Class of 2014." http://ticas.org/sites/default/files/pub_files/classof2014.pdf

The Institute for College Access and Success. 2014b. "Quick Facts about Student Debt." March. http://ticas.org/sites/default/files/pub_files/Debt_Facts_and_Sources.pdf

The Institute for College Access and Success. 2016. "Student Debt and the Class of 2015." October. http://ticas.org/sites/default/files/pub_files/classof2015.pdf

Intergenerational Commission. 2016. "Stagnation Generation: The Case for Renewing the Intergenerational Contract." July. http://www.intergencommission.org/wp-content/uploads/2016/07/Intergenerational-Commission-launch-document.pdf

Ipsos-MORI. 2014. *Global Trends 2014*. http://www.ipsosglobaltrends.com/index.html

Ipsos Public Affairs. 2016. "Rock the Vote/ USA Today Millennial Survey." August. http://www.ipsos-na.com/download/pr.aspx?id=15852

Jacobson, Louis. 2016. "Yes, Donald Trump Did Call Climate Change a Chinese Hoax." *Politifact*. June 3. http://www.politifact.com/truth-o-meter/statements/2016/jun/03/hillary-clinton/yes-donald-trump-did-call-climate-change-chinese-h/

Jacoby, Jeff. 2015. "American Millennials Rethink Abortion, for Good Reasons." *The Boston Globe*. June 9. https://www.bostonglobe.com/opinion/2015/06/09/millennial-americans-rethink-abortion-for-good-reasons/ZCmZNJuCWKVr5brzVfaiuI/story.html

Jelen, Ted G., and Clyde Wilcox. 2003. "Causes and Consequences of Public Attitudes toward Abortion: A Review and Research Agenda." *Political Research Quarterly* 56 (4): 489–500.

Jesdale, Bill M., Rachel Morello-Frosch, and Lara Cushing. 2013. "The Racial/Ethnic Distribution of Heath Risk-Related Land Cover in Relation to Residential Segregation." *Environmental Health Perspectives* 121 (7): 811–17.

Johnson, Anne, Tobin Van Ostern, and Abraham White. 2012. "The Student Debt Crisis." *Center for American Progress*. October 25. https://www.americanprogress.org/wp-content/uploads/2012/10/WhiteStudentDebt-5.pdf

Joint Economic Committee. 2014. "The Millennials: Economic Challenges and Opportunities." *US Senate*. December. http://www.jec.senate.gov/public/_cache/files/a1633d07-c22b-4720-aca6-8c2cf0d06f82/millennials-report.pdf

Joireman, Jeff, Heather Barnes Truelove, and Blythe Duell. 2010. "Effect of Outdoor Temperature, Heat Primes and Anchoring on Belief in Global Warming." *Journal of Environmental Psychology* 30 (4): 358–67.

Jones, Jeffrey M. 2015. "In U.S., 58% Back Legal Marijuana Use." *Gallup*. October 21. http://www.gallup.com/poll/186260/back-legal-marijuana.aspx

Jones, Jeffrey M. 2016. "More Favor Major Government Role in Assisting Minorities." *Gallup*. September 9. http://www.gallup.com/poll/195407/favor%ADmajor%ADg overnment%ADrole%ADassisting%ADminorities.aspx?version=print

Jones, Robert, and L. Carter. 1994. "Concern for the Environment among Black Americans: An Assessment of Common Assumptions." *Social Science Quarterly* 75 (3): 560–79.

Jones, Robert E., and Shirley A. Rainey. 2006. "Examining Linkages between Race, Environmental Concern, Health, and Justice in a Highly Polluted Community of Color." *Journal of Black Studies* 36 (4): 473–96.

Jones, Robert P. and Daniel Cox. 2015. "How Race and Religion Shape Millennial Attitudes on Sexuality and Reproductive Health." *Public Religion Research Institute*. March 27. http://publicreligion.org/site/wp-content/uploads/2015/03/ PRRI-Millennials-Web-FINAL.pdf

Jones, Robert P., Daniel Cox, Eugene J. Dionne Jr., and William Galston. 2011. "What IT Means to Be American: Attitudes in an Increasingly Diverse America Ten Years after 9/11." *Public Religion Research Institute*. September 6. http://www. prri.org/research/what-it-means-to-be-american/

Jones-Correa, Michael A., and David L. Leal. 2001. "Political Participation: Does Religion Matter?" *Political Research Quarterly* 54: 751–70.

Jusko, Karen. 2016. "Safety Net." In *Pathways: The Poverty and Inequality Report 2016*, edited by David Grusky, Charles Varner, and Marybeth Mattingly, 25–31. Stanford: Stanford Center on Poverty and Inequality.

Kadlec, Dan. 2014. "Millennials Put Their Surprising Stamp on the American Dream." *Time*. February 6. http://time.com/5074/ millennials-put-their-surprising-stamp-on-the-american-dream/

Kahan, Dan M., Hank Jenkins-Smith, and Donald Braman. 2011. "Cultural Cognition of Scientific Consensus." *Journal of Risk Research* 14 (2): 1–28.

Kahan, Dan M., Ellen Peters, Maggie Wittlin, Paul Slovic, Lisa Larrimore Ouellette, Donald Braman, and Gregory Mandel. 2012. "The Polarizing Impact of Science Literacy and Numeracy on Perceived Climate Change Risks." *Nature Climate Change* 2: 732–35.

Kahn, Matthew E., and Matthew J. Kotchen. 2011. "Business Cycle Effects on Concern about Climate Change: The Chilling Effect on Recession." *Climate Change Economics* 2 (3): 257–73.

Keeter, Scott, Juliana Horowitz, and Alec Tyson. 2008. "Young Voters in the 2008 Election." *Pew Research Center*. November 13. http://www.pewresearch.org/2008/ 11/13/young-voters-in-the-2008-election/

Kennedy, Caitlyn, and Rebecca Lindsey. 2015. "What's the Difference between Global Warming and Climate Change?" *NOAA Climate.gov*. June 17. https:// www.climate.gov/news-features/climate-qa/whats-difference-between- global-warming-and-climate-change

Kennedy, Courtney, Andrew Mercer, Scott Keeter, Nick Hatley, Kyley McGeeney, and Alejandra Gimenez. 2016. "Evaluating Online Nonprobability Surveys." *Pew Research Center*. May 2. http://www.pewresearch.org/2016/05/02/evaluating- online-nonprobability-surveys/

Khalid, Asma. 2016. "Millennials Just Didn't Love Hillary Clinton the Way They Loved Barack Obama." *NPR*. November 14. http://www.npr.org/2016/11/14/501727488/millennials-just-didnt-love-hillary-clinton-the-way-they-loved-barack-obama

Kiley, Jocelyn, and Michael Dimock. 2014. "The GOP's Millennial Problem Runs Deep." *Pew Research Center*. September 25. http://www.pewresearch.org/fact-tank/2014/09/25/the-gops-millennial-problem-runs-deep/

Kim, Hyoun K., and Patrick C. McKenry. 1998. "Social Networks and Support: A Comparison of African Americans, Asian Americans, Caucasians, and Hispanics." *Journal of Comparative Family Studies* 29 (2): 313–34.

Kincheloe, Joe L. 2004. *Critical Pedagogy Primer*. New York: Peter Lang, Inc.

Kinder, Donald R., and David O. Sears. 1985. "Public Opinion and Political Action." In *The Handbook of Social Psychology*, edited by Lindzey Gardner and Elliot Aronson, 657–741. New York: Random House.

Kochhar, Rakesh. 2014. "Wealth Inequality Has Widened along Racial, Ethnic Lines since End of Great Recession." *Pew Research Center*. December 12. http://www.pewresearch.org/fact-tank/2014/12/12/racial-wealth-gaps-great-recession/

Kott, Lidia J. 2014. "For These Millennials, Gender Norms Have Gone Out of Style." *NPR*. November 30. http://www.npr.org/2014/11/30/363345372/for-these-millennials-gender-norms-have-gone-out-of-style

Kreutz, Liz, and Josh Haskell. 2016. "Campaigning with Hillary Clinton, Al Gore Warns of 'Climate Catastrophe' and Third-Party Risks." *ABC News*. October 11. http://abcnews.go.com/Politics/campaigning-hillary-clinton-al-gore-warns-climate-catastrophe/story?id=42735234

Krogstad, Jens M. 2015. "Hispanics More Likely than Whites to Say Global Warming Is Caused by Humans." *Pew Research Center*. February 27. http://www.pewresearch.org/fact-tank/2015/02/27/hispanics-more-likely-than-whites-to-say-global-warming-is-caused-by-humans/

Krogstad, Jens M., and Richard Fry. 2014. "Dept. of Ed. Project Public Schools Will Be 'Majority-Minority' This Fall." *Pew Research Center*. August 18. http://www.pewresearch.org/fact-tank/2014/08/18/u-s-public-schools-expected-to-be-majority-minority-starting-this-fall/

Krogstad, Jens M., Mark H. Lopez, Gustavo Lopez, Jeffrey S. Passel, and Eileen Patten. 2016. "Millennials Make Up Almost Half of Latino Eligible Voters in 2016." *Pew Research Center*. January 19. http://www.pewhispanic.org/2016/01/19/millennials-make-up-almost-half-of-latino-eligible-voters-in-2016/

Krosnick, Jon A., Allyson L. Holbrook, Laura Lowe, and Penny S. Visser. 2006. "The Origins and Consequences of Democratic Citizens' Policy Agendas: A Study of Popular Concern about Global Warming." *Climatic Change* 77: 7–43.

Kurtzleben, Danielle. 2014. "Study: Income Gap between Young College and High School Grads Widens." *U.S. News and World Report*. February 11. http://www.usnews.com/news/articles/2014/02/11/study-income-gap-between-young-college-and-high-school-grads-widens

Lakoff, George. 2002. *Moral Politics: How Liberals and Conservatives Think*. Chicago: University of Chicago Press (2nd Edition).

Lee, Don. 2016. "Millennials Aren't Big Spenders or Risk-Takers, and That's Going to Reshape the Economy." *Los Angeles Times*. October 10. http://www.latimes.com/business/la-fi-the-millennial-factor-20161010-snap-story.html

Leiserowitz, Anthony, Edward Maibach, Connie Roser-Renouf, Geoff Feinberg, and Seth Rosenthal. 2015. *Climate Change in the American Christian Mind: March, 2015.* New Haven: Yale Project on Climate Change Communication, Yale University and George Mason University. http://environment.yale.edu/climate-communication/files/Global-Warming-Religion-March-2015.pdf

Lindaman, Kara, and Donald P. Haider-Markel. 2002. "Issue Evolution, Political Parties, and the Culture Wars. 2002." *Political Research Quarterly* 55 (1): 91–110.

Lindquist, John H. 1964. "Socioeconomic Status and Political Participation." *The Western Political Quarterly* 17 (4): 608–14.

Liu, Xinsheng, Arnold Vedlitz, James W. Stoutenborough, and Scott Robinson. 2015. "Scientists' Views and Positions on Global Warming and Climate Change: A Content Analysis of Congressional Testimonies." *Climatic Change* 131 (4): 487–503.

Lopez, Mark H., Jens Manuel Krogstad, Eileen Patten, and Ana Gonzalez-Barrera. 2014. "Chapter 2: Latinos' Views on Selected 2014 Ballot Measure Issues." *Pew Research Center Hispanic Trends*. October 16. http://www.pewhispanic.org/2014/10/16/chapter-2-latinos-views-on-selected-2014-ballot-measure-issues/

Lyons, Sean, and Lisa Kuron. 2014. "Generational Differences in the Workplace: A Review of the Evidence and Directions for Future Research." *Journal of Organizational Behavior* 35 (S1): S139–57.

MacCoun, Robert J., and Susannah Paletz. 2009. "Citizens' Perceptions of Ideological Bias in Research on Public Policy Controversies." *Political Psychology* 30 (1): 43–65.

Macias, Thomas. 2015. "Environmental Risk Perception among Race and Ethnic Groups in the U.S." *Ethnicities*. DOI 10.177/1468796815575382.

Maggiotto, Michael A., and Eugene R. Wittkopf. 1981. "American Public Attitudes toward Foreign Policy. *International Studies Quarterly* 25 (4): 601–31.

Malka, Ariel, Jon A. Krosnick, and Gary Langer. 2009. "The Association of Knowledge with Concern about Global Warming: Trusted Information Sources Shape Public Thinking." *Risk Analysis* 29 (5): 633–47.

Margolin, Madison. 2016. "Millennials' Marijuana Usage Has Rise but Pales in Comparion to Baby Boomers' Hazy Days." *LA Weekly*. September 15. http://www.laweekly.com/news/millennials-marijuana-usage-has-risen-but-pales-to-baby-boomers-hazy-days-7386719

Masci, David. 2016. "Where Major Religious Groups Stand on Abortion." *Pew Research Center*. June 21. http://www.pewresearch.org/fact-tank/2016/06/21/where-major-religious-groups-stand-on-abortion/

Matthews, Steve. 2015. "Here's Evidence That Millennials Are Still Living with Their Parents." *Bloomberg Business*. September 18. http://www.bloomberg.com/news/articles/2015-09-18/here-s-evidence-that-millennials-are-still-living-with-their-parents

Maxwell, Lesli A. 2014. "U.S. School Enrollment Hits Majority-Minority Milestone." *Education Weekly* 34 (1): 1, 12, 14–15. http://www.edweek.org/ew/articles/2014/08/20/01demographics.h34.html

Mayer, Alexander K. 2011. "Does Education Increase Political Participation?" *Journal of Politics* 73 (3): 633–45.

McCarthy, Justin. 2016. "One in Eight U.S. Adults Say They Smoke Marijuana." *Gallup*. August 9. http://www.gallup.com/poll/194195/adults-say-smoke-marijuana.aspx

McClain, Paula D., Jessica D. Johnson Carew, Eugene Walton, Jr., and Candis S. Watts. 2009. "Group Membership, Group Identity, and Group Consciousness: Measures of Racial Identity in American Politics?" *Annual Review of Political Science* 12: 471–85.

McClain, Paula D., and Steven Tauber. 1998. "Black and Latino Socio-Economic Political Competition: Has a Decade Made a Difference?" *American Politics Quarterly* 26 (2): 237–52.

McCright, Aaron M., and Riley E. Dunlap. 2011. "The Politicization of Climate Change and Polarization in the American Public's Views of Global Warming, 2001–2010." *The Sociological Quarterly* 52 (2): 155–94.

McDonald, Michael P. 2017. "Voter Turnout Demographics." *United States Elections Project*. http://www.electproject.org/home/voter-turnout/demographics

McGlone, Teresa, Judith Winters Spain, and Vernon McGlone. 2011. "Corporate Social Responsibility and the Millennials." *Journal of Education for Business* 86 (4): 195–200.

McHale, Brandee. 2015. "Why Are So Many Millennials Unemployed?" *CNBC*. December 3. http://www.cnbc.com/2015/12/03/why-are-so-many-millennials-unemployed-commentary.html

Media Insight Project. 2015. "How Millennials Get News: Inside the Habits of America's First Digital Generation." March. http://www.mediainsight.org/PDFs/Millennials/Millennials%20Report%20FINAL.pdf

Miller, Arthur H., Patricia Gurin, Gerald Gurin, and Oksana Malanchuk. 1981. "Group Consciousness and Political Participation." *American Journal of Political Science*, 25 (3): 494–511.

Miller, Ben. 2014. "The Student Debt Review: Analyzing the State of Undergraduate Student Borrowing." *New America, Education Policy Program*. February 17. https://www.newamerica.org/education-policy/policy-papers/the-student-debt-review/

Mislinkski, Jill. 2015. "Millennials and the Labor Force: A Look at Trends." *Advisor Perspectives*. July 29. http://www.advisorperspectives.com/dshort/updates/millennials-and-employment

Mohai, Paul, and Bunyan Bryant. 1998. " 'Race' Effect on Concern for Environmental Quality?" *The Public Opinion Quarterly* 62 (4): 475–505.

Mohai, Paul, and Robin Saha. 2007. "Racial Inequality in the Distribution of Hazardous Waste: A National-Level Reassessment." *Social Problems* 54 (3): 343–70. Environmental Studies Faculty Publications. Paper 2.

Molyneux, Guy, and Ruy Teixeira. 2010. "The Generation Gap on Government: Why and How the Millennial Generation Is the Most Pro-Government Generation and What This Means for Our Future." *Center for American Progress*. https://cdn.americanprogress.org/wp-content/uploads/issues/2010/07/pdf/dww_millennials.pdf

Monchinski, Tony. 2007. *The Politics of Education: An Introduction*. Rotterdam: Sense Publishers.

Moore, Peter. 2016. "Poll Results: Trump and the Pope." *Huffington Post*. February 23. https://today.yougov.com/news/2016/02/23/poll-results-trump-and-pope/

Morello-Frosch, Rachel, Manuel Pastor, Jim Sadd, and Seth Shonkoff. 2009. *The Climate Gap: Inequalities in How Climate Change Hurts Americans & How to*

Close the Gap. Los Angeles, CA: PERE Publications, University of Southern California.

Morin, Rich. 2009. "Different Age Groups, Different Recessions." *Pew Research Center*. May 14. http://www.pewsocialtrends.org/2009/05/14/different-age-groups-different-recessions/

Morin, Rich. 2016. "Behind Trump's Win in Rural White America: Women Joined Men in Backing Him." *Pew Research Center*. November 17. http://www.pewresearch.org/fact-tank/2016/11/17/behind-trumps-win-in-rural-white-america-women-joined-men-in-backing-him/

Motel, Seth. 2015. "6 Facts about Marijuana." *Pew Research Center*. April 14. http://www.pewresearch.org/fact-tank/2015/04/14/6-facts-about-marijuana/

Mottaz, Clifford. 1984. "Education and Work Satisfaction." *Human Relations* 37 (11): 985–1004.

Mzezewa, Tariro, and Jessica DiNapoli. 2015. "African-Americans Still Favor Gun Control, But Views Are Shifting." *Reuters*. July 15. http://www.reuters.com/article/us-africanamerican-guns-idUSKCN0PP2N320150715

Nakamura, David. 2017. "Trump Administration Releases Hard-line Immigration Principles, Threatening Deal on 'Dreamers." *Washington Post*. October 8. https://www.washingtonpost.com/news/post-politics/wp/2017/10/08/trump-administration-releases-hard-line-immigration-principles-threatening-deal-on-dreamers/?utm_term=.daa90c0e24a4

The Nation. 2016. "We Still Need a Future to Believe In." July 18. https://www.thenation.com/article/we-still-need-a-future-to-believe-in/

National Center for Education Statistics. 2000. "Monitoring School Quality: An Indicators Report." Statistical Analysis Report. https://nces.ed.gov/pubs2001/2001030.pdf

National Center for Education Statistics. "Fast Facts on Enrollment." Accessed July 1, 2017. https://nces.ed.gov/fastfacts/display.asp?id=98

National Conference on Citizenship. 2008. "Two Special Generations: The Millennials and the Boomers." http://ncoc.net/226

National Oceanic and Atmospheric Administration. "Global Summary of the Month Dataset."Accessed June 1, 2017. https://www.ncdc.noaa.gov/cdo-web/datasets#GSOM

National Surveys on Energy and the Environment. 2015. "The Fall 2015 National Surveys on Energy and the Environment." http://closup.umich.edu/national-surveys-on-energy-and-environment/nsee-2015-fall.php

New York Times. 2016. "Transcript of Donald Trump's Immigration Speech." *New York Times*. September 1. https://www.nytimes.com/2016/09/02/us/politics/transcript-trump-immigration-speech.html?_r=1

Nielsen. 2014. "Millennials: Much Deeper than Their Facebook Pages." *Millennials: Breaking the Myths*. January 27. http://www.nielsen.com/us/en/insights/reports/2014/millennials-breaking-the-myths.html

Norman, Jim. 2016. "Millennials Like Sanders, Dislike Election Process." *Gallup*. May 11. http://www.gallup.com/poll/191465/millennials-sanders-dislike-election-process.aspx

Nussbaum, Martha C. 1996. "Patriotism and Cosmopolitanism." In *For Love of Country?* edited by Martha Nussbaum and Joshua Cohen. Boston: Beacon Press.

Oblinger, Diana. 2003. "Boomers, Gen-Xers, & Millennials: Understanding the New Students." *EDUCAUSE Review* July/August 38 (4): 37–47.

OECD. 2014. "United States: Tackling High Inequalities. Creating Opportunities for All." June. https://www.oecd.org/unitedstates/Tackling-high-inequalities.pdf

On The Issues. "Republican Party on Education." *Ontheissues.org.* Accessed July 1, 2017. http://www.ontheissues.org/celeb/Republican_Party_Education.htm

On The Issues. "Democratic Party on Education." *Ontheissues.org.* Accessed July 1, 2017. http://www.ontheissues.org/Celeb/Democratic_Party_Education.htm

The Opportunity Agenda. 2014. "The Opportunity Survey: Understanding the Roots of Attitudes on Inequality." http://opportunity-survey.opportunityagenda.org/userfiles/Opportunity_Survey_Report.pdf

Oreopoulos, Philip, Till von Wachter, and Andrew Heisz. 2012. "Short-and Long-term Career Effects of Graduating in a Recession." *AEJ: Applied Economics* 4 (1): 1–29.

Oyserman, Daphna. 1993. "The Lens of Personhood: Viewing the Self and Others in a Multicultural Society." *Journal of Personality and Social Psychology*, 65 (5), 993–1009.

Page, Susan, and Karina Shedrofsky. 2016. "Poll: How Millennials View BLM and the Alt-right." *USA Today.* October 31. https://www.usatoday.com/story/news/politics/onpolitics/2016/10/31/poll-millennials-black-lives-matter-alt-right/92999936/

Page, Susan, and Jenny Ung. 2016. "Poll: Millennials Still Optimistic about Success and the American Dream." *USA Today.* March 14. http://www.usatoday.com/story/news/politics/elections/2016/03/14/poll-millennials-american-dream-trump-obama/81621030/

Paquette, Danielle. 2016. "The Stark Difference between Millennial Men and Their Dads." *The Washington Post.* May 26. https://www.washingtonpost.com/news/wonk/wp/2016/05/26/the-stark-difference-between-millennial-men-and-their-dads/?utm_term=.54756569fc5f

Pascarella, Ernest T., and Patrick Terenzini. 2005. *How College Affects Students, Vol. 2: A Third Decade of Research.* San Francisco: John Wiley & Sons.

Passel, Jeffrey S., and Michael Fix. 1994. "Myths about Immigrants." *Foreign Policy* 95 (summer): 151–60.

Patten, Eileen, and Richard Fry. 2015. "How Millennials Today Compare with Their Grandparents 50 Years ago." *Pew Research Center.* March 19. http://www.pewresearch.org/fact-tank/2015/03/19/how-millennials-compare-with-their-grandparents/

Pew Research Center. 2008. "Do Blacks and Hispanics Get Along?" *Pew Research Center Social and Demographic Trends.* January 31. http://www.pewsocialtrends.org/2008/01/31/do-blacks-and-hispanics-get-along/

Pew Research Center. 2010a. "A Pro-Government, Socially Liberal Generation." February 18. http://www.pewresearch.org/files/old-assets/pdf/1497.pdf

Pew Research Center. 2010b. "Almost All Millennials Accept Interracial Dating and Marriage." February 1. http://www.pewresearch.org/2010/02/01/almost-all-millennials-accept-interracial-dating-and-marriage/

Pew Research Center. 2010c. "Public Knows Basic Facts about Politics, Economics, but Struggles with Specifics." November 18. http://www.pewresearch.org/2010/11/18/public-knows-basic-facts-about-politics-economics-but-struggles-with-specifics/

Pew Research Center. 2011. "The Generation Gap and the 2012 Election." November 3. http://www.people-press.org/2011/11/03/the-generation-gap-and-the-2012-election-3/

Pew Research Center. 2012a. "The Gender Gap: Three Decades Old, as Wide as Ever." March 29. http://www.people-press.org/2012/03/29/the-gender-gap-three-decades-old-as-wide-as-ever/

Pew Research Center. 2012b. "Young, Underemployed, and Optimistic: Coming of Age, Slowly, in a Tough Economy." Washington, DC: Pew Research Center. February 9. http://www.pewsocialtrends.org/files/2012/02/young-underemployed-and-optimistic.pdf

Pew Research Center. 2014a. "Millennials in Adulthood: Detached from Institutions, Networked with Friends." March 7. http://www.pewsocialtrends.org/files/2014/03/2014-03-07_generations-report-version-for-web.pdf

Pew Research Center. 2014b. "Political Polarization Survey." March 16. http://www.people-press.org/2014/03/16/2014-political-polarization-survey/

Pew Research Center. 2014c. "The Rising Cost of Not Going to College." Washington, DC: Pew Research Center. February 11. http://www.pewsocialtrends.org/2014/02/11/the-rising-cost-of-not-going-to-college/

Pew Research Center. 2014d. "Growing Public Support for Gun Rights." http://www.people-press.org/2014/12/10/growing-public-support-for-gun-rights/

Pew Research Center. 2015a. "Changing Attitudes on Gay Marriage." July 29. http://www.pewforum.org/2015/07/29/graphics-slideshow-changing-attitudes-on-gay-marriage/

Pew Research Center. 2015b. "Beyond Distrust: How Americans View Their Government." November 23. http://www.people-press.org/2015/11/23/beyond-distrust-how-americans-view-their-government/

Pew Research Center. 2015c. "A Different Look at Generations and Partisanship." April 30. http://www.people-press.org/2015/04/30/a-different-look-at-generations-and-partisanship/

Pew Research Center. 2015d. "A Deep Dive into Party Affiliation." April 7. http://www.people-press.org/2015/04/07/a-deep-dive-into-party-affiliation/

Pew Research Center. 2015e. "Comparing Millennials to Other Generations." March 19. http://www.pewsocialtrends.org/2015/03/19/comparing-millennials-to-other-generations/

Pew Research Center. 2016a. "A Wider Ideological Gap between More and Less Educated Adults." April 26. http://www.people-press.org/2016/04/26/a-wider-ideological-gap-between-more-and-less-educated-adults/

Pew Research Center. 2016b. "The Parties on the Eve of the 2016 Election: Two Coalitions, Moving Further Apart." September 13. http://www.people-press.org/2016/09/13/the-parties-on-the-eve-of-the-2016-election-two-coalitions-moving-further-apart/

Pew Research Center. 2016c. "Demographic Trends and Economic Well-Being." *Views of Race and Inequality, Blacks and Whites Are Worlds Apart.* June 27. http://www.pewsocialtrends.org/2016/06/27/1-demographic-trends-and-economic-well-being/

Pew Research Center. 2016d. "Campaign Exposes Fissures over Issues, Values and How Life Has Changed in the U.S," March 31. http://www.people-press.org/2016/03/31/campaign-exposes-fissures-over-issues-values-and-how-life-has-changed-in-the-u-s/

Pew Research Center. 2016e. "Top Voting Issues in 2016." July 7. http://www.people-press.org/2016/07/07/4-top-voting-issues-in-2016-election/

Pew Research Center. 2016f. "Changing Attitudes on Gay Marriage." http://www.pewforum.org/2016/05/12/changing-attitudes-on-gay-marriage/

Pew Research Center. 2017. "Public Opinion on Abortion: Views on Abortion 1995-2016." http://www.pewforum.org/2017/01/11/public-opinion-on-abortion-2/

Pilkington, Ed. 2015. "Donald Trump: Ban All Muslims Entering the U.S." *The Guardian*. December 7. http://www.theguardian.com/us-news/2015/dec/07/donald-trump-ban-all-muslims-entering-us-san-bernardino-shooting

Porter, Eduardo. 2014. "Seeking New Tools to Address a Wage Gap." *The New York Times*. November 4. https://www.nytimes.com/2014/11/05/business/economy/seeking-new-tools-to-address-income-inequality.html

Powell, John A. "Six Policies to Reduce Economic Inequality." *Haas Institute*. Accessed June 1, 2017. http://haasinstitute.berkeley.edu/six-policies-reduce-economic-inequality

Public Religion Research Institute. 2014. "Religion, Values & Climate Change Survey." http://www.prri.org/data-vault/?topic%5B%5D=&meta_year%5B%5D=2014

Putnam, Robert D., and David E. Campbell. 2010. *American Grace: How Religion Divides and Unites Us*. New York: Simon and Schuster.

Rainie, Lee, Aaron Smith, Kay L. Schlozman, Henry Brady, and Sidney Verba. 2012. "Social Media and Political Engagement." *Pew Internet and American Life Project, Pew Research Center*. October 19. http://www.pewinternet.org/files/old-media//Files/Reports/2012/PIP_SocialMediaAndPoliticalEngagement_PDF.pdf

Rampbell, Catherine. 2010. "The Recession Has (Officially) Ended." *The New York Times*. September 20. https://economix.blogs.nytimes.com/2010/09/20/the-recession-has-officially-ended/

Reason-Rupe. 2014. "Millennials: The Politically Unclaimed Generation." *The Reason Foundation*. July 10. https://reason.com/assets/db/2014-millennials-report.pdf

Reece, Robert L., and Heather A. O'Connell. 2016. "How the Legacy of Slavery and Racial Composition Shape Public School Enrollment in the American South." *Sociology of Race and Ethnicity* 2 (1): 42–57.

Republican Views on the Issues. 2014. "Republican Views on Education." April 3. http://www.republicanviews.org/republican-views-on-education/

Richmond, Emily, Mikhail Zinshteyn, and Natalie Gross. 2016. "Dissecting the Youth Vote." *The Atlantic*. November 11. https://www.theatlantic.com/education/archive/2016/11/dissecting-the-youth-vote/507416/

Riley, Matilda W. 1973. "Aging and Cohort Succession: Interpretations and Misinterpretations." *Public Opinion Quarterly* 37 (1): 35–49.

Robillard, Kevin. 2012. "Study: Youth Vote Was Decisive." *Politico*. http://www.politico.com/story/2012/11/study-youth-vote-was-decisive-083510

Roosevelt Institute. 2013. "Government by and for Millennial America." http://rooseveltinstitute.org/government-by-and-millennial-america-3/

Roppolo, Michael. 2014. "Americans More Skeptical of Climate Change than Others in Global Survey." *CBS News.* July 23. http://www.cbsnews.com/news/americans-more-skeptical-of-climate-change-than-others-in-global-survey/

Rosenstone, Steven J., and John M. Hansen. 2002. *Mobilization, Participation and Democracy in America.* New York: Longman Publishing Group (Longman Classics Edition).

Ross, Ashley D., and Stella M. Rouse. 2015. "Economic Uncertainty, Job Threat, and the Resiliency of the Millennial Generation's Attitudes toward Immigration." *Social Science Quarterly* 96 (5): 1363–79.

Rouse, Stella M., Kei Kawashima-Ginsberg, and Ben Thrutchley. 2015. "Latino Civic Health Index." *National Conference on Citizenship.* http://ncoc.net/LatinosCHI

Ryan, Camille L., and Kurt Bauman. 2016. "Educational Attainment in the United States: 2015." U.S. Census Bureau, Population Characteristics, Report number P20–578. https://www.census.gov/content/dam/Census/library/publications/2016/demo/p20-578.pdf

Saad, Lydia. 2013. "Republican Skepticism toward Global Warming Eases." *Gallup.* April 9. http://www.gallup.com/poll/161714/republican-skepticism-global-warming-eases.aspx

Saad, Lydia. 2014. "One in Four in U.S. Are Solidly Skeptical of Global Warming." *Gallup.* April 22. http://www.gallup.com/poll/168620/one-four-solidly-skeptical-global-warming.aspx?g_source=CATEGORY_CLIMATE_CHANGE&g_medium=topic&g_campaign=tiles

Saad, Lydia and Jeffrey Jones. 2016. "US Concern about Global Warming at Eight-Year High." *Gallup.* March 16. http://www.gallup.com/poll/190010/concern-global-warming-eight-year-high.aspx

Salyer, Kirsten. 2016. "The Racial Wage Gap Has Not Changed in 35 Years." *Time.* July 1. http://time.com/4390212/race-wage-gap-pew-analysis/

Sanchez, Gabriel. R. 2006. "The Role of Group Consciousness in Political Participation among Latinos in the United States." *American Politics Research* 34 (4): 427–50.

Santhanam, Laura. 2015. "Here's Why It's So Hard to Figure Out How Millennials Feel About Racism." *PBS Newshour.* March 19. http://www.pbs.org/newshour/updates/data-reveal-complex-millennial-attitudes-race/

Scheve, Kenneth F., and Matthew J. Slaughter. 2001. "Labor Market Competition and Individual Preferences over Immigration Policy." *The Review of Economics and Statistics* 83 (1): 133–45.

Schuman, Howard, and Amy Corning. 2012. "Generational Memory and the Critical Period: Evidence from National and World Events." *Public Opinion Quarterly* 76 (1): 1–31.

Schwadel, Philip, and Christopher R.H. Garneau. 2014. "An Age-Period-Cohort Analysis of Political Tolerance in the United States." *The Sociological Quarterly* 55: 421–52.

Scott, Ryan. 2015. "New Report on Millennials Shows Link between Engagement and Cause Work." *Forbes.* May 5. http://www.forbes.com/sites/causeintegration/2015/05/05/new-report-on-millennials-shows-link-between-engagement-and-cause-work/#323d25df2341

Shames, Shauna L. 2017. *Out of the Running: Why Millennials Reject Political Careers and Why It Matters.* New York: New York University Press.

Shin, Laura. 2015. "The Racial Wealth Gap: Why a Typical White Household Has 16 Times the Wealth of a Black One." *Forbes.* March 26. https://www.forbes.com/sites/laurashin/2015/03/26/the-racial-wealth-gap-why-a-typical-white-household-has-16-times-the-wealth-of-a-black-one/#1e1db661f45e

Shingles, Richard D. 1981. "Black Consciousness and Political Participation: The Missing Link." *The American Political Science Review* 75 (1): 76–91.

Shushok Jr., Frank, and Vera Kidd. 2015. "Millennials in Higher Education: As Students Change, Much about Them Remains the Same." In *Positive Psychology on the College Campus,* edited by John C. Wade, Lawrence I. Marks and Roderick D. Hetzel. New York: Oxford University Press.

Smith, Adam. 1982. *Correspondence of Adam Smith, Glasgow Edition of the Works and Correspondence of Adam Smith.* Vol. 2a, p. 456. Oxford: Oxford University Press.

Solt, Frederick. 2008. "Economic Inequality and Democratic Political Engagement." *American Journal of Political Science* 52 (1): 48–60.

Sommeiller, Estelle, Mark Price, and Ellis Wazeter. 2016. "Income Inequality in the U.S. by State, Metropolitan Area, and County." *Economic Policy Institute.* June 16. http://www.epi.org/publication/income-inequality-in-the-us/

Spence, Alexa, Wouter Poortinga, and Nick Pidgeon. 2012. "The Psychological Distance of Climate Change." *Risk Analysis* 32 (6): 957–72.

Spence, Edward. 2001. "Cosmopolitanism and the Internet." In *Selected Papers from the Second Australian Institute of Computer Ethics Conference (AICE2000),* edited by J. Weckert, 88–93. Canberra: Australian Computer Society.

Spitzer, Robert. J. 2015. *The Politics of Gun Control.* New York: Routledge.

Stahl, Ashley. 2016. "New Study Reveals That Millennial Employment Is on the Rise." *Forbes.* May 18. http://www.forbes.com/sites/ashleystahl/2016/05/18/new-study-reveals-that-millennial-underemployment-is-on-the-rise/#40bf28d15201

Stein, Joel. 2013. "The New Greatest Generation: Why Millennials Will Save Us All." *Time.* May 20.

Steverman, Ben. 2016. "Millennials Still Want Kids, Just Not Right Now." *Bloomberg.* May 3. https://www.bloomberg.com/news/articles/2016-05-03/millennials-still-want-kids-just-not-right-now

Stoker, Laura, and Kent M. Jennings. 1995. "Life-Cycle Transitions and Political Participation: The Case of Marriage." *American Political Science Review* 89 (2): 421–33.

Stokes, Atiya Kai. 2003. "Latino Group Consciousness and Political Participaiton." *American Politics Research,* 31 (4): 361–78.

Stone, Will. 2016. "A 'Lost Generation of Workers': The Cost of Youth Unemployment." *NPR.* July 2. http://www.npr.org/2014/07/02/327058018/a-lost-generation-of-workers-the-cost-of-youth-unemployment

Stratford, Michael. 2016. "What the Republican Platform Says about Education." *Politico.* July 19. http://www.politico.com/tipsheets/morning-education/2016/07/what-the-republican-platform-says-about-education-215401

Strauss, Anselm L., and Juliet Corbin. 1998. *Basics of Qualitative Research: Techniques and Procedures for Developing Grounded Theory.* London: Sage (2nd Edition).

Strauss, Valerie. 2012. "What GOP Platform Says on Education." *The Washington Post.* August 28. https://www.washingtonpost.com/blogs/answer-sheet/post/what-gop-platform-says-on-education/2012/08/28/4b993bce-f15a-11e1-892d-bc92fee603a7_blog.html?utm_term=.b2ca25875604

Strauss, Valerie. 2016. "Democrats Make Education Revisions to 2016 Platform—and a Key Reformer Is Furious." *The Washington Post.* July 12. https://www.washingtonpost.com/news/answer-sheet/wp/2016/07/12/democrats-make-key-education-revisions-to-2016-platform-and-a-key-reformer-is-furious/?utm_term=.28f5807c0132

Tajfel, Henri, M.G. Billing, R.P. Bundy, and Flament Claude. 1971. "Social Categorization and Intergroup Behaviour." *European Journal of Social Psychology* 1 (2): 149–78.

Talbot, Margaret. 2015. "The Populist Prophet: Bernie Sanders has Spent Decades Attacking Inequality. Now the Country is Listening." *The New Yorker.* October 12. https://www.newyorker.com/magazine/2015/10/12/the-populist-prophet

Talty, Alexandra. 2015. "More Millennials Living at Home Than Ever Before." *Forbes.* July 31. http://www.forbes.com/sites/alexandratalty/2015/07/31/more-millennials-living-at-home-than-ever-before/#61ea9ce01702

Tam Cho, Wendy K., James G. Gimpel, and Tony Wu. 2006. "Clarifying the Role of SES in Political Participation: Policy Threat and Arab American Mobilization." *Journal of Politics* 68 (4): 977–91.

Taraborrelli, Angela. 2015. *Contemporary Cosmopolitanism.* New York: Bloomsbury.

Taylor, Adam. 2014. "Was #Kony2012 a Failure?" *The Washington Post.* December 16. https://www.washingtonpost.com/news/worldviews/wp/2014/12/16/was-kony2012-a-failure/

Taylor, Andrea, Wandi Bruine de Bruin, and Dessai Suraje. 2014. "Climate Change Beliefs and Perceptions of Weather-Related Changes in the United Kingdom." *Risk Analysis* 34 (11): 1995–2004.

Taylor, Paul. 2014. *The Next America: Boomers, Millennials, and the Looming Generational Showdown.* New York: Public Affairs.

Telhami, Shibley. 2015. "What Americans (especially Evangelicals) Think about Israel and the Middle East." Paper presented at Center for Middle Eastern Policy, Brookings Institute, December 4, Washington, D.C.

Telhami, Shibley and Katayoun Kishi. 2015. "The Arab Uprising and the Rise of Cosmopolitan Identity." Discussion Paper at *Brookings Institute,* May 31.

Thompson, Derek. 2012. "Adulthood, Delayed: What Has the Recession Done to Millennials?" *The Atlantic.* February 14. http://www.theatlantic.com/business/archive/2012/02/adulthood-delayed-what-has-the-recession-done-to-millennials/252913/

Thompson, Derek. 2013. "The Best-Educated Generation in American History Isn't Educated Enough." *The Atlantic.* December 12. https://www.theatlantic.com/business/archive/2013/12/the-best-educated-generation-in-american-history-isnt-educated-enough/282302/

Thompson, Derek. 2015. "Millennials: $2,000 Poorer than Their Parents Were at the Same Age." *The Atlantic*. January 31. http://www.theatlantic.com/business/ archive/2015/01/young-adults-poorer-less-employed-and-more-diverse-than-their-parents/385029/

Thompson, Derek. 2016. "The Liberal Millennial Generation." *The Atlantic*. February 29. https://www.theatlantic.com/politics/archive/2016/02/the-liberal-millennial-revolution/470826/

Thrall, Trevor. 2016. "Millennials Not Scared of Outside World." *CNN*. March 16. http://www.cnn.com/2016/03/16/opinions/millennials-foreign-policy-views-thrall/

Thrall, Trevor A., and Erik Goepner. 2015. *Millennials and U.S. Foreign Policy: The Next Generation's Attitudes toward Foreign Policy and War (and Why They Matter)*. Washington, DC: Cato Institute.

Tichenor, Daniel J. 2002. *Dividing Lines: The Politics of Immigration Control in America*. Princeton: Princeton University Press.

Tieku, Thomas Kwasi. 2012. "Collectivist Worldview: Its Challenge to International Relations," in *Africa and International Relations in the 21st Century*, edited by Cornelissen S., Cheru F., Shaw T.M. International Political Economy Series. London: Palgrave Macmillan.

Time. 2015. "Here's Donald Trump's Presidential Announcement Speech." *Time*. June 16. http://time.com/3923128/donald-trump-announcement-speech/

Timm, Jane C. 2014. "Millennials: We Care More about the Environment." *MSNBC*. March 22. http://www.msnbc.com/morning-joe/millennials-environment-climate-change

Tooely, Melissa. 2015. "No Child Left Behind Is Gone, but Will It Be Back?" *The Atlantic*. December 24. https://www.theatlantic.com/education/archive/2015/12/ no-child-left-behind-is-gone-but-will-it-be-back/421329/

Twenge, Jean M. 2014. *Generation Me - Revised and Updated: Why Today's Young Americans Are More Confident, Assertive, Entitled--and More Miserable than Ever Before*. New York: Atria Books.

Twenge, Jean M., William K. Campbell, and Elise C. Freeman. 2012. "Generational Differences in Young Adults' Life Goals, Concern for Others, and Civic Orientation, 1966–2009." *Journal of Personality and Social Psychology* 102 (5): 1045–62.

Tyson, Alec, and Shiva Maniam. 2016. "Behind Trump's Victory: Divisions by Race, Gender, Education." *Pew Research Center*. November 9. http://www.pewresearch.org/ fact-tank/2016/11/09/behind-trumps-victory-divisions-by-race-gender-education/

U.S. Bureau of Labor Statistics. 2012. *BLS Spotlight on Statistics: The Recession of 2007–2009*. February. https://www.bls.gov/spotlight/2012/recession/pdf/recession_bls_spotlight.pdf

U.S. Bureau of Labor Statistics. 2014. "Employee Tenure in 2014." September 18. http://www.bls.gov/news.release/pdf/tenure.pdf

U.S. Bureau of Labor Statistics. 2016. "Characteristics of Minimum Wage Workers, 2015." *BLS Reports*. April. https://www.bls.gov/opub/reports/minimum-wage/ 2015/home.htm

U.S. Bureau of Labor Statistics. 2017. "Labor Force Statistics from the Current Population Survey." https://www.bls.gov/cps/tables.htm#nempstat_m

U.S. Census Bureau. 2010. "The Foreign Born Population in the United States." May 2012. https://www.census.gov/prod/2012pubs/acs-19.pdf

U.S. Census Bureau. 2014. "CB14–219: New Census Bureau Statistics Show How Young Adults Today Compare with Previous Generations in Neighborhoods Nationwide." December 4. http://www.census.gov/newsroom/press-releases/2014/cb14-219.html

U.S. Census Bureau. 2015a. "CB15-113: Millennials Outnumber Baby Boomers and Are Far More Diverse, Census Bureau Reports." June 25. https://www.census.gov/newsroom/press-releases/2015/cb15-113.html

U.S. Census Bureau. 2015b. "Young Adults, Then and Now." January 30. http://www.census.gov/content/dam/Census/newsroom/c-span/2015/20150130_cspan_youngadults.pdf

Uslaner, Eric M., and Mitchell Brown. 2005. "Inequality, Trust, and Civic Engagement." *American Politics Research* 33 (6): 868–94.

Vega, Tanzina. 2016a. "Blacks Still Far Behind Whites in Wealth and Income." *CNN Money*. June 27. http://money.cnn.com/2016/06/27/news/economy/racial-wealth-gap-blacks-whites/

Vega, Tanzina. 2016b. "Why the Racial Wealth Gap Won't Go Away." *CNN Money*. January 26. http://money.cnn.com/2016/01/25/news/economy/racial-wealth-gap/

Verba, Sidney, and Norman H. Nie. 1972. *Participation in America: Political Democracy and Social Equality*. New York: Harper & Row.

Verba, Sidney, Kay Schlozman, and Henry Brady. 1995. *Voice and Equality: Civic Voluntarism in American Politics*. Cambridge: Harvard University Press.

Vertovec, Steven, and Robin Cohen. 2002. "Introduction: Conceiving Cosmopolitanism." In *Conceiving Cosmopolitanism: Theory, Context and Practice*, edited by Steven Vertovec and Robin Cohen, 1–22. Oxford: Oxford University Press.

Wagaman, Andrew. 2016. "For Millennials, 9/11 and Its Aftermath Shaped Their View of the World." *The Morning Call*. September 11. http://www.mcall.com/news/local/mc-911-millenials-worldview-15-years-anniversary-20160911-story.html

Wagner, John. 2016. "Clinton Turns to Al Gore and Climate Change to Excite Millennials in Florida." *The Washington Post*. October 11. https://www.washingtonpost.com/politics/clinton-appears-in-florida-with-gore-to-promise-action-on-climate-change/2016/10/11/db8745d4-8fc9-11e6-9c85-ac42097b8cc0_story.html?utm_term=.e55fef4936a7

Wardekker, Arjan J., Arthur C. Petersen, Jeroen P. van der Sluijs. 2009. "Ethics and Public Perception of Climate Change: Exploring the Christian Voices in the US Public Debate." *Global Environmental Change* 19: 512–21.

Weber, Elke U. 2006. "Experience-based and Description-based Perceptions of Long-term Risk: Why Global Warming Does Not Scare Us (Yet)." *Climatic Change* 70: 103–20.

Weber, Elke U., and Paul C. Stern. 2011. "Public Understanding of Climate Change in the United States." *American Psychologist* 66 (4): 315–28.

Weir, Kirsten. 2013. "More than Job Satisfaction." *American Psychological Association* 44 (11), December. http://www.apa.org/monitor/2013/12/job-satisfaction.aspx

White House. 2014. "15 Economic Facts about Millennials." *The Council of Economic Advisers*. October. https://www.whitehouse.gov/sites/default/files/docs/millennials_report.pdf

Whitemarsh, Lorraine. 2011. "Scepticism and Uncertainty about Climate Change: Dimensions, Determinants and Change over Time." *Global Environmental Change* 21 (2): 690–700.

Wilkinson, Katherine K. 2012. *Between God and Green: How Evangelicals Are Cultivating a Middle Ground on Climate Change*. New York: Oxford University Press.

Williams, Timothy. 2014. "Poll Finds That More Americans Back Gun Rights than Stronger Controls." *The New York Times*. December 11. https://www.nytimes.com/2014/12/12/us/gun-control-gun-rights-pew-survey.html

Winograd, Morley and Michael Hais. 2017. "President Obama, the Millennial Whisperer." *Los Angeles Times*, January 16. http://www.latimes.com/opinion/op-ed/la-oe-winograd-hais-obama-the-millennial-president-20170116-story.html

Winton, Jesse. 2016. "Why Millennials Are Skeptical of Gun Control." *The Washington Times*. September 20. http://www.washingtontimes.com/news/2016/sep/20/why-millennials-are-skeptical-of-gun-control/

Witkin, Rachel. 2016. "Millennials Are Less Likely to Support Gun Control than You'd Think." *NBC News*. July 24. http://www.nbcnews.com/news/us-news/millennials-are-less-likely-support-gun-control-you-d-think-n610546

Wittkopf, Eugene R. 1990. *Faces of Internationalism: Public Opinion and American Foreign Policy*. Durham: Duke University Press.

Wolfgang, Ben. 2016. "Hillary Clinton Blows Chance to Win over Millennials with Slow Evolution on Pot." *The Washington Times*. October 6. http://www.washingtontimes.com/news/2016/oct/6/hillary-clintons-marijuana-legalization-stance-ali/

Wolfinger, Raymond, and Steven J. Rosenstone. 1980. *Who Votes?* New Haven: Yale University Press.

Wong, Janelle S., Pei-Te Lien, and M. Margaret Conway. 2005. "Group-Based Resources and Political Participation among Asian Americans. *American Politics Research* 33 (4): 545–76.

Wood, Dan B., and Arnold Vedlitz. 2007. "Issue Definition, Information Processing, and the Politics of Global Warming." *American Journal of Political Science* 51 (3): 552–68.

World Bank. 2015. "The State of Social Safety Nets 2015." *The World Bank Group*. http://documents.worldbank.org/curated/en/415491467994645020/pdf/97882-PUB-REVISED-Box393232B-PUBLIC-DOCDATE-6-29-2015-DOI-10-1596978-1-4648-0543-1-EPI-1464805431.pdf

World Meteorological Association. "Understanding Climate." Accessed June 1, 2017. https://www.wmo.int/pages/themes/climate/understanding_climate.php

Yale Program on Climate Change Communication. 2016. "Global Warming's Six Americas." http://climatecommunication.yale.edu/about/projects/global-warmings-six-americas/

Zaller, John. 1992. *The Nature and Origins of Mass Opinion*. Cambridge: Cambridge University Press.

Zogby, John, and Joan S. Kuhl. 2013. *First Globals: Understanding, Managing, & Unleashing the Potential of Our MillennialGeneration*. https://www.amazon.com/Understanding-Unleashing-Potential-Millennial-Generation-ebook/dp/B00DE3N19W

Index

abortion rights, support for, 175–76,
179–83, 186–90, 255n7, 278
income differences and, 189
inter-generational differences in, 176,
179, 181
Millennial Generation and, 175–76,
179–83, 186–90, 192, 229–30,
278, 295n16
race and ethnic differences in, 182–83,
188, 230
religion and, 189–90, 295n16
Affordable Care Act (Obamacare),
70, 232–33
African Americans, 6–7
abortion rights and, 182–83, 188, 230
belief in a rigged system, 220–21, 232
belief in climate change, 161, 164, 168
belief in government economic
intervention, 57, 59–61, 98, 227
economic optimism of, 21
education and, 88–89
foreign policy beliefs of, 117–24, 126
gun control and, 182–85, 192, 230
healthcare cost reform and, 72, 74
immigration attitudes of, 138–40, 144
income inequality and, 55, 200
marijuana legalization and, 182–83,
186–87, 192, 230
Millennial Generation and, 7–8,
33, 35–36
minimum wage and, 63–65, 74

political engagement and, 199–201,
209–10, 231
racial tolerance and, 9
Social Security reform and, 67–68
standardized testing beliefs of, 94–96
student loan debt and, 98–101, 227
unemployment and, 20, 48, 51

Baby Boomers, 4, 19–20, 131, 296n1
generational identity of, 5
healthcare costs and, 70
international politics and, 106–7, 127
political views of, 9, 14–16, 173
socioeconomic status of, 200
"Black Lives Matter" movement, 9, 295n6
border security, 12, 136–37, 139, 228
presidential election of 2016 and,
129–30, 198, 232–33
Trump administration and, 136, 148
Brownstein, Ronald, 22
Brulle, Robert J., 155

Civil Rights Movement, 5, 201
climate change beliefs, 149–72, 274–75.
See also Millennial Generation,
climate change beliefs and
economic assessments and, 154–55
election of 2016 and, 149–50
factors explaining belief in, 159–66
inter-generational differences in, 150,
158, 164–69, 229